PRACTICAL GLOBAL FAMILY LAW

CAROLINA ACADEMIC PRESS CONTEXTUAL APPROACH SERIES
ANDREW J. MCCLURG, SERIES EDITOR
JANET LEACH RICHARDS, FAMILY LAW EDITOR

Practical Global Tort Litigation
United States, Germany, and Argentina
Andrew J. McClurg, Adem Koyuncu, Luis Eduardo Sprovieri

Practical Global Family Law
United States, China, and Italy
Janet Leach Richards, Chen Wei, Lorella dal Pezzo

PRACTICAL GLOBAL FAMILY LAW

UNITED STATES, CHINA, AND ITALY

Janet Leach Richards

Chen Wei

with Lei Wenbi, Pi Xijun, and Ran Qiyu

Lorella dal Pezzo

CAROLINA ACADEMIC PRESS

Durham, North Carolina

Library of Congress Cataloging-in-Publication Data

Richards, Janet.
  Practical global family law : United States, China, and Italy / Janet Leach
Richards, Chen Wei (with Lei Wenbi, Pi Xijun, and Ran Qiyu), Lorella dal
Pezzo.
    p. cm. -- (Contextual approach series)
  Includes bibliographical references and index.
  ISBN 978-1-59460-434-8 (alk. paper)
  1. Domestic relations--United States. 2. Domestic relations--China. 3.
Domestic relations--Italy. I. Chen, Wei. II. Dal Pezzo, Lorella. III. Title. IV.
Series.

  K670.R53 2009
  346.01'5--dc22

                                              2009001609

CAROLINA ACADEMIC PRESS
700 Kent Street
Durham, North Carolina 27701
Telephone (919) 489-7486
Fax (919) 493-5668
www.cap-press.com

Printed in the United States of America

To my family.
JLR

To my family.
CW

To my son Marco Giorgio.
LdP

CONTENTS

SERIES EDITOR'S PREFACE

The Contextual Approach Series (CAS) had its genesis at the Florida International University College of Law, South Florida's public law school, where I taught as a member of the founding faculty from 2002–06. The FIU College of law is one of the most international of all U.S. law schools, drawing its students from many diverse cultures and nations. Uniquely, the FIU College of Law curriculum requires that all courses, including domestic law courses, include a comparative and/or international law component. Comparative law is the study of similarities and differences in the law and legal traditions of different nations. International law is the "law of nations." It covers the entire field of both public and private transnational relationships.

To satisfy the comparative/international law requirement in my Torts and Products Liability courses, I searched long and hard for manageable, self-contained materials comparing the U.S. common law tort litigation system with tort systems of other countries. While the search turned up a large body of outstanding comparative law scholarship, only a sliver of it addressed tort law and litigation. A wider discovery was that most comparative law literature is historical, theoretical or thematic in nature. Not many materials attempt to explain how law "really works" in other countries as compared to the U.S. common law system.

One obvious explanation for this gap is the sheer enormity of the task. To say that comparing legal systems is difficult is euphemistic. Think how impossible it would be, for example, to "compare the law" of New York and Texas, then consider the proportions of comparing different legal systems of different countries. As a byproduct of this obstacle, comparative law coverage tends to be either very broad or very narrow. Survey-type materials offer wide geographic and subject matter coverage, but do not convey any sense of how law really functions in other countries. Analyses of specific topics give much greater depth, but the subject matter often has only narrow application.

Like many faculty members at the FIU College of Law, I tried both the macro and micro approaches to teaching comparative/international law in Torts and Products Liability, with underwhelming success. In Torts, I distrib-

uted a nifty chart attempting to compare common law and civil law systems
in six pages, assigned a lengthy law review article about the Alien Tort Claims
Act, and invited guest speakers such as the Chief Justice of the Costa Rica
Supreme Court and a distinguished lawyer from Argentina. I made my Products Liability students do presentations about Latin American products liability law. All of these endeavors were interesting, but my students weren't
learning much about comparative or international law. There had to be a balance between "Today we're going to compare the law of the entire world," and
"Today we're going to explore interpretations of article 1(c)(ii) of the Convention on International Liability for Damage Caused by Space Objects." Feed-
back from students at FIU confirmed that my difficulties in trying to integrate
comparative and international law were not unique.

It occurred to me that one way to strike a breadth-depth equilibrium and
also help bring comparative law to life would be to *contextualize* it by applying the substantive and procedural law of different nations to the same set of
case facts. A case-based approach offers unique advantages. Foremost, it gives
students a contextual foundation to which they can attach what they're learning. Legal principles mean little in isolation from facts, which is a principal
reason U.S. law students learn most subject matter by the "case method." Applying law to facts promotes analysis that is not only more focused, precise,
and accurate, but more accessible and retainable. It is one thing to recite a
general rule about, for example, the burden of proof in a given legal system,
and quite another to unweave the intricacies of how proof burdens apply to a
concrete set of facts.

Applying the law of different nations to a consistent fact pattern also serves
to highlight both similarities and differences more dramatically than a purely
expository approach. A case approach would not intuitively occur to lawyers
in other legal systems, such as those following the civil law tradition, where
lawyers are trained to think in terms of codes rather than cases, but a "problem approach"—essentially the same thing—probably would. Regardless of
the system, lawyers around the world are engaged in the same task: solving
legal problems, many of them universal in nature.

Thus, I came up with the idea for a series of comparative law books in different subject areas based on sets of problem facts designed to raise fundamental issues of law and policy at the heart of each respective subject—issues
that all peoples in all nations and legal systems must face. Each book in the
CAS compares how these issues would be addressed by the law of the U.S. and
two other nations representing different legal systems and different regions of
the world. To enhance the "on the ground" accuracy and perspective of the
books, each series entry relies on "inside" experts in the particular subject area

from each of the three countries rather than on U.S.-trained comparative law experts. "As every comparatist knows," writes Mathias Reimann, "it is difficult, and sometimes outright impossible, for an outsider fully to understand the law of a foreign country." Mathias Reimann, *Liability for Defective Products at the Beginning of the Twenty-First Century: Emergence of a Worldwide Standard*, 51 AM. J. COMP. L. 751, 755 (2003).

The first entry in the CAS was *Practical Global Tort Litigation: U.S., Germany, and Argentina* (2007), which I co-authored with Adem Koyuncu (Cologne, Germany) and Luis Sprovieri (Buenos Aires, Argentina). Currently, books are underway in a variety of subject areas involving many different countries.

Accessibility is a guiding principle of the CAS. The goal is to craft texts accessible to people without a prior background or expertise in comparative law, and which can be understood by readers lacking knowledge of any of the three legal systems discussed, including the U.S. CAS books are designed for any reader, in or outside the U.S., interested in learning about how the legal systems of different nations would attack, both procedurally and substantively, the same set of universal legal issues in a subject area as raised by the problem facts of the particular book. The books are structured to provide a true side-by-side comparison of the law, as applied, in the three countries.

The primary utilities of CAS books in law school are as supplemental texts in domestic law courses for professors who want to expose their students to a comparative legal perspective, or as primary or supplemental texts in comparative law courses or advanced courses in the particular subject.

The CAS is offered as a contribution to what should become a growing body of "contextual comparative law."

Andrew J. McClurg
Herbert Herff Chair of Excellence in Law
The University of Memphis
Cecil C. Humphreys School of Law

Practical Global Family Law
Editor's Preface

It has been a wonderful learning experience to work on this book with my talented co-authors. I learned so much from the experience. I was surprised both at the similarities and the differences between our three countries.

Family Law is a difficult topic to cover from a U.S. perspective, as the law is heavily state oriented. Consequently, I have focused on the law in Tennessee and have tried to mention alternative approaches from other states, where appropriate.

I considered selecting marriage, adoption, domestic violence, and any number of other interesting topics for our fact pattern, but ultimately chose a simple divorce fact pattern, both for its simplicity and for its universal applicability.

I was tempted to choose a number of different countries for this text because family law seems to be so different in other parts of the world. I finally settled on China, because of its large population, vast history, communist influence, and civil law background; and Italy, because of its long history of not recognizing divorce, its membership in the E.U., and the influence of the Holy See.

In this book, we will follow Mario, an Italian-American, and Lily, a Chinese-American, as they seek to obtain a divorce in the U.S., China, and Italy, respectively.

This book is designed as a student reader, to provide a comparative family law experience for students in a basic family law class or a comparative law class.

The initial chapters draw heavily on the format of the original book in this series, giving a basic overview of common law and civil law, a bit of background about each country, and the facts on which our divorce is based.

The remaining chapters focus directly on the divorce itself, covering such topics as divorce procedure, grounds for divorce, child custody and visitation, child support, property division, spousal support, spousal agreements, appeals, and attorney fees.

Charts are inserted at the end of the substantive chapters to highlight and summarize the similarities and differences between the countries. The original manuscripts from my co-authors have been edited to make the material more easily read and understood by American law students, while attempting to retain the voice of each author and the rich cultural differences of each country. In many instances, translations or definitions are supplied in parentheses to aid in this effort.

I hope you will enjoy reading this book and will gain a greater understanding and appreciation of comparative law in the process. I think the book demonstrates that we can certainly learn alternative ways to approach legal issues by studying the law of our global neighbors.

Janet Leach Richards
Cecil C. Humphreys Professor of Law
The University of Memphis
Cecil C. Humphreys School of Law

ACKNOWLEDGMENTS

This book would not have been possible without the unselfish efforts of many people. We would like to acknowledge them below as a small sign of our great gratitude.

In the U.S., Richards would first like to thank her friend and colleague, the Herbert Herff Chair of Excellence at the University of Memphis Cecil C. Humphreys School of Law, Professor Andrew J. McClurg, for initiating this comparative law series and inviting her to edit the Family Law book in the series. Writing a book like this is very much a collaborative effort and would not have been possible without the professional dedication and cooperation of her two co-authors, Professor Chen Wei and attorney Lorella del Pezzo. Richards was extremely fortunate to have Ms. Cong Ding, a Chinese citizen, as her research assistant. Ms. Ding was tireless in her efforts and precise and thorough in her research. In short, she was essential to the success of this project. Finally, an enormous debt must be acknowledged to Mrs. Linda Hayes who formatted all the chapters, more than once, and meticulously edited every page. The Plough Foundation provided support for this project through the author's Cecil C. Humphreys Professorship.

In China, while writing this book, Chen and her colleagues referred to many works, papers, social investigation reports, cases, and other proposed legislative materials written by distinguished Chinese experts, scholars, and lawyers, including Wu Changzhen, Yang Dawen, Wang Deyi, Xu Mingxian, Cao Yisun, Jiang Wei, Zeng Yi, Liu Shijie, Liu Yalin, Du Jun, Hu Kangsheng, Liang Shuwen, Wang Shengming, Sun Lihai, Rong Weiyi, Song Meiya, Xia Yinlan, Xie Jingjie, Chen Min, Wang Jing, Cui Li, Sun Xiaomei, Lv Guohua, Gu Xiulian, Wen Zhe, Song Jianchao, Sun Changshan, Ye Wenzhen, Lin Qingguo, and Jian Chun'an. They also consulted some published foreign laws translated by scholars such as Chen Mingxia, Xu Jihua, Luo Jiezhen, Chen Weizuo, and Qu Tao, etc. Wu Yu and other librarians in the library of Southwest University of Political Science and Law, China offered considerate services and assistance to them when they consulted some materials and borrowed related books. Professor Zhao Wanyi, the dean in the Civil and Commercial

Law School, gave much support to this project in the copy fees for the Chinese and English manuscripts. We are most appreciative to them for all their help!

PRACTICAL GLOBAL FAMILY LAW

CHAPTER 1

ROADMAP TO A CONTEXTUAL COMPARATIVE LAW JOURNEY

This is a story about an ordinary divorce case between a Chinese-American, Lily Chou and an Italian-American, Mario Penna. It is possible that they might have married and divorced in the United States, China, or Italy. In this book, we will assume, alternately, that Lily and Mario did marry and divorce in each of these three countries. In doing so, we will compare and contrast the divorce law in all three countries, highlighting the similarities and the differences among them. This book tracks the *Lily Chou v. Mario Penna* (hereafter *Lily v. Mario*) hypothetical divorce as it progresses through the legal system of each country. Like all stories, this one requires "back story"—in our case, to provide a contextual anchor for Lily's and Mario's multinational legal journey. Before meeting Lily and Mario, we'll give you some background about the legal systems of the U.S., China, and Italy, and the sources of law in common law and civil law systems, both generally and as they pertain to divorce law.

This book is intended as a basic primer on comparative divorce law and litigation in the U.S. common law system and in two major civil law systems from Europe (Italy) and Asia (China), using one simple divorce case as the vehicle for exploration. The emphasis is on clear, concise explanation and analysis of these topics:

- Court Systems, Judges, and Legal Professions (chapter two);
- Sources of Law in Civil and Common Law Countries, concentrating on Sources of Divorce Law (chapter three);
- Whether to Divorce: The Divorce Process (chapter five);
- Grounds for Divorce (chapter six);
- Child Custody and Visitation (chapter seven);
- Child Support (chapter eight);
- Property Division (chapter nine);
- Spousal Support (chapter ten); and

- Antenuptial Agreements, Settlement Agreements, Appeals, Attorney Fees (chapter eleven).

Even though the focus is on a single set of facts, considerable generalizing is required in a book that attempts to cover concisely an entire litigated divorce case in three countries. Volumes could be, and in many cases have been, written about the myriad topics and doctrines discussed. Moreover, within each country, different legal systems function simultaneously, with many variations among them. The U.S., for example, is comprised of not one, but fifty-one legal systems: the federal system and a separate system for each of the fifty states. On the other hand, both China and Italy have unitary court systems.

The book attempts to deliver a big picture overview of a litigated divorce case while at the same time not skimping on important details. We do not delve deeply into historical, cultural, or other explanations for why legal rules developed the way they did. Any such effort in a book intended as a basic primer would have come up far short or, alternatively, would have converted the project into a much different book or set of books. Several excellent existing works explore the historical and social evolution of common and civil law traditions, while others provide in-depth analysis of divorce law in specific countries or states. Readers interested in learning more detail should consult those works, some of which are listed in the bibliography.

One consequence of these omissions is that readers should be cautious in assessing the many convergences in doctrinal rules among the three countries highlighted herein, realizing that they may obscure underlying non-apparent differences. Similarly, with regard to differences, Basil Markesinis cautions that simply because a particular legal feature appears to be missing in one system does not mean it is not accounted for in other ways. *See* BASIL MARKESINIS ET AL., COMPENSATION FOR PERSONAL INJURY IN ENGLISH, GERMAN AND ITALIAN LAW 198 (2005).

Because the book is intended to survey an entire litigated case, dispute resolution mechanisms such as mediation and settlement, by which most cases are resolved in all nations, are discussed only tangentially.

To facilitate coherent side-by-side comparisons, we opted in most places for a compartmentalized format in which the law of our respective nations is set forth under separate subheadings, beginning with the U.S., followed by China, and then Italy. We considered and rejected as too unwieldy and confusing the alternative approach of trying to weave together the intricacies of the law in all three nations line by line.

We strived to construct a neutral comparative account. The purpose is to inform, not persuade. Except for brief editorial comments in the final chapter, we leave it to others, including readers, to pass judgment on the relative merits of any particular aspect of the legal systems studied.

Here is some other useful advance information:

Abbreviations. The sources below, mentioned often, are abbreviated as indicated. However, full titles are used from time to time as appropriate to refresh readers' memories.

China
    National People's Congress—NPC
    Supreme People's Court—SPC
Italy
    European Union—E.U.
    Italian Civil Code—C.c.
    Italian Civil Procedure Code—C.p.c.
    Italian Code of Criminal Procedure—C.p.p.
    Italian Constitution—Cost.
    Italian Constitutional Court—C.Cost.
    Italian Penal Code—C.p.
    Pubblico Ministero—PM
    Examining Magistrate—GI

Monetary and Statistical Comparisons. We generally resisted the temptation to make a direct monetary comparison of the support and property awards in each country. Comparatists avoid making direct monetary comparisons among nations, for good reason. Money figures become outdated because of inflation, deflation, and other reasons. Moreover, without accounting for all of the social and other factors that influence monetary awards in different countries, which is probably impossible, comparisons can take on an "apples and oranges" appearance. We recognize the limited value of attempting to estimate and compare awards in a hypothetical divorce case for three countries, but thought readers would want to know "the ending" to Lily's and Mario's story. As a compromise, we decided to assign monetary values of the parties' assets in relation to each other. For example, "Lily's ring is worth ten times as much as Mario's watch." To the extent that money is discussed, Yuan (China) and Euros (Italy) are exchanged for U.S. dollars using the following 2008 approximate average currency exchange rates:

$100 U.S. = 683.40 Yuan
100 Yuan = $14.63 U.S.

$100 U.S. = 77.72 Euros
100 Euros = $128.68 U.S.

Currency exchange rates fluctuate, of course, and some currencies are more stable than others. Again, the figures are used only to provide a general comparative perspective.

Some statistics are cited, usually to support generally accepted propositions. Statistical evidence in a concise work such as this one is necessarily incomplete, omitting conflicting data and explanation as to how the figures were determined. As with the monetary references, readers should not put too fine a point on precise statistical figures. Many of the figures were rounded to the nearest whole numbers for easier consumption.

Translations. Quotations of Chinese and Italian legal sources in this book were translated to English from Chinese and Italian by co-authors Chen and dal Pezzo and by Richards' research assistant, Ms. Cong Ding. To enhance accuracy, these translations were compared to other translations, where available. One truth confirmed many times during the composition of this book is that there is no such thing as a single accurate translation of a legal principle or legalese from one language to another. When one consults multiple translations to English of a particular Chinese or Italian legal principle, one encounters differences in the translations. All convey the same substance, but, invariably, differences appear in the precise words and sentence structure.

Summary Charts. Beginning with the comparison of specific areas of procedural and substantive law in chapter five, charts are inserted at the end of each chapter highlighting key similarities and differences discussed in the chapter. Intended only as handy reference guides, the charts do not contain detailed explanation or qualifications to make them precisely accurate.

With all of the above disclaimers and limitations, this book is unique in its problem approach to comparative law. By contextualizing comparative law—that is, by applying the substantive and procedural law of different countries to a consistent set of facts—the intention is to showcase similarities and differences among the U.S. common law divorce system and the civil law divorce systems of China and Italy in a way that is understandable, interesting, and digestible. We seek to *show* in addition to tell. So what are we waiting for? To continue our journey metaphor, it's time to crank the ignition and begin the trip.

CHAPTER 2

LEGAL SYSTEMS ON THREE CONTINENTS—THE UNITED STATES, CHINA, AND ITALY

Most comparative law study, including this book, focuses on the two most influential worldwide legal traditions: common law and civil law. The common law—a system in which judge-made precedent traditionally formed the primary source of law—developed in England beginning at the time of the Norman Conquest in 1066 A.D. and was carried to other nations, including the U.S., through British territorial expansion. Other notable common law countries include Australia, Canada, Ireland, and New Zealand. Civil law—a system in which codes and other statutes are the primary source of law—is rooted in Roman law dating back to 450 B.C. The underpinnings of modern civil law are found in the French Civil Code of 1804, often called the Napoleonic Code, and the German Civil Code of 1896. The civil law traditions of these two countries have played a dominant role both in the distribution and shaping of civil law throughout the world.

Civil law is both much older and more widely distributed than the common law tradition. All of Western Europe and Latin America operate under civil law systems, as do parts of Africa and Asia. The legal systems of Eastern Europe also were built on a foundation of civil law. Following World War II, socialist law was overlaid on those systems by the former Soviet Union. With the fall of Soviet socialism, the civil law foundation of Eastern European countries is re-emerging. *See generally* JOHN HENRY MERRYMAN, THE CIVIL LAW TRADITION: AN INTRODUCTION TO THE LEGAL SYSTEMS OF WESTERN EUROPE AND LATIN AMERICA 1–5 (2d ed. 1985) (discussing worldwide distribution of common law and civil law systems).

It's not possible to differentiate common law and civil law systems in anything approaching black and white terms. The variations among the legal systems of different nations, even nations that fall under the same classification as "common law nations" or "civil law nations," are enormous. They include

7

differences in both procedural and substantive rules of law, as well as fundamental structural differences such as the extent to which a system adheres to the principle of judicial review. Even in countries following similar legal traditions, social and economic differences dramatically impact how those rules are applied in practice and the results that flow from their application. It has been observed, for example, that the modern version of England's common law system has more in common with civil law systems on the European continent than with the U.S.

Complicating categorization further, many legal systems are mixed systems combining elements of both Anglo-American common law and European civil law, and, in some cases, Islamic law. South Africa's legal system is a combination of Roman-Dutch civil law and English common law. Pakistan's legal system is grounded in English common law mixed with elements of Islamic law, while India's is a combination of common law and Hindu law. The U.S. state of Louisiana is a mixed civil law-common law jurisdiction. In some civil law countries, U.S. law has been particularly influential. This is true in many Latin American countries.

With 192 nations on the planet, and so many variations among their legal traditions, selecting any three countries for comparative study is susceptible to criticism as being arbitrary. Nevertheless, the U.S., China, and Italy are fitting subjects for a tri-continent "common law versus civil law" comparative study of divorce law. The U.S. is the largest common law system in the world and the U.S. litigation system is the most intricately developed and oft-used, while Italy and China are major civil law systems on their respective continents.

Similar to the Italian legal system, Chinese law follows the basic rules of the civil law, but with several distinct characteristics. As one of the oldest legal systems in the world, modern Chinese law is a mixture of traditional Chinese legal approaches and Western civil law influences. Meanwhile, Chinese law still retains a few socialist law vestiges. A comparison of the family laws of the U.S., China, and Italy provides a unique perspective of the different evolutionary paths of culture and history between Eastern and Western civilizations. During its 2000 year history of being a slave and feudal society, China's family laws were used to support arranged marriages and implement a patriarchal social system. Starting from the middle of the nineteenth century, the systematic introduction of Western law provided the building blocks for modern Chinese law. The Civil Law Kinship Volume, enacted in 1931, was modeled after the kinship volume of civil laws of Germany, Japan, and Switzerland from the continental legal system. The Civil Law Kinship Volume abolished the system of arranged marriages that was popular in China during the past thousands of years and instituted a system basing marriage on the mutual consent of both parties. This Civil Law Kinship Volume effected the transformation from the old Chinese law to modern Chinese law in form, which was considered to be progressively significant at the time. However, the law still maintained some provisions of the Draft of Civil Law of the Qing Dynasty, leaving some remnants of the feudal family and marriage system.

After the Chinese Communist Party came to power in 1949, the first Marriage Law of the People's Republic of China (hereinafter Marriage Law 1950) was promulgated, with the goal of eliminating the remnants of feudal marriage customs, by prohibiting arranged and coerced marriages, concubinage, polygamy, and child neglect. It also upheld the principles of freedom of marriage, monogamy, gender equality, and protection of children's interests. Thirty years later, with the start of economic reform and the need for reconstructing a legal system, Marriage Law 1980 was enacted as an amendment to Marriage Law 1950. While further strengthening the principles of Marriage Law 1950, Marriage Law 1980 is influenced by a family planning policy, which promotes late marriage and late reproduction. On April 28, 2001, Marriage Law 1980 was amended by the legislature to address several new situations. The 2001 amendments will be referred to herein as the current Marriage Law, as they represent the most current version of the Marriage Law. The current Marriage Law amended the requirements for marriage, *e.g.*, it provides that marriage shall be prohibited where either the man or the woman is suffering from any disease that is regarded by medical science as rendering a person unfit for marriage; it adds void and voidable marriage systems; and it supplements marital property systems by narrowing the scope of matrimonial joint property, and defining both matrimonial joint property and the separate property of a spouse. It supplements the divorce system, such as recognizing the visitation rights of one parent to the child after divorce and the right of the housekeeper in the family to claim economic compensation. Recognition of legal liabilities for domestic violence, maltreatment, and desertion of family members were added. *See* CHEN WEI, LEGAL SCIENCE OF MARRIAGE, FAMILY AND SUCCESSION 18–23 (Beijing: Publishing House of the Masses) (2005).

In addition to the unique history and characteristics of Chinese family law, the skyrocketing divorce rate in recent years makes China an interesting choice for comparative family law study. Once rare in China, divorce is becoming more common than ever. After thirty years of rapid economic growth and the influence of Western ideology, as more and more women gain financial independence and start to embrace individualism, fewer and fewer women chose to cherish traditional values and tolerate an unhappy marriage. Meanwhile, the liberal divorce law has also contributed to the rising divorce rate. The law now provides for a "no fault divorce." Though in practice, judges tend to maintain marriages instead of ending them, the liberal divorce law makes divorce much easier to obtain today than in the past.

Comparing Italian and U.S. family law offers a unique opportunity to contrast common law evolution with the reform approach typical of a civil law system, while providing a civil law example of the driving force of constitutional principles in family law reform, enhanced by the unique historical influence of the Holy See and the emergent influence of the European Union (E.U.).

First, a comparison between U.S. and Italian family law is singularly illustrative of how common law systems and civil law systems respond to the evolutionary pressures of the social and cultural needs of the society they reflect. In the U.S., historically, each state dealt independently with family law matters, primarily through common law evolution resulting in fragmentation and asymmetries at times difficult to reconcile into a cohesive system. For example, while fault based divorce was introduced relatively early in many states, no fault divorce was not accepted as the predominant dissolution procedure at the same time in every jurisdiction. California was the first state to adopt no fault divorce grounds in 1969, but New York, the last state to adopt no fault grounds, still permits a no fault divorce only by consent, meaning that the parties must enter into a separation agreement and live separately for one year. By contrast, Italian family law typifies the legal evolution of a civil law system driven by legislation and codification, where decisional trends take a back seat. Indeed, since unification in 1861, the law reflected a paternalistic system, the product of an agrarian society, with an emphasis on maintaining a concentration of land ownership, and on promoting the effective management of the family enterprise under a single rule, that of the husband. Francesco Parisi & Gianpaolo Frezza, *The Evolving Principles of Italian Family Law*, 9 DIGEST 1, 2 (2001). The system survived almost without a wrinkle through two Civil Codes enactments (the 1865 Civil Code and the innovative 1942 Civil Code) and the promulgation of the 1948 Constitution, heralding a new form of government (The Italian Republic as opposed to the Constitutional Monarchy which had been in place since Italy's birth as a modern nation-state after World War II (WWII)). Italian family law remained relatively simple: there was no divorce or separation. Finally, starting in the 1970s, Italy began to respond to the extraordinary pressures for change to its archaic legal order, by then hopelessly out of sync with its modern social structure post-WWII and with the 1948 Constitution, through sweeping legislative reforms. With respect to family law, a quantum leap took place, aligning the Italian legal system to those of other industrialized nations. Thus, major portions of the 1942 Civil Code regulating family relationships were rewritten, and separation and no fault divorce were introduced. *See e.g.* C.c. Arts. 143, 144, 149 *et seq.* The resulting unitary and largely cohesive system is in harmony with Italian constitutional principles, until then not reflected in the law, of the equality between the spouses, the preeminence of the interests of children, and the protection of individual liberties within family life in what has been called the "privatization of family relationships." MICHELE SESTA, CODICE DELLA FAMIGLIA 8 (Giuffrè Ed. 2007) (hereinafter, Sesta).

Second, the comparative study of U.S. and Italian family law illustrates a parallelism between the systems in that constitutional law, albeit in different ways, plays a central role in family law reform on both sides of the Atlantic. In the U.S., court decisions with respect to family matters have been constantly expounding principles of equality between spouses under the Equal Protection Clause, and the respective role of divorced spouses in child rearing. In Italy, on the other hand, the initially unheeded mandates of COST. Art. 29 (equality between the spouses) and Art. 30 (equality between legitimate and illegitimate children) became the cornerstone of the sweeping family law reform of the 1970s, while the doctrinal discourse centers around the interpretation and refinement of the new Civil Code provisions in light of the constitutional norms regarding the family.

Third, Italy is an interesting choice for comparative study particularly with respect to divorce because of the notable peculiarity that the legal development of the subject area cannot be understood without reference to the influence (some may say interference) of what amounts to a politically foreign sovereign: the Holy See. Italian family law is uniquely connected to this legal and religious system through the device of an international treaty known as the New Concordat. *See* NEW CONCORDAT, TREATY BETWEEN THE ITALIAN REPUBLIC AND THE HOLY SEE, February 18, 1984. At the risk of stating the obvious, the Holy See does not recognize divorce as a valid method of rescission of the matrimonial sacrament, which can only be terminated through the ecclesiastical procedure of annulment available in a relatively short list of situations. *See* NEW CONCORDAT, Art. 8(2). Since the ceremonial marriage before a catholic priest perfects both a religious sacrament and a legal contract and status, the introduction of separation and divorce created a quandary in this area of the law.

Fourth, Italy represents a uniquely valid choice for comparative analysis because its family and divorce law is now rapidly evolving under the influence of yet another supranational sovereign, the E.U. The pervasive "presence" of the E.U., whose original mission was mainly economic in nature, with its consistent attempts to foster legislative uniformity among its ever increasing member base, is now extending to matters traditionally reserved to each member state, adding layers of complexity in comparative analysis. E.U. family law makes the U.S./Italy comparative study even more fertile. Indeed, the E.U.'s more or less gentle, more or less paternalistic, more or less persuasive interference in family law matters in Italy echoes U.S. federal interventions vis-à-vis the individual states.

Including a civil law nation from Asia and one from Europe adds an extra comparative dimension. While both China and Italy are civil law countries, large cultural, religious, political and social differences exist between them and between their continents that influence their legal traditions, particularly in the area of divorce law.

Comparing Geographic and Demographic Data

Not sure exactly where Shapingba, Chongqing is located? Wondering if Bologna, Italy has anything to do with the development of the similarly named lunchmeat? Can't remember where the U.S. ranks in worldwide population? No problem. To give readers at least a barebones frame of reference, some demographic and geographic statistical information is offered about the respective countries and cities where our hypothetical divorce will be filed. Most of the information below comes from THE WORLD FACT BOOK compiled by the U.S. Central Intelligence Agency (available at https://www.cia. gov/library/publications/the-world-factbook/index.html).

Although some might be reticent about relying on information provided by the notorious American spy agency, THE WORLD FACT BOOK is regarded as a reliable, up-to-date source, collecting information from U.S. agencies and organizations such as the Bureau of the Census, Department of Defense, Department of Labor, and the National Science Foundation. Readers need to consult history, sociology, and anthropology texts for a deeper cultural understanding and travel guides for more colorful descriptions. Borrowing from Sgt. Joe Friday in the 1960s U.S. television series, *Dragnet*, these are "just the facts," and very basic ones at that.

United States

Located in North America between Canada and Mexico, the United States has a population of approximately 301 million people, including a labor force of 151.4 million, and a land area of 9,161,923 square kilometers. It is the world's third largest country both in size (after Russia and Canada) and population (after China and India). The U.S. is comprised of fifty states, including Alaska and Hawaii, and the District of Columbia, where the capital is located.

The U.S. has the largest economy in the world. The Gross Domestic Product (GDP) in 2006 was $12.98 trillion, or $43,500 per capita. Twelve percent of the population lives below the poverty line. While highly diversified, the economy is primarily service-based, with 78.6% of the GDP coming from services, 20.4% from industrial processes, and 0.9% from agriculture.

The U.S., of course, imports and exports massive quantities of consumer products and other goods and materials. Exports break down on a percentage basis by type of product as follows: 9% agricultural products, 27% industrial supplies, 49% capital goods (*e.g.,* aircraft, computers, telecommunications equipment), and 15% consumer goods. Imports are divided as follows: 5% agricultural products, 33% industrial supplies (including oil), 30% capital goods, and 32% consumer goods.

Ethnically, the U.S. population is roughly 69% non-Hispanic white, 13% Hispanic, 13% black, 4% Asian, and 1% Native American and Alaska native. Religiously, the population is divided as follows: 52% Protestant, 24% Roman Catholic, 2% Mormon, 1% Jewish, 1% Muslim, 10% other, and 10% either nonreligious or no religious preference. English is the dominant language (82%), with Spanish being the second most prevalent language (11%). Ninety-nine percent of the U.S. population over the age of fifteen can read and write.

The United States is also known for having the world's highest divorce rate (4.95 per 1000 population), whereas China and Italy both have much lower divorce rates (1.46 and .27 per 1000 population, respectively).

Memphis, Tennessee, where our hypothetical case will be filed, is the largest city in Tennessee, with a population of more than 680,000, and is also the seventeenth largest city in the United States. The greater Memphis metropolitan area includes more than 1.2 million persons. Located on the mighty Mississippi River, the city is probably best known for Graceland, the home of Elvis Presley; the Lorraine Motel, the site of Dr. Martin Luther King's Assassination; Beale Street, the home of the blues; and the Memphis in May, month-long outdoor celebration, honoring a different country each year and including the World Championship Bar-B-Q Cook-off.

China

Located in Eastern Asia, the People's Republic of China is the most populous country in the world with 1.3 billion people, including a labor force of

803.3 million, and a land area of 9,326,410 square kilometers, slightly smaller than the U.S. China is comprised of twenty-one provinces, five autonomous regions, and four municipalities, including Shanghai, Chongqing, and Beijing, where the capital is located.

China's economy has changed gradually from a centrally planned system to a market system since 1978. The economic reform has stimulated a double-digit growth rate for nearly thirty years. In 2007, China stood as the second largest economy in the world, after the U.S. The GDP in 2007 was $6.991 trillion, or $5,300 per capita. Unlike the U.S., where the economy is primarily service-based, in China, 48.6% of the GDP comes from industry, 40.1% from services, and 11.3% from agriculture.

As a country with the largest population and limited natural resources, China imports machinery and equipment, oil and mineral fuels, plastics, LED screens, optical and medical equipment, organic chemicals, and copper. In 2007, China imported $901.3 billion in such products and materials. China had $1.217 trillion in exports in 2007, in commodities, including machinery, electrical products, apparel, textile, steel, and mobile phones. The 2007 account balance is $360.7 billion.

Ethnically, 91.5% of China's population is Han Chinese, and 8.5% is Zhuang, Manchu, Hui, Miao, Uyghur, Tujia, Yi, Mongol, Tibetan, Buyi, Dong, Yao, Korean, and other nationalities. Religiously, China is officially atheist, with 3%–4% population Daoist, Buddhist, and Christian, and 1%–2% population Muslim. Mandarin is the dominant language, although large populations speak Cantonese, Shanghainese, Taiwanese, Xiang, Gan, Hakka dialects, and other minority languages.

Chongqing, the city where our hypothetical case will be filed, is the largest and most populous provincial-level municipality, with a population of 31 million. Until March 14, 1997, Chongqing was a sub-provincial city within Sichuan Province in Southeast China. Although the majority of the population is ethnic Han, numerous minority groups including Tibetan, Miao, Qiang, and Tujia reside in the city. Founded 3000 years ago, Chongqing is a port city located in the upper reaches of the Yantze River, which cuts through nearby Mount Wushan to create the world famous Three Gorges. The unique Three Gorges Dam is the focal point of Chongqing's tourist attractions. Chongqing is also famous for its spicy Sichuan Cuisine and hotpot delicacy.

Italy

Located in the South of Europe, Italy has a population of 58.1 million people, including a labor force of 24.6 million and a land area of 301,230 square kilometers, roughly the size of Florida and Georgia combined. This uniquely boot shaped peninsula stretching across the Mediterranean Sea, with annexed islands of Sicily and Sardinia is bordered by France to the Northwest, Switzerland and Austria to the North, and Slovenia to the Northeast. The peninsula also includes the two foreign sovereigns of San Marino and the Holy See. Italy is a parliamentary republic since June 2, 1946, when the preceding monarchic form of government was abolished by popular referendum. Administratively, the Republic is divided into twenty Regions, five of which are administered by special statute.

After WWII, Italy underwent a radical structural, social, political, and economic change. From a largely agrarian and static society, Italy became a major player in the world economy within a few decades, currently claiming sixth place among the industrialized nations of the world. The Gross Domestic Product (GDP) in 2006 was $1.756 trillion, or $30,200 per capita, even though it is estimated that as much as 27% of the economy is underground, which does not contribute to the correction of the budget deficit which continues to elude any administration.

Like the U.S. and other leading European nations, Italy has a primarily service-based economy, counting for 69% of the GDP, while industry and commerce make up 29.1%, and agriculture 2%. Italy's largely mountainous terrain is unsuitable for large scale farming. The North produces primarily grains, sugar beets, meat, and dairy, while the South produces vegetables, fruits, oil, and wine, employing 1.4 million people altogether. The country remains a net food importer. Italy is also a net energy importer, counting for internally produced natural resources only the natural gas extracted in the Po Valley and off-shore in the Adriatic Sea. Italy also imports most of the raw materials for its manufacturing and processing industries, which are mostly comprised of small and medium sized firms. Italy's most prominent industries produce precision machinery, motor vehicles, chemicals, pharmaceuticals, fashion, and clothing.

Ethnically, Italy's population has been largely homogeneous until recent years when massive immigration waves have posed unprecedented challenges to the receiving centers at the major ports of entry and to the infrastructures trying to accommodate the newcomers from North Africa, and Eastern Europe. Still, over 90% of the population is Italian, with significant and rapidly changing percentages of Germans and Albanians. The country's predominant religion is Roman Catholic. Literacy stands at 98% of the adult population.

Bologna, where the divorce will be filed, is the "*Capoluogo*" (administrative center, similar to a U.S. state capital) of the Region Emilia-Romagna, with 400,000 inhabitants (swelling to 500,000 when the university is in session) and over 1 million in the greater metropolitan area, a thriving commercial and industrial hub at the foot of the Appennini Mountains overlooking the Po Valley. Founded by the Etruscans, at one point the second most populous city of the Roman Empire along the Via Emilia, and later the fourth largest city in Europe, Bologna sits at the natural intersection of thoroughfares connecting the major centers of the North of Italy and Europe with the Center and South of Italy, for which it has developed a competitive infrastructure, including the Airport Guglielmo Marconi, fifth largest in Italy, and the Fiera Center, the fourth largest exhibition area in Europe. Nicknamed "*la dotta*" (the learned one) the city boasts the oldest University in Europe, dating to 1088, particularly known to this day for its School of Law. Another nickname that Bologna earned is "*la ghiotta*" (the gourmand) for its world renown cuisine featuring rich *tortellini* and *tagliatelle alla Bolognese*, (yes, the meat sauce!) and cured meats like *salame, prosciutto*, and *mortadella di Bologna*, a veritable culinary homage to the city's rich historical past.

The city wears proudly its historical vestiges, dating from the Roman times through the Middle Ages and the Renaissance, woven into its modern metropolitan layout, and features a historical center with timeless monuments, cathedrals, and buildings along with miles of unique porticoes as the backdrop to its bustling high-tech twenty-first century life. Likewise, with somber respect, Bologna lives a sad part of its more recent history with the memorial of the ruins, forever embedded in the prompt reconstruction, of the terrorist bomb explosion at its Central Railway Station on August 2, 1980, which killed eighty-five people during the busiest tourist transit month of the year.

Comparing Court Systems, Judges, and Legal Professions

Before one could begin to understand how an automobile transmission works, he or she would have to know what an automobile looks like. Similarly, before attempting to understand how a divorce case is handled in a particular legal system, one needs at least a snapshot of the overall system. Here's an overview of the court structures, judiciaries, and legal professions in the U.S., China, and Italy.

United States

Courts. The U.S. is a federalist system in which a federal, or national, court system operates both independently from and interdependently with separate court systems in each of the fifty states. Each system (that is, the federal judicial system and the judicial system of each state) has a set of trial courts, usually one or more intermediate appellate courts, and a single high court, called the Supreme Court in the federal system and in most states. The classic representational diagram is a triangle or pyramid with the trial courts lining the bottom, a much smaller number of intermediate appellate courts filling a layer in the middle, and a single high court at the top. Most U.S. courts, both state and federal, are courts of general jurisdiction, although specialized federal tax and bankruptcy courts exist, and some states have specialized courts in areas such as family law, juvenile law, and probate law.

The federal court system is made up of ninety-four trial courts known as U.S. District Courts spread across the country, thirteen intermediate appellate courts known as U.S. Courts of Appeal (eleven regional courts of appeal, plus courts of appeal for the Federal Circuit and the District of Columbia Circuit), and the U.S. Supreme Court. Federal district courts and judgeships are allocated roughly according to population and corresponding caseload. Thus, largely rural Idaho and North Dakota have only one federal district court with two judges each, whereas populous Tennessee (home to our divorce case) has three district courts and nineteen district court judges. Our divorce, however, will not be heard in the federal court. It will be heard in the state court system.

Civil subject matter jurisdiction in the federal court system is primarily limited to cases involving federal questions (*e.g.*, a dispute involving a federal statute or a provision of the U.S. Constitution) or those where the opposing parties are citizens of different states and the amount in controversy exceeds $75,000. *See* 28 U.S.C. § 1331 (federal question jurisdiction); 28 U.S.C. § 1332 (diversity of citizenship jurisdiction). Diversity of citizenship jurisdiction, however, allows some state cases to be brought in federal court when the parties are residents of different states. When federal subject matter jurisdiction is based on diversity of citizenship, federal courts are required to apply the substantive legal rules of the state in which the case arose under the *Erie* doctrine, from *Erie R.R. v. Tompkins*, 304 U.S. 64 (1938). Thus, a federal court hearing a state case filed in Tennessee would be required to apply the substantive common law and statutory rules of the state of Tennessee to the case. Diversity jurisdiction does not apply to divorce cases, however, because of the "domestic relations exception," which precludes federal courts from hearing divorce, alimony, and child custody cases. Family law, including divorce law, has traditionally been a matter of state law and all divorce cases are filed in state courts.

In addition to the federal judicial system, each state has its own unified judicial system, which usually includes trial courts, intermediate appellate courts, and a state high court. Most civil disputes, and, as noted, all divorces, are filed in state court.

Contrary to the view of the American justice system generated by movies and television, very few civil cases that are filed actually go to trial in the U.S. Most cases settle or are dismissed. With regard to divorce cases, estimates suggest that more than 90% of the cases settle prior to trial. Trials are very expensive for the parties. Many courts encourage or require the parties to engage in alternative dispute resolution techniques, such as mediation, in order to encourage settlements prior to trial.

Trials are presided over by a single judge in both the federal and state systems. The right to a trial by jury, a fundamental distinguishing feature from civil law systems, is guaranteed by both the federal and forty-seven of the fifty state constitutions. Again running contrary to public perception, a majority of civil cases that go to trial in the U.S. are "bench" trials; that is, trials before judges rather than juries. Although the right to jury trial is constitutionally guaranteed in some cases, one of the parties must demand a jury or the right will be deemed waived. In a majority of divorce cases, the parties are content with a trial before a judge only. In other types of civil cases, such as personal injury cases, for instance, plaintiffs almost always demand a jury trial.

Assuming that a party can point to an alleged error in the trial court, an appeal, as of right, exists to an intermediate appellate court in the federal and most state systems. The percentage of divorce cases that are appealed is obviously going to be higher in states that permit an appeal as of right. The number will also be higher in those states in which the appellate courts are perceived to be more willing to reverse the trial courts' decisions. As we will see, trial judges have a great deal of discretion in deciding many of the issues in divorce cases. Those decisions involving the greatest amount of judicial discretion are the ones most likely to be reversed on appeal. For instance, the passage of child support guidelines have removed most of the judicial discretion in setting child support, but there are no similar guidelines for spousal support in most states. Thus, one would expect to find more appeals challenging spousal support awards than child support awards. Appeals to the highest court of the state are usually not as of right, in those states with intermediate appellate courts, so there are many fewer divorce cases reviewed by the states' highest courts.

Judges. Federal judges are nominated by the President and must be confirmed by the U.S. Senate. They are appointed for life. A majority of states still rely on popular elections to select some or all of their judges for a term of years, although the trend, particularly for appellate judges, is toward eliminating judicial elections in favor of judicial appointments by governors or legislatures, usually with the help of judicial nominating commissions. Even appointed state judges often are subject to regular retention votes, an arrangement in which citizens are asked to vote "yes" or "no" every few years as to whether the judge should be retained on the bench. Unless the judge has become controversial for some reason, these merit retention votes usually operate as perfunctory stamps of approval.

Judges in the U.S. rarely begin their legal careers as members of the bench. Becoming a judge is an honor usually reserved for a select group of lawyers who have established themselves and their reputations over many years as practitioners.

Given the starring role of judges in a common law system, including the general recognition (if not complete popular acceptance) of the principle of judicial supremacy, U.S. judges stand out much more than their counterparts in civil law countries. Most U.S. law students can rattle off the names of legendary judges such as Benjamin Cardozo, Learned Hand, Oliver Wendell Holmes, and John Marshall, as well as current U.S. Supreme Court justices. Some judges of lesser status become household names among laypersons due to their handling of cases attracting substantial media attention. This is not the case in civil law countries, where most judges labor in obscurity.

Legal profession. Statistics compiled by the American Bar Association show that in 2006 the U.S. had 1,116,967 lawyers, approximately one lawyer for every 270 citizens. Approximately 30.2% of U.S. lawyers are women. Not surprisingly, the majority of lawyers are concentrated in heavily populated areas. New York has the most lawyers (144,599), while North Dakota has the fewest (1,368). In 2006, the U.S. had 195 law schools accredited by the American Bar Association, as well as some unaccredited law schools. Enrollment at accredited law schools stands at about 148,600 students, divided almost evenly between men and women. Law school is a three-year graduate program leading to a Juris Doctor degree. (Warning: If you are a U.S. law student and this comes as news to you, step back and reassess your career plans.) A four-year undergraduate degree is a prerequisite to law school admission. To qualify to practice, a law school graduate must take and pass an intensive state-administered examination known with fear and trepidation among law students as "the bar exam."

China*

Courts. Unlike the federalist system in the U.S., China adopts a unitary system in which a central government is composed of a legislative branch, an ad-

---

* This part is written by Chen Wei, Pi Xijun, and Lai Wenbin.

ministrative branch and a judiciary branch. The legislative branch makes law and is called the National People's Congress (NPC). The administrative branch executes law and exercises the administrative power of the state. The State Council is the highest power of state government. The judiciary branch is further divided into two branches: the court which applies the law to resolve disputes, and the procurator which prosecutes criminal offenses and oversees the activities of the public security and state security agencies, people's courts, and prisons to ensure that proper laws and procedures are being applied.

In China, the judicial organs are called "people's courts." Similar to the U.S. system but with one additional level, people's courts are classified into four levels: 1) the Supreme People's Court (SPC); 2) high people's court, provincial level; 3) intermediate people's court, between provincial and country level; 4) basic people's court, country or municipal level. People's courts also include special courts such as military courts, railway transport courts, forestry courts, farm courts, petroleum courts, and other special courts. However, no family court is established in China.

As the highest judicial organ, the SPC supervises the judicial work of people's courts in all lower levels and special people's courts. The people's court at higher levels supervise the judicial work of the people's court at the next-lower level. Basic people's courts are county and municipal level courts which adjudicate criminal and civil cases of first instance. However, criminal cases carrying the death penalty or life imprisonment are excluded from basic people's courts' jurisdiction. In its discretion, the basic people's courts can request cases of major importance to be transferred to higher-level courts. The intermediate people's courts have first instance jurisdiction over cases transferred from basic people's court, cases dealing with foreign parties, and criminal cases subject to life or death sentences. The courts of this level can also, in their discretion, request that important cases be transferred to high people's courts. The high people's courts hear, in the first instance, major criminal cases which impact the entire province, cases transferred from lower courts, and cases appealed from lower courts' judgments.

The people's court follows the principle of openness in the adjudication of cases. Article 7 of the LAW ON THE ORGANIZATION OF PEOPLE's COURTS provides that all cases in the people's courts shall be heard in public, except for those involving state secrets, private affairs of individuals, and crimes involving minors. Some civil cases, such as divorce cases, may be heard in private sessions if the parties concerned so request.

In the administration of justice, the people's courts adopt the system whereby the second instance is the last instance. This means a case is closed after going through two levels of trial. Within the time period prescribed by law, the party concerned has the right to appeal to the people's court at a higher level from the judgment made by a local people's court in a case of first instance. If the party concerned does not appeal against the judgment, the judgment will become final once the time period for appealing expires. The judgment made by a higher people's court is final for the appealed case. However, cases involving the death penalty need to be reviewed by the Supreme People's Court. Although second instance is usually final, all rulings and judgments made by the Supreme People's Court, even in the first instance, are final.

Compared with the United States, China's divorce rate is not high. However, with the continuous development of China's society and economy, significant changes have taken place in people's opinions regarding marriage and family. The divorce rate is rising year by year. In 2003, the national divorce rate was 0.105%, 0.015% more than in 2002. In 2004, the national divorce rate was 0.128%, an increase of 0.025%, compared with that in 2003. In 2005, the national divorce rate was 0.137%, growing by 0.009% over the last year. In 2006, 1,913,000 couples got divorced in the Chinese mainland, increasing by 128,000 pairs those in the previous year; the national divorce rate was 0.146%, a rise of 0.009% over the previous year. In addition, in 2005, among the 4,360,184 civil cases handled by basic people's courts at various levels, cases concerning marriage, family, and succession totaled 1,132,458, accounting for 25.97% of all civil cases. In addition, in 2006, the basic people's courts handled 4,382,407 civil cases, among which, 1,159,437 were cases concerning marriage, family, and succession, making up 26.46% of all civil cases.

Judges. The system of people's congress is the organ through which the people exercise state power. The people's congresses at all levels are constituted through democratic elections, and they are responsible to the people and subject to people's supervision. The President of the Supreme People's Court is elected by the National People's Congress. The vice-presidents, chief judges, associate chief judges, and judges are appointed or removed by the Standing Committee of the National People's Congress, which is the permanent body of the NPC and exercises the power of the highest state organ when the NPC is not in session. Similarly, Presidents of local people's courts at various levels are elected by the local people's congresses at corresponding levels. Their vice-presidents, chief judges, associate chief judges, and judges are appointed and removed by the standing committees of the local people's congresses at corresponding levels.

First-hearing minor criminal cases and economic dispute cases handled by the basic people's court could be tried by a one-judge court. Other first-hearing criminal and civil cases are heard by collegiate panels consisting of an odd number of at least three judges or a combination of judges and people's assessors. Citizens who have the right to vote, have never been deprived of political rights, and have reached the age of twenty-three are eligible to be elected people's assessors. The people's assessors are considered as members of the divisions of the courts in which they participate, and enjoy equal rights with the judges, during the period in which they are functioning as people's assessors. The collegiate panel is a basic form of the people's court. When collegiate panels cannot reach a unanimous opinion, the majority opinion controls. The opinion of the minority should also be recorded in the court record with signatures of the panel members.

People's courts at all levels may, according to their needs, be staffed with assistant judges, who are appointed or removed by the people's courts themselves. Assistant judges help the judges do their work. Upon the recommendation of the president of the court and with the approval of the judicial committee, an assistant judge may provisionally exercise the functions of a judge.

People's courts at all levels have clerks to keep records of the court proceedings and to take charge of other matters concerning the trials. Local people's courts at various levels have marshals to carry out the execution of judgments and orders in civil cases and the execution, in criminal cases, of the parts of judgments and orders concerned with property. Local people's courts at various levels have forensic physicians. People's courts at all levels have a certain number of judicial policemen who provide security and maintain order.

Legal Profession. Similar to Italy, and different from the U.S. three-year full-time post-graduate J.D. program, the Chinese legal education system is a regular undergraduate education in colleges and universities. To practice law, a person must acquire a judicial qualification and a lawyer's practice certificate. For judicial qualification, anyone who fulfills the academic legal course requirement in a law major or other majors of universities may acquire the judicial qualification by passing the national judicial examination, which is similar to the "bar exam" in the U.S. For a lawyer's practice certificate, a person must practice in a law firm for a full year, and must be a person of good character and conduct.

According to the latest statistics, the number of practicing lawyers has reached about 150,000, and more than 10,000 law firms have been set up in China. Eighty percent of lawyers mainly act as litigators; the others provide services in non-litigation legal affairs. The proportion of lawyers is 1 for every 10,000 citizens in China. More and more enterprises recognize the significant role of lawyers in their business, and engage lawyers as legal counsel. The lawyer profession is promising. L Guohua, *The Gap Between Lawyers and Enterprisers in China, at*: http://www.wn315.com/shop_info_view.asp?id=2598.

A lawyer in China is required to join his local lawyers' association. A lawyers association is the lawyers' self-disciplinary organization. The All-China

Lawyers Association is national level lawyer association, while local lawyers associations are established in provinces, autonomous regions, and municipalities. Local lawyers associations may be established according to the need of each city. A lawyer who has joined his local lawyers association is automatically a member of the All-China Lawyers Association.

Italy

Courts. Italy operates under a system of courts of general jurisdiction, supplemented by courts of special jurisdiction for administrative, auditing, military, and fiscal matters. General jurisdiction courts include the Justice of the Peace, the (Ordinary) Tribunals, the Monitoring Tribunals (overseeing the execution of penal sentences), Juvenile Courts, Court of Appeals, and the Court of Cassation, which is the supreme court of last resort, located in Rome. Additionally, there are special Assizse Tribunals, composed of two career judges and six lay judges, who have jurisdiction over the most heinous criminal cases. Laterally, and with special review functions, there is also a Constitutional Court, also located in Rome, composed of fifteen judges selected through a constitutionally mandated process by the highest representatives of the three branches of government, whose mandate is to decide on the constitutionality of all laws and decrees promulgated by the legislative branch.

The courts of general jurisdiction handle most civil and criminal cases including family and divorce matters. Among them, jurisdiction for divorce cases belongs to the Ordinary Tribunals of first instance. The independence of the judiciary, constitutionally mandated, is safeguarded by the *Consiglio Superiore della Magistratura*, (the Superior Council of the Judiciary). The judiciary is an autonomous and independent organ not subject to any other power of the state. *See* Cost. Art. 104. Administrative jurisdiction is vested in the Regional Tribunals (*Tribunali Amministrativi Regionali*), known as the TAR. Each of the twenty regions has its own TAR.

The tribunals of general jurisdiction, however, belong to a unitary system of administration of justice which functions on a three tier basis. There are currently 159 Ordinary Tribunals handling civil and most criminal matters in the first instance. Appeal is taken to the twenty-two District Courts of Appeal located, for the most part, in the cities *Capoluogo di Regione* (administrative centers for each Region, similar to a U.S. state capitals).

Judges. Unlike in the U.S., in Italy, as in other civil law countries, judges are relatively low profile civil servants. A career on the bench is one of the many options open to law school graduates (see below under **Legal Profession** for a general description of the legal education curriculum). To become a judge, the candidate enters into a judicial clerkship type program which lasts a couple of years, then sits for a state exam very similar to the Italian bar exam. Because this career path is in the public sector, scores in university exams, dissertation scores, and pass scores in the two-tiered written and oral sessions of the admission exam become crucially important to compete for the finite available posts. Academic performance is uniquely important to this career choice not only to be admitted to the judgeship exam, but also to qualify for a particular judgeship in the area of one's preference. In point of fact, the first appointment for the newly admitted judge may very well be to some remote area removed from her place of origin. Later transfers to different, more coveted locations must be postponed until one has satisfactorily completed the initial probationary period. Approval of a transfer request is based mostly on seniority and subject to post availability.

This unadorned description obscures the tremendous importance and prestige of a career in the pubic sector in Italy, as in most civil law systems. Although generally commanding a lower pay as compared to a successful career as a lawyer in private practice or even as a lawyer employee in the private sector, the bench attracts some of the best students and best minds because of its competitiveness, and because of the many advantages it offers: life tenure, government benefits, personal prestige, respect, opportunities for advancement, and promotions based on service and seniority.

While the profession of judge in Italy commands the respect of the private legal community and of society at large, the function of the judge remains that of application of the law. The judge has a great deal of discretion in the interpretation and application of the law especially where, as in family matters, the black letter law is in the form of broad brush principles or literally relies on the judge's expertise to reach the best solution, keeping in mind the objectives of the code provisions, the supplementary statutes and decrees, and the overarching principles enunciated in the Constitution. However, only occasionally a judge will forge new interpretive paths, and even if and when he does, he is just as likely to go in a different direction the next time around, in the interest of justice, without having or causing a problem with the legal system. Different judges will use more or less of the "wiggle room" the law gives them to create the law of the case and to achieve justice in the case at hand. On the other hand, uniformity of training, the possibility of reversal on appeal, and the impact of career aspirations are all factors contributing to produce consistency of application and interpretation.

Legal Profession. As of 2006, there were approximately 180,000 lawyers licensed to practice in Italy, of which about 73,000 were women, although just over 121,000 were in active practice. Most law schools in Italy are public. Legal education follows the patterns of most civil law countries. While in the U.S. legal education starts after the undergraduate studies as a specialized post-graduate three-year program (four years for part time programs), academic legal education in Italy is a regular university program to which students gain access after completing a five-year high school preparation. The program is four years full time of intensive university studies geared at familiarizing the students with the theory and philosophy of law, as well as the basic tenets of the relevant areas of law encompassed by the codes, the Constitution, and the most prominent laws and decrees in effect. However, most students do not qualify for graduation within the four years but take at least five to graduate. This is because, besides meeting the very demanding program requirements in terms of class work, to qualify for graduation, the students are required to prepare and "defend" one major and two minor dissertations, like in most U.S. Ph.D. programs. The university program confers a Doctorate in Jurisprudence, which in turn is the prerequisite to a mandatory practical training for both the career paths of lawyers and judges (See **Judges** above.) This mandatory practical training is similar to a clerkship (whether judicial in preparation for the state exam for judgeship, or in a law office in preparation for the state bar exam for private practice) generally with little or no pay, during which graduates receive practical training and actively partake in legal work, drafting legal documents, negotiating settlements, working with clients, becoming involved in case preparation and presentation in court, or in support work for the court, as the case may be.

As it pertains to the postgraduate training for private practice, after two years, the graduate, generally already admitted provisionally to practice under the tutelage of the training lawyer, can sit for the written portion of the state bar exam, a two day ordeal not unlike a U.S. bar exam, consisting of essays in multiple subject areas. After successfully passing the written state bar exam (the pass rate is quite low as compared to U.S. state bar exams), in another six months, the candidate faces the last tribulation before permanent admission to practice, consisting of a two to three hour oral exam in front of a panel of seven judges. Passing the second (oral) part of the exam allows the candidate full admission to the local Bar, under the auspices of the District Court of Appeals for the attorneys. Currently, the training program and state exams are bifurcated for preparation and admission to either private practice or judgeship. Both paths present similarities of approach and training, and, therefore, the graduate could conceivably sit for both state exams if he so chooses, although he would have to do so at least one year apart from each other, in order to have potentially a private practice and a public service career path open to him.

La *"dottrina"* (the doctrine). A concept and an aspect of the legal profession which deserves mention in the Italian legal system is the doctrine, a term that will appear repeatedly in this book. The doctrine is at any given time the latest interpretation and application trend of the law in a given area as embodied in the writings of respected scholars and teachers of law (*diritto*). It is, in other words, the work product of another portion of the legal profession: teaching and scholarship. Albeit somewhat elusive, the doctrine is apparently well understood and accepted both conceptually and practically by scholars, judges, and private law practitioners alike. Indeed, all "actors" in the legal scene are known to refer profusely to the doctrine in their writings, including legal briefs and court opinions, at times quoting the source specifically, and other times by general reference without further specification.

Indeed, traditionally, in civil law systems, scholars, teachers and professors of law have been shrouded with great clout, and their opinions expressed in their writings and in their lectures relative to the meaning of the black letter law, or the "true" intention of the "legislator" (legislature) in enacting this or that norm, has been held in the highest esteem, and, as such, it has been and is the object of deference in legal practice. This is because, historically, from the time of Justinian all the way to modern times, to be admitted to the scholarly circles of professors and analytical thinkers worthy of a teaching assignment in a renown university (*"titolare di cattedra,"* literally "owning title to the desk") was a highly coveted position to be achieved only by the best and the brightest, normally as the culmination of a successful career in law practice and after lengthy mentoring by other renown scholars. The rewards of this alternative second career lie not so much in financial rewards, or in the practical accomplishment of helping clients, but in the prestige afforded by research and scholarly work, in the respect it elicits in all legal professionals, in the intellectual challenge, and in the opportunities for achievement, recognition, and participation in shaping the evolution of the law.

CHAPTER 3

Sources of Law

The last preliminary stage before setting forth and analyzing Lily's and Mario's hypothetical divorce case is to gain insight into the sources of law in common law versus civil law countries, as well as the specific sources of divorce law in the U.S., China, and Italy. "Where does law come from?" is a question that goes to the heart of the core differences between common law and civil law traditions. As will be seen throughout this book, the answers in real life are quite different from popular perception. Scholars have been researching and writing about common and civil law legal traditions for hundreds of years. The discussion below is an over-simplified thumbnail review of the sources of law in the two traditions, followed by a more detailed discussion of the sources of divorce law in the U.S., China, and Italy.

Where Does Law Come From? — An Overview

Common Law: As the Case May Be

It is regularly said that the central distinguishing feature of a common law tradition is that the primary source of law is a body of case law developed by judges known as "precedent." The inventory of judicial precedent in the U.S. is large. West's National Reporter System, which publishes judicial opinions of both state and federal courts, contains more than 11,000 volumes of precedent from more than six hundred U.S. courts. The system adds more than 130,000 decisions each year. Theoretically, under the doctrine of *stare decisis*, if a case is "binding precedent," the rule of the case must be followed by a court confronted with similar facts in a subsequent case.

Simplistically, binding precedent in state systems consists of cases decided by a higher court of the same jurisdiction that cannot be distinguished from the case at bar. Thus, the decision of a state supreme court is binding precedent on all other courts in that state, including trial courts and intermediate appellate courts. Contrarily, a decision of the high court of a different state would not be binding, although it might be considered persuasive. Similarly, a federal court decision interpreting state law might be considered persuasive, but would not be binding on a state court. In the federal system, decisions by the U.S. Courts of Appeal are binding on the federal district courts in the same federal circuit. Decisions of the U.S. Supreme Court interpreting federal law are "the law of the land," binding in all state and federal courts.

Reality diverges from theory with regard to the binding nature of judicial precedent in the U.S. common law system. Although a system in which precedent controls the outcome of cases would seem to assure a degree of certainty and predictability in adjudicating cases, in practice, common law decision-making allows for great flexibility in reaching decisions.

The conventional view of judging in a common law system is a simplistic one: decisions are arrived at by applying existing rules of law from similar cases to known facts. In the early twentieth century, a school of critical analysis known as legal realism emerged in the U.S. that challenged this conventional view, a view Roscoe Pound labeled "mechanical jurisprudence." Legal realism served as an ancestor to the critical legal studies movement of the late twentieth century. Without embracing everything the realists had to say, their critique of formulaic judging is useful for our overview of common law decision making.

Realists rejected the notion that judges act only as "living oracles" of the law who merely apply rather than make law. They believed that neither legal rules nor the process of judicial fact determination is certain enough to provide a sound basis for predicting the outcome of litigation, controlling judicial discretion, or evaluating judges and the bases for their decisions. In other words, they essentially argued that there is little precedent that is truly binding. Though the realists did not always make the distinction clear, a rough dichotomy of philosophy existed between "fact skeptics" and "rule skeptics." Jurist and expositor of realist thought Jerome Frank elaborated on the difference in his book, *Law and the Modern Mind* (1963). The fact skeptics were concerned primarily with trial court decisions and the elusive nature of fact determination. Because the judge or jury chooses which facts to believe, and because such selection is frequently based on either conscious or unconscious prejudices, the fact skeptics believed there is little to constrain a trial court from reaching whatever decision it chooses. Because appellate courts have limited power in common law systems to disturb fact findings made by trial courts, the realists asserted that many trial court mistakes go uncorrected at the appellate level. Precedent, they argued, thus becomes of small value because the determination of the facts by the trial court, either the judge or jury, already has determined which precedent will control.

Rule skeptics focused on appellate court decisions. They were skeptical of the notion that the rules articulated by judges in a written decision provide reliable guidance in predicting the results of future cases, or even that the written decisions represent the true reasons for why the court reached the result it did. Their view was that judges do not decide cases by applying precedential rules to facts to reach a decision, but rather, operate in reverse by first arriving at a decision and then working backwards, searching for rules to support their conclusions. The rule skeptics believed that the rules expressed in judicial opinions mask the true reasons for the decision, including the mores, customs, social, economic, and political backgrounds of the judge.

The realists' basic points must be appreciated. The notion that all, or even most, decisions in common law systems are controlled by the mechanical application of "binding precedent" is not accurate. Even setting aside the cynical views held by some realists regarding the motivations of judges, few cases are identical to one another. A change in a single fact may command a different result from a prior, otherwise similar case. Thus, it should come as no surprise that judges in common law systems are required to make new law on a regular basis despite an ample body of precedent.

Moreover, one must remember that case law constitutes only one slice of the total law-pie in common law jurisdictions. Constitutions, statutes, and administrative regulations fill in the rest of the pie and they are each large slices indeed. The United States Code, the body of federal legislation binding in all fifty states, fills more than 34,000 pages, excluding tables and indices. John Merryman has observed that individual U.S. states have as much legislation in force as most civil law countries. Of course, constitutions, statutes, and regulations invariably require interpretation by courts in common law and, as seen below, civil law systems, adding another vast layer of judicial precedent.

Civil Law: An Ode to Codes

Whereas conventional wisdom holds that the primary source of law in common law systems is a body of binding judicial case precedent, the same wisdom holds that the *only* sources of law in civil law systems are codes and other legislation. This orthodoxy took root following the French Revolution in the late eighteenth century, which triggered the emergence of nation-states in Continental Europe and a belief in state sovereignty, both externally and inwardly, as a fundamental concept. Inwardly, this included the view that only the state, not individuals, could make law, a view that was reflected in a belief in the strict separation of power between legislatures and courts. Only the former had the power to make law for the state. *See generally* MERRYMAN, at 19–25.

Legislative power found its primary expression in codes. Codes form the basic blueprint of law in civil law countries. Codes are essentially books of statutes that set forth, in an organized fashion, the law in different subject areas. However, this description, while technically accurate, does not do justice to the importance of codes in civil law nations. In the way they are venerated, codes may be better analogized for common law students to constitutions rather than statutes. While U.S. statutes tend to be unsystematic, topical, specific, and prolix, codes purport to be organized and complete, yet succinct and rich in meaning. Organization is the key. That is what a code is supposed to do: place legal categories in order so that solutions to practical problems can be identified by the lawyers, sanctioned by the judges, and adhered to by everyone else. This helps explain why codes tend to be maintained even when they fall out of pace with the needs of modern societies.

Most civil law countries have separate codes addressing civil law, commercial law, criminal law, and civil and criminal procedure. Rights and obligations of ordinary citizens are addressed in the civil code, as well. Civil codes generally are arranged under headings such as the law of persons, family law, property law, succession law, and the law of obligations. With respect to family law, generally civil code provisions define the capacity to enter into a marriage, the ceremonial requirements, the rights and obligations of spouses relative to each other and their children, and the bases for separation and divorce. The civil code provisions are supplemented by a multitude of special laws dealing with specific sub-areas and by legislative decrees (*decreti legge*), generally dealing with yet narrower sub-topics in greater detail. The applicability of both code provisions and special laws pertaining to family and divorce generally extends uniformly throughout each country, whereas in the U.S. the law of divorce is particularly a state matter, with each of the fifty states having their own statutes and cases addressing the rights and obligations of the parties in a divorce proceeding. Increasingly, though, the federal government is becoming involved in divorce matters through federal statutes designed to address primarily the support and welfare of children (*i.e.*, Parental Kidnapping Prevention Act, PKPA), and the preference for heterosexual marriages (Federal Defense of Marriage Act DOMA). The federal statutes are binding on all the states. In addition, decisions by the U.S. Supreme Court that interpret the U.S. Constitution are binding throughout the country (i.e., *Loving v. Virginia*, 388 U.S. 1 (1967), striking down Virginia's antimiscegenation law).

The idea of a civil code, one that defines the rights and obligations of persons under various circumstances, is one most U.S. law students would find appealing. Frustrated by the indefiniteness of the common law, students frequently offer classroom comments such as, "Why don't they just write all the rules down in one place? That way, we'd know what the law is!" Without realizing it, they're advocating the ideology of a civil law system.

But can any body of statutory law really provide all the answers to the infinite variety of cases that arise day to day? Civil codes vary in their detail. The widely imitated French Napoleonic Code of 1804 was purposely written concisely so that it could be read and understood by ordinary citizens. Most of its provisions represent broad statements of general principle rather than specific rules of law. A utopian product of the French Revolution, one motivation for the code was to eliminate the need for lawyers by setting forth the law in a simple and straightforward way that could be read and understood by the masses.

At the other end of the spectrum is the Prussian Territorial Law of 1794. It stands as an attempt to implement what so many U.S. law students desperately wish for: a detailed compendium of rules intended to foresee and govern the entire range of human conduct. Enacted under Frederick the Great, the Prussian Code contained more than 17,000 provisions setting forth specific rules intended to govern specific fact situations. In theory, judges were prohibited from interpreting the code. Any questions of interpretation were to be referred to a special commission. It didn't work that way in practice. Even 17,000 provisions proved to be insufficient to cover all varieties of human conduct. Seventeen million provisions might not be enough. The Prussian Code broke down under its own weight. It was a failure. As an aside, Prussia eventually became part of Germany and the Prussian Territorial Law can be regarded as a predecessor to the national codification of German law that occurred after the unification of the formerly independent German states in 1871.

The highly influential German Civil Code (GCC) of 1896, discussed more extensively below, stands somewhere in between the user-friendly French Code and the unwieldy Prussian Code. The product of twenty years study and crafting in the late nineteenth century, the GCC is a "scientifically" thought-out code that, while it does not attempt to regulate the specific details of human conduct, is more precise and cohesively organized than the French Code. Whereas the goal of the French and other codes was to wipe out and replace preexisting law, the German code was based on a thorough study of the history of German law with the goal of implementing the lessons and essential principles of that history in a way that fit together systematically. *See generally* MERRYMAN, at 26–33 (discussing the French, Prussian, and German civil codes).

In addition to the codes, civil law countries regularly adopt other statutes or acts that are not part of the codes. Acts tend to address more specific subject matters and contain narrower provisions than codes. Acts in civil law countries are no different than legislative acts passed by Congress or state legislatures in the U.S. Nor is there any difference in legal effect between an act and a code provision, as they occupy the same level in the hierarchy of sources of law. If an act specifically addresses a matter, the act applies. In cases where an act leaves room for interpretation or does not answer a specific private law question, the more general provisions of the codes can be consulted. Of course, both code and act provisions often apply in the same case.

Under the strict view of separation of powers that is part of the foundation of the civil law tradition, judges are neither trusted to nor supposed to make law. Only legislators make law. The role of a judge is simply to *apply* the law — code or other statutory provisions — promulgated by the legislators. There is no doctrine of *stare decisis* or notion of binding precedent in civil law systems. In theory, the lowliest trial court judge in a civil law system can ignore decisions of the high court of last resort. To implement this philosophy, the goal is to create a body of statutory law so clear and comprehensive that there is no room for judicial interpretation. Whereas certainty is only one of many competing values in a common law system, it is a primary value of a civil law system.

But just as there is a divergence between theory and reality regarding the nature of precedent in common law systems, the above paragraph, while sound in theory, does not accurately describe the way civil law systems work. Civil law judges make law every day, just like common law judges.

Code provisions in particular usually are written in broad language. The provisions simply do not answer most of the questions that arise from case to case. In some cases, there might not be any directly applicable code provision, or just as problematic, more than one conflicting provision might apply. In these instances, there is no escaping that judges have to make law to resolve the case. While all case decisions must be rooted in a code or other statutory provision, it is common to find judicial decisions in civil law nations in which the court reaches a conclusion by stringing together deductions from a series of broadly worded code provisions, none of which says precisely what the court ends up deducing from them.

The simplistic view that civil law judges mechanically apply clear code or other statutory provisions to reach decisions is myth along the same lines as the myth that common law judges mechanically apply binding precedent to reach decisions. While it is true that, unlike in common law systems, judicial opinions in civil law countries are not binding in other cases, even in the same court, they are very influential. Despite the absence of any principle of *stare decisis*, civil law judges frequently rely on and cite to prior judicial decisions in resolving cases. Merryman writes that the civil law "judge may refer to a precedent because he is impressed by the authority of the prior court, because he is persuaded by its reasoning, because he is too lazy to think the problem through himself, because he does not want to risk reversal on appeal, or for a variety of other reasons." MERRYMAN, at 47. As will be seen herein, in family and divorce matters Italian lawyers and judges refer to the applicable code provisions, constitutional norms, and maxims extracted from the decisions of higher courts, particularly the Supreme Court of Cassation for explanation, interpretation, and concrete application of the rather terse legislative norms. As compared to the analysis and application prevailing in a common law system such as the U.S., Italian legal analysis starts at the code provision, or special law, as the only black letter, mandatory norm to apply in the concrete case, relying on doctrinal interpretation and judicial precedent only as a persuasive interpretive tool to help decide the case at hand.

Unlike in the U.S., in Italy, a case decision is not intended to change the law in any way, but only to apply existing law to a particular situation. In doing so, an opinion of the highest court may contribute to legal interpretation, but interpretive trends are only produced by consistent decisions of higher courts found persuasive by other courts and practitioners and sanctioned by doctrinal analysis. However, neither doctrinal distillation, nor case decisions—even if instructive or consistently followed—create law other than for the case at hand, as application remains susceptible of change in the next case.

Having noted that case law is highly influential in both common and civil law systems, this is an instance where merely observing the "sameness" glosses over deeper differences. Civil law judges do make law every day and some of their decisions, particularly those of high courts, may be influential, but there will likely always be a vast difference in the way common law judges make law and civil law judges make law. Civil law judges are concerned only with making the "law of the case." Their purpose is to solve the case before them, not shape the law generally, a function that is left to the legislators, and in the legal profession, to the scholars. Unlike in the U.S., court decisions in civil law countries often are not published in full format in easily accessible reporting systems. Scores of decisions give little explanation of their reasoning and receive very little or no attention. Judicial decisions often do not trace a cohesive development of the law. Rather, they constitute a sea of specific-to-the-case applications of legal principles. In one sense, interesting because it cuts against the grain of civil law ideology, civil law judges have more freedom than common law judges to apply whatever law best resolves the case, in part because their decisions need not be constrained by their possible effect on future cases.

Sources of Divorce Law

The hypothetical case we crafted to use as the vehicle for exploring divorce law in the United States, China, and Italy is a simple divorce case. One reason for pursuing a case-based approach in this book is to narrow the level of abstraction at which comparative law is often discussed. Thus, having addressed generally the sources of law in the U.S. common law system and civil law systems, we turn more specifically to the sources and development of divorce law in our three nations of study. Expanding on the points above, what follows turns upside down some of the traditional notions of the sources of law in common and civil nations. Far from being exclusively a case-based system, U.S. divorce law is becoming increasingly dominated by legislative controls, whereas it could be said that a trend in the opposite direction is slowly emerging in Italy where a relatively unitary and cohesive system of family law is being increasingly integrated by case law, commanding respect at least until *il legislatore* (the legislator, meaning the legislative branch) specifically intervenes. In China's civil law system, however, because only a small number of cases are published and available to the public, the interpretation of the divorce law is mainly carried out by the judge hearing the case. Although the Supreme People's Court occasionally interprets ambiguous issues of family law, such instances are much less frequent than in the common law jurisdictions of the U.S.

The sections below do not explain in detail the substantive theories of divorce law and how they function. That is left for later chapters. Rather, these paragraphs focus on the origins of those theories and their roots in the law.

United States

As previously mentioned, there is no comprehensive national divorce law. Instead, each of the fifty states has its own divorce law, including state constitutional provisions, statutes, and case law. Despite the local nature of divorce law, there is a great deal of similarity among the states in some instances. There are three principal reasons for the similarities.

First, the original states drew on the law of England, which was in effect at the time the colonies became states. States that were later created often drew on the divorce law of the state out of which they were formed. For instance, Tennessee used to be a part of North Carolina and many of Tennessee's first divorce laws were patterned on the laws of North Carolina in effect at that time.

Second, there are two groups, the National Conference of Commissioners on Uniform State Laws (NCCUSL) and the American Law Institute (ALI), who draft uniform laws and principles for adoption by the states in order to promote uniformity among the states. A number of states have adopted versions of some of the divorce provisions promulgated by these groups, although not always in the uniform version, leading to continuing disparities among the states.

Third, Legislators and lobbying groups often draw on legislation passed in one state and urge its adoption in other states, particularly where there is strong public support for such legislation. The no fault divorce laws that started in California and swept across the country are the best example of this phenomenon.

The second source of divorce law comes from the federal government in the form of case law interpreting provisions of the United States Constitution, as it pertains to divorce law; statutes passed by Congress related to divorce law, including the numerous tax provisions related to divorce; and treaties such as the Hague Convention which addresses international child abduction. Nonetheless, divorce law is still considered primarily a matter of state concern, as borne out by the refusal of the federal courts to hear state family law matters under its diversity jurisdiction. *Ankenbrandt v. Richards*, 504 U.S. 689 (1992).

Divorce law, probably more than any other area of the law, is influenced by the religious and moral values of the citizens in each state. Predictably, the marriage and divorce laws are more liberal in some states and more conservative in others. The outcome in any given case can differ, depending on the state in which the divorce is heard.

There has been an increasing effort on the part of Congress to create some uniformity among the states in recent years, regarding child custody jurisdiction, child support jurisdiction and child support amounts. For example, the Parental Kidnapping Prevention Act (PKPA) was enacted to discourage parental kidnapping and forum shopping for custody orders by attempting to limit child custody jurisdiction to one state at a time.

Congress has also injected itself in the debate over recognition of same sex marriages, which indirectly affects divorce law. If the marriage is not recognized, the parties don't need a divorce. Nor can the financially dependent "spouse" turn to the divorce court for spousal maintenance or to the federal government for spousal benefits. Congress passed the federal Defense of Marriage Act (federal DOMA) which provides that states do not have to give full faith and credit to homosexual marriages entered into in another state. The federal DOMA also limits the definition of spouse to heterosexual marriages for purposes of qualifying for any federal benefits given to "spouses."

Originally, divorces in the United States were granted either by the colonial legislatures or courts of equity. Today, each state legislature grants divorce jurisdiction to designated state courts to hear divorces, pursuant to state divorce statutes and cases, preempted in certain circumstances by federal laws and cases, as outlined above.

China*

Unlike the U.S., China embraces a unitary system of law. China's Constitutional Law, as the supreme law of the land, provides the basic principles of family law. Article 49 of CONSTITUTIONAL LAW states: "Marriage, the family and mother and child are protected by the state. Both husband and wife have the duty to carry out [China's] family planning policy. Parents have the duty to rear and educate their underage children, and children who have come of age have the duty to support and assist their parents. Violation of the freedom of marriage [arranged marriage] is prohibited. Maltreatment of old people, women and children is prohibited."

Further, unlike Italy, which has enacted Civil Codes addressing marriage and family relationships, China has not enacted a civil code regarding family law, except for the General Principles of Civil Law, which contains provisions concerning guardianship of minors and family property ownership. These provisions are supplementary to the Marriage Law, a separate act enacted in 1950 with amendments in 1980 and 2001. The contents of the Marriage Law is essentially devoted to family law and is the main source of law for our study.

As mentioned previously, in traditional China, marriages were contracts arranged between the couple's families rather than between two individuals. Similarly, the couple's families also were responsible for resolving divorces. Although divorce was available in theory, it was very rare in practice because, in ancient China, the social system did not allow women to achieve economic independence. There were no work opportunities outside the family for women. In an unhappy marriage, the husband could purchase a secondary wife without divorcing his first wife. The woman, on the other hand, did not have such choice. In addition, because divorce was associated with disgrace of the family, families often tried their best to disprove and prohibit divorces. Chinese families had a strong conception of marriage permanency.

The marriage and divorce patterns began to change after the foundation of People's Republic of China in October 1949. As one of the first laws promulgated by the newly founded state, the Marriage Law 1950 abolished the thousand-year practice of arranged marriages. Three decades later, China imple-

---

* This part is written by Chen Wei, Pi Xijun, and Ran Qiyu.

mented the Marriage Law 1980. Marriage Law 1980 further emphasized the free choice of partners, and prohibited arranged marriage and other acts of interfering with the freedom of marriage. In addition, because China was facing a serious population growth problem, family planning was encouraged in the Marriage Law 1980. The essential elements of family planning are late marriage and late childbirth.

In 1978, China initiated market economic and political structural reforms. Great changes have taken place in people's ideological concepts ever since. Especially in the 1990s, some new situations and new problems arose in the field of family and marriage. For example, conduct damaging the monogamy system, such as bigamy, concubinage and cohabitation with members of the opposite sex outside of marriage have increased dramatically. These actions have had significant negative impacts on marriage stability. Under the Marriage Law 1980, the rights and interests of the divorced women were not guaranteed, the support and education of the children in divorced families were not properly addressed, support of the elderly was not required, and domestic violence increased, which resulted in the increase of female crimes. Because of these problems, the broad masses of people were eager to amend the Marriage Law 1980 to deal with the new problems presented by the market economy. In response, in 2001, the legislature amended the Marriage Law. The Marriage Law 2001 (the current Marriage Law) contains six chapters and fifty-one articles.

Chapter I of the current Marriage Law contains five foundations of Marriage Law, namely, freedom of marriage, monogamy, equality between men and women, protection of the rights and interests of the children and the old people, and family planning. Chapter II is entitled marriage contract. It describes the legal requirements and the procedures of entering marriage, the grounds for void and voidable marriages, and the legal consequences when a marriage is invalidated or avoided. Chapter III states that family relations can be classified into the wife-husband, parent-child, grandparent-grandchild and brother-sister relations. Chapter IV provides for divorce requirements and procedures. Chapter V addresses remedies and legal liabilities. Chapter VI contains supplementary provisions.

Another important source of divorce law comes from judicial interpretations by the Supreme Court. In the 1950s, the National People's Congress (NPC) bestowed the power of judicial interpretation to the Supreme People's Court, when interpretations involving the specific application of laws and decrees in court trials are needed. The judicial interpretation is treated like a formal source of law in China. The Supreme Court has issued several judicial interpretations to assist the lower courts in carrying out the Marriage Law:

(1) Several Opinions on the Disposition of Property in the Trial of Divorce Cases by the Supreme Court (effective November 3, 1993);

(2) Several Opinions on the Support of Children in the Trial of Divorce Cases by the Supreme Court (effective November 3, 1993);

(3) Judicial Interpretation I of Several Issues on the Application of Marriage Law by the Supreme Court (effective December 27, 2001.); and

(4) Judicial Interpretation II of Several Issues on the Application of Marriage Law by the Supreme Court (effective April 1, 2004).

When dealing with marriages and family issues concerning foreigners, any treaties that China has contracted, or taken part in, can be applied. Where the provisions of the conventions are inconsistent with Chinese law, the international treaties are applied, unless such right is reserved otherwise in the treaty.

The last source of divorce law is national or local administrative regulations. The State Council of China promulgated a series of administrative regulations concerning divorce law. These national regulations include Regulations of Marriage Registration (effective October 1, 2003), and Several Provisions on Marriage Registration between Chinese and Foreigners (effective August 1983). Additionally, local administrative regulations are mainly local adaptations of marriage law. The local administrative regulations may also reflect the local implementation of national administrative regulations, *i.e.*, the Regulations of Marriage Registration, at the provincial level.

Italy

Unlike the U.S. but like China, Italy has a cohesive unitary system of family and divorce law starting with, in hierarchical order, constitutional norms enunciating general principles at the foundation of the relationship created by marriage and identifying the very nature of marriage. *See* Cost. Arts. 29–30. Next are the Civil Code provisions spelling out the rights and duties of the spouses and the protections afforded to spouses and children during marriage and in case of separation and divorce. *See* C.c. Arts. 143 *et seq.* The current content of these Civil Code provisions was extensively modified by the Family Law Reform, in 1975, which completely rewrote most of the dispositions of the 1942 Civil Code dealing with family and separation, the most common predicate to a divorce decree. *See* Law 24 May 1975 n. 151, Gazz. Uff. 23 mag. 1975 ed. str. Divorce is dealt with by special law, known as the Law of Divorce, of the same hierarchical level among sources of law as the Civil Code, marking an historical break with a legal and social tradition that simply ignored the institution of divorce. *See* Law 1 December 1970 n. 898, Gazz. Uff. 3 dic. 1970 n. 306.

Italian law traces its origin directly to Roman law and the Codification of Justinian. After centuries of barbarian invasions, conquest, and destruction known as "*i secoli bui*," in the early eleventh century a creative elaboration emerged that, blending the Roman and the Germanic tradition, eventually produced Italian law and the Italian language, marked the rebirth of the arts, commerce, and the freedoms of prosperous city-states, making Italy (the peninsula, not the modern political subdivision) the fulcrum of European civilization for over four centuries. This period of cultural and economic bliss was in turn followed by centuries of economic and political disarray, extending until after the formation of the Italian nation-state. MAURO CAPPELLETTI, JOHN H. MERRYMAN, & JOSEPH M. PERILLO, THE ITALIAN LEGAL SYSTEM: AN INTRODUCTION, 1–2 (Stanford University Press) (1967).

The present state of family and divorce law in Italy is the result of a tormented, if relatively short, national history. After the Reform of 1975, family law still is undergoing a constant process of legislative refinement, change, and adaptation to a rapidly evolving social landscape. In the recent past, this evolution also reflects the influence of the international governance entities of the European Union which are taking an ever increasing role in shaping the internal laws of member states in all areas of law, including family law.

The evolutionary problem in family law in Italy was never the lack of uniformity, which was resolved via the positivist approach of the legal system recognizing in the legislative branch the only legitimate seat of the power to make laws. Rather, the problem since national unity in 1861 up until the 1970s, was the inability of the legal order to evolve at the same pace as the social, political, and moral changes prevalent among the majority of the population.

On one hand, Italian legal evolution stalled and lost its direct connection with the country's social reality between WWI and WWII under the dark political cloud of the totalitarian regime of Mussolini. After the demise of the fascist regime, the political and legal landscape was reconstructed at the end of WWII with the birth of the modern Republic of Italy. The post-WWII legal order inherited the history and institutions of the previous regimes, yet it represented essentially a new beginning heralded by the choice of a republican form of government, expressed by popular referendum, and the promulgation of the 1948 Constitution.

On the other hand, the unfolding of a complex relationship between Church and State deeply affected the evolution of family law in Italy. Upon political unification, in line with the prevailing ideals of the time favoring complete separation between the religious sphere vis-à-vis the state, the Civil Code of 1865 imposed the civil marriage as the only form of matrimony recognized by the state, supplanting the earlier exclusivity of the Church in matters of matrimony. The ensuing chasm between sovereigns was corrected only during the fascist epoch when the 1929 Concordat, essentially an international treaty between the then existing Italian government and the Holy See, sanctioned the commitment of the State to recognize religious marriages as valid within the secular sphere. Today, pursuant to the New Concordat of 1984, Italy has a dual rite marriage system: the civil rite conducted by a laic public official, with effect only within the secular system, and the religious rite celebrated before a Catholic priest under Canon Law, which also produces effects in the secular system, so long as the priest informs the spouses of the civil consequences of marriage by reading to them the appropriate dispositions of the Civil Code, and then causes the act to be transcribed in the Register of Vital Statistics within a prescribed number of days. *See* NEW CONCORDAT, Art. 8(1). While under the 1929 Concordat, the Ecclesiastical Courts maintained exclusive jurisdiction over the marriages celebrated by a Catholic priest notwithstanding their secular effects, the New Concordat of 1984 eliminates the exclusive jurisdiction of the religious tribunals. The Supreme Court of Cassation has confirmed, exceptionally for a civil law legal order creating law out of whole cloth in the absence of a clear legislative reference, concurrent jurisdiction of secular and religious tribunals in keeping with the recognition that Italy is no longer a Catholic state, but is a non-confessional secular state. Mario Ventura, *The Permissible Scope of Legal Limitations on the Freedom of Religion or Belief in Italy*, 19 EMORY INT'L L. REV. 913, 918 (2005); Cass. CC SU 13 Feb. 1993/1824, DE, 1992, I, 315.

Between 1929 and the New Concordat of 1984, the introduction of divorce (by special law in 1970) had to contend with the additional wrinkle that the special relationship between the State and the Church had since been elevated to Constitutional import: "The State and the Catholic Church are each in its order, independent and sovereign." COST. Art. 7. The Christian Democrats, the Monarchists and the Neo-Fascists, the center and right wing political parties that affirmed their power after WWII, for decades strenuously opposed efforts to introduce divorce. The Church naturally was vociferously averse to the introduction of divorce, seen as an inadmissible secular interference with the sanctity and indissolubility of the sacrament of marriage. The opposition to the institution of divorce did not even subside after the passage of the Law of Divorce, and the issue was eventually tested by popular referendum in 1974, confirming, to the chagrin of the referendum promoters, that the Parliament, in promulgating the Law of Divorce, had in fact interpreted the prevailing popular will a few years earlier. The task of reconciling the principle of indissolubility of the religious marriage, with the legally sanctioned cessation of the legal effects of the rite through divorce fell on the Constitutional Court.

The Court, in multiple decisions between 1971 and 1974 recognized the constitutionality of divorce and emphasized the dichotomy between the act of marriage and the status thereby created. MICHELE SESTA, CODICE DELLA FAMIGLIA [THE FAMILY LAW CODE], 6 (Giuffrè Ed. 2007).

The Law of Divorce operated its own compromise recognizing the extant reality of a dual marriage rite, and choosing to forgo the use of the popular all-encompassing term "divorce," in favor of a more precise politically acceptable dual dissolution process, each producing substantially the same result with respect to the legal system. Hence, Art. 1 addresses the "dissolution of the matrimonial bond" for marriages celebrated by civil rite, while Art. 2 addresses marriages celebrated by religious rites and duly transcribed, and provides that the judge can pronounce the "cessation of their civil effects." It should be noted that the same dignity and the same opportunity of producing a valid marriage in the legal order is afforded to all religious rites of matrimony through the administrative procedure of registration, construed in essence as the operative link between the religious sphere and the secular sphere. SESTA, 3210–3211.

CHAPTER 4

CASE FACTS

Lily Chou v. Mario Penna

Lily Chou was born in the United States. Her mother, an American flight attendant, met her father, a Chinese businessman, on an overseas flight. Lily's future husband, Mario Penna, was also born in the United States, to an Italian father and an American mother. Lily and Mario met when they were both students, and married twelve years ago. Lily chose to retain her maiden name. They have two children. Jade, who is nine years old, and Dino, who is five years old. Lily, age thirty-six, has not worked since Jade was born. Prior to Jade's birth, Lily worked as a human resources director. She completed her university education prior to marrying, but she has not kept current with her business and technical skills.

Mario, age forty, finished the last few years of his Ph.D. program in biology after he and Lily were married. Lily supported them during this time, working in the human resources department of the local electric company, and Mario obtained some educational loans. Mario has worked as a research biologist for a large lab for the past four years. This year, he will net approximately twice what Lily last earned, after taxes and other mandatory deductions. Despite the fact that Mario's salary has steadily increased, Mario thinks the family needs more money to continue its current standard of living and he has been insisting that Lily return to work, now that both children are in school. Mario's employer furnishes health and life insurance, as well as a pension plan, at no cost to the employee. The health insurance plan covers the entire family.

The parties have not accumulated much wealth or property during the marriage. The only things of value are Mario's pension, the equity in the home, the antique coin collection that he inherited when his father died two years ago, Lily's diamond engagement ring, which originally belonged to Mario's great-grandmother, and Mario's gold watch that Lily bought with funds from their joint savings account, as a graduation present for Mario when he received his Ph.D. The amount of the pension and the equity in the home are roughly equal in value. Lily's ring is worth ten times as much as Mario's watch, and the coin collection is worth as much as the pension and home equity combined. The home furnishings are mostly thrift store purchases. Their debts include Mario's educational loans, the mortgage on the home, and credit card debts for general living expenses.

Mario and Lily have been facing increasingly serious marital problems. Each partner has a different view regarding the cause of the marital strife, as noted below.

The parties have entered into a trial separation. Mario rented an apartment a few minutes away. They have only one car, which is titled in Mario's name and is four years old. He took the car when he moved out, but allows Lily to use it occasionally. Right now, she needs the car for medical appointments, grocery shopping, and the children's birthday parties and play dates—all the ordinary activities of a household with children. Mario has been increasingly uncooperative about letting Lily use the car for the past two months, and has kept it at his apartment. He insists that he needs it for work, but Lily thinks he is deliberately being mean and controlling because the bus passes right in front of his place and he could take it to work, if he would. When she suggested the bus to Mario, he said he needed the car "because he is the only one working to support the family."

Lily's Story

Lily attributes these difficulties to the couple's different attitudes about child-rearing. The troubles surfaced when Dino was born deaf. Lily feels that Mario has never been able to totally accept Dino. While Lily, as well as Dino's older sister Jade, have put considerable effort into learning sign language and teaching Dino to communicate, Mario has not been supportive and believes that Dino should learn to read lips and communicate in writing as he matures. Lily says she can tell that Mario is embarrassed by Dino's unusual speech and has been insistent that Dino's hearing can be "fixed." Mario is certain that some surgical procedure exists that will restore the child's hearing, and has persisted in taking Dino to a variety of specialists, who have all concurred that it is unlikely that anything can be done. The doctors have recommended that Dino should not be put through painful and potentially dangerous surgery that is unlikely to produce any favorable results. Lily is certain that Mario is deeply disappointed that his son will not be able to participate in all the activities that Mario enjoys.

Mario has recently been pushing Jade into a number of athletic activities, although his daughter is a reluctant participant, having little interest or ability in sports. She often cries or pretends to be ill when it is time to go to practice. Lily has pleaded with Mario to allow Jade to drop out of the various sports programs, but Mario refuses. Lily is afraid that Jade will develop an ulcer or possibly an eating disorder if she is forced to continue playing sports.

Lily has received considerable support from her neighbor, Alex Lee, a child psychologist who moved into the neighborhood after his own recent divorce. Alex has spent considerable time with both children and has offered Lily some advice on how to deal with both Dino's deafness and Jade's increasing resentment over being pressured to play sports. Instead of appreciating Alex's help, Mario feels Alex is interfering with his family and has become increasingly jealous of the time Lily spends with their neighbor. Mario has become irrational about the topic and has accused Lily of flirting with Alex. Although she had not initially been interested in any physical or romantic involvement with Alex, Lily felt demeaned by Mario's accusations and turned to Alex for emotional support. One thing led to another and she recently began having a sexual relationship with Alex, but Lily believes Mario does not know this.

Mario and Lily's situation has deteriorated to the point that divorce now seems inevitable. Lily thinks she should have sole custody of both children. She feels strongly that Mario's contact with them should be as limited as possible, believing that his attitudes towards them, in addition to his clear dislike of Alex, would be dangerous to their healthy development. Because of Mario's inability to communicate effectively with Dino, Lily wants to forbid any overnight visits, because the child is too young to cope with his father's unreasonable expectations and always seems distraught by his father's impatience and unreasonable demands. She fears that the stress of these interactions could trigger health problems. Because their differences of opinion regarding the children's upbringing are so great, Lily wants to make all decisions about their welfare herself, without consulting Mario about anything regarding the children. She has encouraged Mario to start an investment account for the children's education, but he has refused, and she is afraid he will not pay for their higher education.

Lily also thinks she should get full title to the house. Although it is a bit larger than she needs, she doesn't want the children to suffer any additional disruption to their lives that would result from moving at this time. To meet expenses, she will need both spousal support and child support. At some later date, she is willing to go back to work, but with Dino's special needs, she is insistent that she needs to be at home for at least a few more years until Dino has developed better skills. Lily is worried about the effect of the divorce on the kids. She thinks they should have the same opportunities to go to camp, participate in activities, and go to college as she did, but she can't afford to pay for these expenses. Although Lily is an agnostic, she wants the children to have some religious exposure. She had originally agreed that the children would be raised Catholic, like their father, but she is reluctant to send the children to mass or religious instruction without a Catholic adult in the home to bolster their religious upbringing.

Lily is worried about her own future as well. When she stopped working to care for Jade and then Dino, Mario supported her belief that a mother should be at home with the children. Now, not only have they fought so bitterly about the children, he is demanding that she needs to work, to carry her part of the financial burden—as if quitting work had been her idea all along. Lily knows that it will be difficult to get back into the job market and make up for lost time. She is concerned that she'll never be able to save enough for a comfortable retirement. What she'd really like to do is to go back to school to become a lawyer, but she would require a great deal of financial assistance, and Mario is totally opposed to the idea. She did apply, however, without telling Mario, and has been admitted. The only bit of good news in the financial area is that she won the jackpot at the nearby casino last week. She hasn't told Mario and doesn't plan to let him know. She plans to use the money to take the kids on a great vacation to help them deal with the stress of the impending divorce.

Lily wants out of this marriage, but she also wants financial security. She doesn't want to be in the situation of some of her divorced friends who are looking for new husbands because they can't support themselves. She also wants Mario to have as little involvement with the children as possible. She says that when they are older they can decide whether they want more contact with their father, but right now Lily feels that Mario's involvement with the children will do more harm than good, especially since she has heard that he may be having his new girlfriend spend the night at his apartment.

Mario's Story

Mario believes that he and Lily were happier than most married couples until the birth of his son, Dino. Mario wants Dino to learn to read lips so he will be able to function more freely in the world. Mario also wants to explore possible medical advances that could offer the hope of restoring Dino's hearing. Lily opposes both of these approaches, choosing, instead to use sign language, which Mario believes will limit Dino's ability to get a job and live independently. Mario thinks that Lily feels that Dino's deafness may somehow be her fault and that keeping him dependent on her is her way of coping with her guilt. Mario worries that Lily is over-protective of Dino, and that this "smothering" may prevent him from developing into a fully functioning adult.

Mario's preference is to obtain custody of both children. Rather than put them through a bitter court fight, he will settle for less, but insists that he have substantial time with both—not a brief Saturday visit, but several overnights a week, alternate weekends, alternate holidays and half of all school vacations. He doesn't think that having his new girlfriend spend the night is a problem. The kids like her and everyone gets along. Lily will just have to accept the fact that they are getting divorced and he will have someone new in his life.

He also wants to be involved in all major decisions concerning the children. He realizes that he and Lily can't consult on every little thing; but he does want to be part of major medical and school decisions. He is particularly anxious that the kids should continue attending church with him, stating that he and Lily agreed that the children would be raised as Catholics. Mario believes strongly in his obligation to tithe (10% of his salary).

Mario wants to make sure that Jade continues playing sports. He thinks that playing team sports will teach her discipline and make her more competitive in school. She complains a little about having to play, but he knows what is good for her and is sure that she will be glad, in the long run, that he made her stick it out.

Although Mario is willing to provide what is necessary for the children, he doesn't want to pay Lily anything. He blames her for the breakdown of the marriage and regrets that he was such a chump and didn't realize sooner that she was more interested in the neighbor than in working on her marriage. Mario wants the children to have special things, such as summer camp, but he wants to be able to do such things as gifts, rather than as part of a court order or agreement, so that the children will know he does it out of affection, not simply because he is forced to do so. This is particularly true regarding college tuition. Besides, he doesn't want to be committed to pay for these things if he can't afford them and Lily should have to pay her share, too.

Mario feels strongly that Lily should be contributing something to the family's financial needs which are considerable, but she has refused to work outside the home. He didn't mind her staying at home when the kids were little, but he sees no reason why she can't work now. He also wants to get his equity out of their home within the next four or five years, at the latest. He is willing to trade off higher support payments in the short run to speed up the sale of the house. He has found a small apartment, where he has lived for six weeks, but he does not want to remain there indefinitely.

He is willing to split the equity in the house, but believes that the pension and antique coin collection belong to him, along with the car, which is titled in his name.

He has no present plans to remarry. He worries that Lily is seeing far too much of the neighbor, Alex. His worst fear is that Lily will get the house and kids and let Alex move in with her to enjoy it all while subverting his relationship with the kids, or, worse, that Lily will marry Alex and move away, taking the kids with her.

Three Countries, Three Lawsuits

Based on their mixed cultural heritage, we will assume, alternately, that Lily and Mario chose to live in the United States, China, and Italy, during their marriage and divorce. We will now explore the law of all three countries to learn how similar or different the divorce procedures and outcomes would be, based on the same facts, in each of the three countries.

U.S.

The state where the parties were married is not necessarily the state that will have jurisdiction to grant the divorce. The Supreme Court has determined that domicile can be a sufficient basis for subject matter jurisdiction over the status of the marriage. *Williams v. North Carolina*, 317 U.S. 287 (1942). If one of the parties is domiciled in Tennessee at the time the divorce petition is filed, Tennessee can exercise subject matter jurisdiction over the *res* or status of the marriage. If the two spouses are domiciled in different states, it is possible for the divorce to be filed in two different states. In such cases, the first court to enter a final divorce decree dissolves the marriage, depriving the other court of subject matter jurisdiction. The final decree of the first court is entitled to full faith and credit in the second state and all other states as well. If the determination of domicile by the foreign state court is based on an *ex parte* hearing, the forum state court may disregard such finding in the face of cogent evidence to the contrary. *Williams v. North Carolina*, 325 U.S. 226 (1945). State courts are not required to recognize divorce decrees of foreign countries but generally do so under the doctrine of comity, unless doing so will offend the strong public policy of the state.

In addition to the domicile requirement, most states impose a residency requirement if the acts giving rise to the divorce petition occur outside of the state and the petitioner is a nonresident at that time. In Tennessee, the residency requirement is six months, but may be satisfied by either the plaintiff or defendant. Tenn. Code Ann. §36-4-104.

Once the attorney determines that the divorce can be filed in Tennessee, the attorney must determine in which county to file, within Tennessee. Venue in Tennessee is proper in the county where the parties lived at the time of the separation or in the county where the defendant resides, if a state resident or in the county where the plaintiff resides if the defendant is a nonresident or convict. Tenn. Code Ann. §36-4-103(a)(2). After determining that the parties' resided in Shelby County at the time of separation, the attorney must determine which court has jurisdiction to hear divorces. In Shelby County, Tennessee, the Circuit and Chancery courts have concurrent jurisdiction to hear divorces. The court clerk will randomly assign the divorce to one of the divisions of Circuit or Chancery Court, in order to balance the case load among the judges and to prevent forum shopping by the attorneys or litigants.

If the divorce is settled during or prior to trial, it cannot be appealed. If the matter remains contested and is decided by the court, it may be appealed to the Tennessee Court of Appeals. Thereafter, appeals to the Tennessee Supreme Court are granted by permission of the court. Jurisdiction over divorces and other family law matters is primarily a matter of state law. Under the "domestic relations exception" to federal subject matter jurisdiction, the federal courts lack jurisdiction to hear family law matters, despite the presence of diversity of citizenship. *Barber v. Barber* 62 U.S. 582 (1858).

China[*]

Similar to the U.S., in China, parties often file for divorces at places different from the one that granted their marriage licenses. There are two approaches for divorce in China, divorce at registry and divorce through action. In either approach, the parties can get divorced in their current domicile.

Article 31 of the Marriage Law provides for the concept of divorce at registry. If both parties desire a divorce and they reach an agreement on issues of child custody and property disposition, divorce certificates must be issued in a divorce registration office and the marital relationship is dissolved. Further, Article 10 of Regulations on Marriage Registration (2003) stipulates that where the parties desire to divorce on a voluntary basis, they should file for divorce at the divorce registration office of the permanent residence of either party. The office designated for filing for a divorce under this approach is the

---

[*] This part is written by Chen Wei, Pi Xijun, and Lei Wenbin.

civil affairs department of the people's government at the county level. The following example illustrates this approach. If the permanent residence of one party is Shaping Ba District, Chongqing Municipality, and that of the other party is Futian District, Shenzhen City, Guangdong province, the parties may go through divorce registration formalities at the civil affairs department of either Shaping Ba District, Chongqing Municipality or Futian District, Shenzhen City, Guangdong province.

The people's court cannot accept a divorce petition where the parties have already obtained a divorce at a divorce registration office. However, within one year of divorce, under this approach, they may file at the people's court to modify the agreement regarding the disposal of property for reasons of fraud or coercion. If the people's court finds that no fraud or coercion existed when the agreement on the partitioning of property was reached, it must dismiss the pleading.

The second approach is divorce through action. Unlike the U.S., where it is possible for the divorce to be filed in the state of either party's domicile, in China, a divorce lawsuit must be brought to the people's court of the defendant's domicile. The defendant's domicile is usually the place where the defendant's residence is registered. If the defendant's domicile is different from his habitual residence, the lawsuit should be under the jurisdiction of the people's court of his habitual residence. Habitual residence refers to the last place where a natural person lives for more than one year after leaving his domicile. For instance, if the plaintiff's domicile is Shaping Ba District, Chongqing, and the defendant's domicile is Futian District, Shenzhen City, Guangdong, the plaintiff must file in the People's Court of Futian District, Shenzhen City, Guangdong to start the divorce proceedings. There are a few exceptions that allow a divorce to be filed in the people's court of plaintiff's domicile:

(1) where the defendant does not reside within the territory of the People's Republic of China;
(2) where the defendant's whereabouts are unknown or the defendant has been declared missing;
(3) where the defendant is undergoing reeducation through labor;
(4) where the defendant is imprisoned;
(5) where the defendant is a soldier, provided that the plaintiff is not;
(6) where the defendant has departed from his or her domicile for more than one year;
(7) where both the plaintiff and the defendant have departed from their domiciles for more than one year and the defendant has no habitual residence.

Where both parties are Chinese citizens but one party lives abroad and files for divorce in the court of the country of residence, and the other party lives in China and files in the people's court, the people's court that accepts the filing has jurisdiction over the case. In addition, in the situation where both parties are Chinese citizens, but living overseas, if the foreign country rejected the divorce petition for jurisdiction reasons, the peoples court where the marriage took place or the last domestic domicile of either party will have jurisdiction over the case. When two or more people's courts have jurisdiction over a lawsuit, the people's court that accepts the case first has jurisdiction and the case cannot be transferred to another court that also has jurisdiction. If a people's court finds that the case was already accepted by another court that also has jurisdiction, it has to decline to accept the case. After accepting a case, the jurisdiction of the people's court will not be influenced by a subsequent change of domicile or habitual residence of either party.

Divorce cases of the first instance (trial level) are usually under the jurisdiction of a basic people's court. However, the following divorce cases must be under the jurisdiction of an intermediate people's court: major cases involving foreign elements; cases that have major impacts on the jurisdiction of the court; and cases under the jurisdiction of the intermediate people's courts as determined by the Supreme People's Court.

Italy

In Italy, like in the U.S., the place of marriage does not necessarily determine where the petition for divorce can be filed. Rather what counts in determining territorial competence (venue) is the place of last residence of the party called into court. C.p.c. Art. 706 (after the recent reform Law 14 May 2005, n. 80, Gazz. Uff. 111, Supp. Ord. 14/05/05 entered into effect on March 1, 2006, eliminating domicile as a territorial competence connection which was used until that date). Subject matter jurisdiction (note that jurisdiction is a term Italian law reserves for issues of conflicts of laws, while subject matter in Italian terminology is an aspect of competence) belongs to the ordinary Tribunal of first instance, commonly its family law sections. C.p.c. Art. 9.

In most cases, a divorce petition is premised on a prior uninterrupted separation period of three years. *See* Law 1970/898, Art. 3 (2)(b). As such, normally, the first step towards divorce is a petition for separation, which, while it does not seek to change the legal status of the spouses as such, formally starts the status of separation. Then the clock starts ticking for a legitimate basis for divorce. Some commentators have called this "divorce subject to condition subsequent," SESTA, at 488.

A brief reference to substantive law is necessary to clarify this stepwise approach where a separate procedure for separation has in fact become an integral part of the divorce process. As we have seen, due to the tormented political evolution of the institution of divorce, rules for separation are found in the codes, while rules on divorce are found in separate legislation, albeit of equal hierarchy. In the thirty-eight years since its enactment, divorce law has not been incorporated in the codes other than by reference. *See, e.g.,* C.c. Art. 149 "Marriage Dissolution: Marriage is dissolved by the death of a spouse or in the cases contemplated by law." On the contrary, separation reform has been integrated into the codes. Before the introduction of divorce, separation was a temporary measure allowing the spouses an opportunity for reflection with the ultimate goal of reconciliation. At that time, separation could and would normally end without formalities. Sesta, at 3227. After the introduction of divorce, separation, although maintaining its intrinsic goal of reconciliation, has become the vestibule for divorce, and in concrete application, the one basis for a divorce petition which obscures all others. *Id.* Inevitably, this scheme results in a somewhat duplicative set of both substantive and procedural norms found in the Civil code, in the Code of Civil Procedure, and in divorce legislation. Constant legislative modification and integration, including the recent changes operated by Law 2005/80, together with multiple decisions of the Supreme Court and the Constitutional Court have focused on harmonizing the system available to the spouses when their marriage undergoes a pathological phase, attempting to make separation and divorce a uniform proceeding, albeit contained in different sources.

As a basis for divorce, separation is subject to waiver only in the presence of a limited number of conditions, such as when one of the spouses is found guilty of a serious criminal offense, or when having obtained a divorce abroad the former spouse has remarried, or when one of the spouses has obtained a final declaration of sex change. In the vast majority of cases, either of the spouses, or both, can file for divorce only when three years have passed, following the judicial decision that starts separation. *See* C.c. Arts. 150 and 151; Law 1970/898, Art. 3 (purporting to contain the exclusive list of admissible bases for dissolution of marriage).

There are two types of separation. The simplest one is called consensual, and it is based on the common will expressed by the spouses in an agreement subject to the approval of the court. *See* C.c. Arts. 150, 158 and C.p.c. Art. 711. This type of separation is considered by some an absolute right (*diritto perfetto*), in line with the tendency towards the privatization of the spousal relationship, thus conceptualized as the realization of individual autonomy both in its physiological and in its pathological state, not the realization of a superior interest of the state. Sesta, at 489. In this view, the individual rights of the spouses to choose their status prevail over the state's interest to regulate status. *Id.* However, other commentators opine that the right to separation cannot be exercised indiscriminately, but only if life in common has become intolerable, otherwise it would constitute an abuse of right. *Id.* In light of the persisting interpretive uncertainties, it is common practice to list the reasons of intolerability of life in common when petitioning the court. Procedurally, in the consensual, the parties have to appear personally before the President of the Tribunal who will attempt reconciliation by first meeting with each spouse, and then by meeting with them together. C.p.c. Art. 708. The second type of separation is called judicial, independent from the will of at least one of the spouses, which is available when circumstances occur that make continuing cohabitation intolerable or such that it would bring grave prejudice to the education of the children. C.c. Arts. 150, 151, and C.p.c. Art. 706. Procedurally, it is for this type of separation that the residence (and before 2006 the domicile) of the spouse called into court is determinative in terms of venue. To be sure, both types of separation require judicial intervention. The consensual requires judicial approval through homologation (official recognition) of the agreement of the spouses, while the judicial goes through an adversary proceeding ending in a decree of separation. On the other hand, an informal separation decided by the spouses and implemented without judicial sanction, does not start the clock ticking towards establishing the predicate for divorce.

After the predicate time has elapsed, the procedurally similar divorce petition can be filed before the tribunal of the last common residence of both spouses, or of the place where the spouse called into court resides. Law 2005/80. A joint petition for divorce can be filed before either the tribunal of last residence of one or the other of the spouses. *Id.* The parties are required to appear personally *and* with counsel as the President of the Tribunal will, once more, attempt reconciliation by meeting with the spouses, one by one, and then together. *Id.* A joint petition also offers the advantage of a speedier resolution through a hearing *in camera.*

Conflict of laws issues (identified in Italian as *guirisdizione*) are commonly dealt with by the norms of International Private Law. *See* Law 31 May 1995, n. 218, Reform of the Italian System of International Private Law, Gazz. Uff. 3 June 1995, n. 128. Art. 32 of Law 1995/218 states that the Italian tribunal has a basis for jurisdiction when one of the spouses is a citizen or when the marriage ceremony took place in Italy. However, International Private Law norms are residual and therefore trumped by E.U. laws, namely Reg. n. 2201, 27 November, 2003, referred to as "Brussels Two *bis*" which considers both habitual residence of one or both spouses and common citizenship. SESTA, at 3250. Notably, the nexus of domicile is not relevant under E.U. law, and the recent civil procedure reform harmonized internal Italian law to E.U. rules in this respect. Also, when the proceeding is initiated by only one spouse and the other resides abroad or cannot be found, the petition is filed before the tribunal of last residence of the petitioner, and when even the petitioner resides abroad, the petition can be filed before any tribunal of the territory. *See* Cass. Civ. Sezioni Unite, 1 December 1989, n. 5293. In the interest of judicial economy, under E.U law, the same tribunal that decided on the spouse's separation retains competence to decide on the subsequent divorce petition, even if it is different than the forum identified by the criteria of connection (jurisdictional grounds) of the E.U. Regulation, member state law permitting. Brussels Two *bis*, Arts. 3 and 5.

For both separation and divorce, the residence of the spouse called into court is ascertained based on the data contained in the Civil Register, and a temporary change of abode by one of the spouses does not count until formally reported. Based on C.p.c Art. 706, and Law 1970/898 (as reformed by Law 2005/80) both petitions for separation and petitions for divorce have to contain the facts on which the petition rests, but need not contain the specificity demanded by prior law. After a petition for separation or divorce is filed, the first step is always an attempt at reconciliation by the President of the Tribunal. Only after the failed attempt at reconciliation, will the President of the Tribunal set the hearing in front of the *Giudice Istruttore* (G.I.), or examining judge, and in that same order, will assign the petitioner a term during which to deposit before the court's registrar a supplemental petition for either separation or divorce, as the case may be. This second document must satisfy the basic elements of a civil petition including, among others, the object of the petition, the facts and the law on which it is based, and the relative conclusions, with an indication of the means of proof the petitioner intends to proffer, particularly documents. C.p.c. Art. 163. In the case of Lily and Mario, the competent tribunal is the ordinary Tribunal of Bologna, the section dealing with family matters, since the couple resides there. The doctrine (respected legal scholarship) points out that any reference to the common residence is problematic at the divorce stage, when after three years of separation it is not only common but necessary that the spouses have different residences. SESTA, at 3275.

CHAPTER 5

WHETHER TO DIVORCE:
THE DIVORCE PROCESS

We start our case at the very beginning, with the decision of whether, and, if so, where to seek a divorce. What factors, cultural and otherwise, influence this decision? The U.S. is viewed, from both within and without, as having a high divorce rare, as compared to other countries. Is it true? If so, what factors help explain why Americans are more likely to divorce than their Asian and European counterparts? Once a decision is made to obtain a divorce, how do people obtain legal representation? Substantively, this chapter examines how lawyers in the respective countries conduct the initial client interview and explores attorneys' fee arrangements. It also discusses the settlement process, the use of ADR (usually mediation), and the pros and cons of a contested trial. Finally, this chapter looks at the gathering and presentation of facts in a contested trial.

Based on our fact pattern in Chapter 4, Lily has American and Chinese ancestry, while Mario has American and Italian ancestry. Our fact pattern does not identify the country in which Lily and Mario met, wed and lived. For our purposes, we will consider the possibility that the facts occurred in each of the three countries under consideration, the United States, China, and Italy.

United States

Factors Influencing the Decision to Divorce

The U.S. is known for its high divorce rate, where, statistically, approximately half of all marriages end in divorce. The high divorce rate is blamed primarily on recognition of no fault grounds for divorce, which, in its pure form, allows a spouse to obtain a divorce without having to prove the fault of or obtain the consent of the other spouse. No fault divorce was first passed in California, in 1969. CAL. CIVIL CODE §2310. Other factors influencing the high U.S. divorce rate include longer life expectancies ("until death do us part" is a lot longer today than it was for our great ancestors), greater economic independence of women (fewer women have to stay in a marriage for purely economic reasons) and changing social mores (divorce does not carry the social stigma that it once did).

Today parties are more likely to proceed cautiously regarding divorce where there are children of the marriage, where the marriage is one of long duration, where one or both parties have strong religious convictions about the impropriety of divorce, where the parties work together or are engaged in a family business or other joint enterprise, and where one party is very dependent on the other, financially or emotionally.

Where to File for Divorce

Family law is, for the most part, a matter of state law. Divorces are decreed by state courts that are granted divorce subject matter jurisdiction by each state's legislature or state constitution. Various religions have limitations on the availability of divorce. These limitations are not legally binding on the parties. If the state court divorces the parties, they are legally divorced and free to remarry in a civil ceremony, even though they may not be considered "divorced" in the eyes of the church or among the other members of their religion. For this reason, some parties obtain both a civil divorce, granted by the state, and a religious divorce, granted by their church.

State courts generally have the authority either to grant an absolute divorce, which dissolves the marriage completely, or to grant a legal separation (divorce from bed and board—*a mensa et thoro*), which requires the parties to live separately but does not allow them to remarry. With legal separation, the parties are considered legally married in all respects except cohabitation.

A state may assume jurisdiction over the *res* or status of the marriage for purposes of dissolving same if either of the parties is domiciled in the state at the commencement of the proceeding. Consequently, it is possible for a divorce proceeding to be filed in two states at the same time if each of the parties is domiciled in a different state. The first court to render a final decree of divorce dissolves the marriage, thus depriving the other state of jurisdiction over the *res* or status of the marriage. In order to address the financial aspects of the divorce, property division, spousal support, and child support, the court must have jurisdiction over the defendant or the defendant's property located in the state. Finally, in order to address child custody and visitation issues, the court must comply with state and federal law that seeks to recognize child custody jurisdiction in only one state at a time, theoretically the state with the most current relevant information about the child. Thus, it is possible that one state might have jurisdiction to dissolve the marriage but might lack jurisdiction to address the financial issues or the custody issues. In such cases, the parties may bifurcate the divorce, resolving some issues in one state and the other issues in another state or states.

Because of the complex jurisdictional issues associated with divorce actions, the attorney must be well versed in the law and interview the client carefully before taking the case to determine whether the divorce should be filed in that state.

Once the attorney determines that her state has subject matter jurisdiction to hear the divorce, the attorney must next consider venue rules that dictate the appropriate county in which to file the divorce and state statutes that govern which court within the appropriate county has jurisdiction to hear divorce cases. Finally, there is also the matter of residency requirements that may apply requiring parties to be residents of a state for some period of time, usually six months to two years, prior to filing a divorce petition.

Obtaining Legal Representation

If Lily and Mario decide to get a divorce, one or both will likely need to hire an attorney. A few states have procedures in place to facilitate *pro se* divorces (where the parties represent themselves), but most states still make it difficult for parties, even those with relatively simple divorces (*e.g.,* uncontested, no minor children, no spousal support issues, and agreement on property division) to proceed without legal representation. Sometimes, only one party will hire an attorney, usually when money is scarce or the divorce is uncontested. If the divorce is contested or the parties have considerable wealth, each will usually hire counsel. Courts allow parties to file for divorce under a pauper's oath, *U.S. v. Boddie,* 91 S. Ct. 780 (1971), but there is no constitutional right to an attorney in a divorce case. Consequently, states that have no *pro se* program in place usually have a large number of indigent citizens who want, but cannot obtain, a divorce. Legal services offices generally give priority to litigants claiming domestic violence or child abuse. There are generally not enough attorneys, paid or *pro bono,* to handle the demand among the indigent for divorces where domestic violence or child abuse is not involved.

Attorneys in the U.S. advertise according to their areas of interest or specialization. The yellow pages of the phone book will invariably list many attorneys who claim to be able and willing to handle divorce cases. Some attorneys advertise on billboards and television as well. Some clients choose attorneys based on referrals from friends or based on the attorney's reputation in the community. Some attorneys develop a reputation as a "bull dog" or "cut throat," who will fight the other side every step of the way. Other attorneys develop a reputation as a cooperative or conciliatory lawyer who seeks to preserve the relationship between the parties post divorce, particularly where there are minor children. Still other attorneys have elected a non-litigation practice where parties are encouraged to resolve their disputes through alternatives to litigation such as mediation, arbitration, and settlement conferences, to name a few. Most attorneys fall somewhere in between these descriptions and vary their approach according to the case, the client's wishes, and the approach of adversary counsel and the other spouse. Some attorneys charge a flat rate for a divorce but most charge an hourly rate and require a substantial retainer upfront. The attorney who handles the initial divorce may or may not handle any appeals or post divorce petitions. In protracted contested divorces, it is not unusual for a client to change attorneys several times.

Initial Client Interview

Attorneys are ethically obligated to represent their clients zealously, but they are also ethically obligated to counsel and advise their clients. This counseling obligation requires the attorney to advise the client about the existence of and possible advantages of alternative dispute resolution procedures such as mediation. In addition, courts increasingly are mandating that divorcing parties give mediation a try, especially where there are minor children involved. Often, attorneys will spend time in the initial client interview attempting to give clients a realistic picture of the divorce process and "life after divorce." This is also a good time to discuss client expectations, attorney expectations, fee structures, and the need for additional experts (financial consultants, appraisers, private investigators, tax experts, psychologists, psychiatrists, etc.).

Most attorneys charge an hourly fee and require a substantial retainer before taking a divorce case. If a party seeking a divorce does not have assets, but the other party does, the court can order alimony *pendente lite*, including attorney fees to enable the non-monied party to prosecute the divorce. The court, in a contested divorce, may also order one spouse to pay a portion of the other spouse's attorney fees as a form of support.

The attorney will develop the facts of the case by interviewing the client and/or having the client complete an extensive questionnaire covering jurisdictional issues, grounds for divorce, assets, expenses, and issues related to child custody and support. Further facts may be developed by presenting written questions (interrogatories, requests for admissions) to the other spouse or by deposing the spouse under oath. It is the responsibility of each spouse to develop and present all the facts that the court will consider in a divorce trial. The court does not play a role in developing the facts except to the extent that the court may appoint a guardian *ad litem* or attorney *ad litem* to represent the interests of the minor children. Infrequently, a judge will direct questions to a witness on the stand, but most judges rely on the attorneys to examine and cross-examine witnesses.

The vast majority of divorce cases settle prior to trial, in part because trials are so expensive, but also because cases that go to trial generally take longer to be heard, and can be appealed, making the process even longer, more expensive and more indeterminate. Divorces that do not settle prior to or during trial are often the most contentious, and take a significant emotional toll on one or both spouses and any children involved, making it very difficult to co-parent effectively post divorce.

Most states do not allow juries in divorce cases, so the identity of the judge assigned to the case is also a factor in whether and how a case will settle. Good divorce attorneys will know the track record of each judge on various issues that may arise in a given case and will use that information to advise their clients on the viability of a settlement offer. Assuming that the case will go to trial, we will next look at the rules and procedures that govern divorce trials in the U.S.

Roles of Lawyers and Judges

Under the U.S. adversarial system of civil litigation, the parties and their lawyers bear exclusive responsibility both for uncovering the facts necessary to support their claims and defenses and for presenting those facts to the court. Judges play no role in the fact development process, except to the extent that they are called on to resolve discovery disputes during the pretrial phase of the proceedings. Even then, the judge's role is simply to resolve the dispute, not to become actively involved in eliciting the facts.

In a trial, U.S. judges serve as neutral referees, not as active participants. The parties determine which evidence to present, how much evidence to present, and in what order to present it. Lawyers conduct all questioning of witnesses. A lawyer who calls a witness conducts direct examination of the witness, after which opposing lawyers are permitted to cross-examine the witness. Although judges have the power to ask questions of witnesses, they rarely exercise that power.

The vast majority of divorce trials are without a jury. Where a jury is allowed, a judge's primary role during the trial is to act as gatekeeper with regard to what evidence the jury will be permitted to hear. Unlike in civil law countries where few evidentiary rules exist, evidence-taking in the U.S. is governed by detailed rules of evidence governing both the content and elicitation of evidence. Because the trial will be conducted in the state court, the state rules of evidence will be applicable. *See e.g.,* TENN. RULES OF EVID., Rule 101 *et seq.* This set of rules, which is very similar to the federal rules of evidence, is in essence an organized, systematic "code" of evidence, that has been intricately refined in a large body of case law. U.S. evidentiary rules stem in large part from a perceived need to prevent juries from hearing or judges from considering evidence that is unreliable or irrelevant.

The rules of evidence are not self-executing. If a particular item of evidence is improper (*e.g.,* hearsay) or a question is framed improperly (*e.g.,* a leading question of a witness on direct examination or a question that calls for speculation), it is up to the opposing attorney to raise a timely, properly articulated objection. The judge usually will not do the lawyers' job for them. In short, in the U.S. common law system, the parties and their lawyers control virtually every aspect of fact development and presentation, while the judge's role is essentially a passive one.

Pretrial Informal Fact Investigation and Discovery

In the U.S., facts are gathered and developed during a clearly defined "pretrial" phase of the proceeding. Lawyers develop facts in two ways: investigation conducted without the aid of formal legal procedures and "discovery" conducted through mechanisms provided for by the rules of civil procedure; in our case, the Tennessee Rules of Civil Procedure.

Informal fact investigation includes interviewing clients and cooperative witnesses and reviewing documents in their possession, retaining experts to furnish opinions on technical matters, conducting Internet and other records research, and sometimes even hiring private investigators to locate witnesses or track down other information. Testimony in U.S. courts is almost always received orally, so a witness's demeanor, appearance and overall "likeability" would all play crucial, if intangible, roles in persuading the jury or in the court's determination of the witness's credibility. This is particularly true in divorce cases where so much of the evidence comes down to "He said. She said."

Given the importance of a spouse's testimony, each spouse's lawyer would carefully review their client's testimony prior to the client's pretrial discovery deposition (discussed below) and court appearance. This is one criticism of the U.S. system of truth finding. By the time a party or other key witness appears at a deposition or in court, she will have "gone over her story" with lawyers perhaps several times. Within proper bounds, there is nothing unethical about a lawyer "preparing" a witness to testify. Indeed, it could be viewed as malpractice not to do so. An unprepared witness might not know to emphasize important facts, or might state a fact in an unfavorable way rather than in a more favorable, but equally truthful way. Psychological studies show that differences in descriptive word choices can have a potent impact on how an event is perceived by an audience.

A competent divorce lawyer also would interview other family members, close friends, teachers, coaches, etc., who have information relevant to the issues that will be determined at trial.

With regard to formal discovery, the Tennessee Rules of Civil Procedure, and similar rules in every state, provide a variety of tools that parties can use to unearth facts, including oral depositions, written interrogatories, requests for the production of documents and other tangible things, physical and mental examinations of persons, and requests for admission. This procedure is contrary to that in civil law countries, where pretrial discovery does not exist.

On the upside, the liberal U.S. discovery system facilitates in-depth fact finding. Since discovery is controlled by the parties, who have financial and other motivations to uncover any fact that might help their cases, the system carries built-in incentives to be thorough. In civil law systems, where judges run the fact-development process, this incentive is missing. Faced with a heavy caseload, a busy judge in a civil law system does not have an incentive to turn over every possible evidentiary stone and the parties have no power to do it on their own. The U.S. discovery system also largely eliminates "trial by ambush." If the parties have taken advantage of available discovery opportunities, very few surprises are left by the time the trial rolls around.

On the other hand, the U.S. discovery system can be inefficient and add enormously to the transactional costs of litigation. It may not be necessary to turn over every stone in a case, and every additional stone that is turned over through a formal discovery mechanism adds more cost. The added costs deplete the very assets over which the parties are fighting. The results are particularly tragic where minor children are involved. The money that the parents spend fighting each other could certainly be better spent on their children.

The system is also susceptible to abuse. The scope of discovery is very broad in divorce actions. Vexatious discovery can wear out opposing parties, financially and otherwise. "Truth" finding can be obstructed by failures to respond promptly and candidly to discovery requests. Unfortunately, lawyers and their clients who play by the rules sometimes end up at a disadvantage compared to those determined to thwart the rules. While remedies exist for abusive discovery in the form of motions to compel discovery, motions for protective orders, and motions for sanctions for frivolous or abusive tactics, pursuing such remedies is itself expensive and can result in further delay.

Interrogatories

In our divorce case, both sides would serve interrogatories (written questions) on the other. States generally limit the number of questions that can be posed in a set of interrogatories, absent permission of the court. Each side is required to provide written answers to each interrogatory under oath, or make objection to it, stating the reasons for the objection. Interrogatories are much less expensive than oral depositions, but also less effective at uncovering information. Skilled lawyers have elevated answering interrogatories and document requests in noncommittal or evasive ways to an art form.

Lily's and Mario's lawyers would serve interrogatories on the other's client, seeking, *inter alia*, information relevant to the issues that will be determined in the divorce: grounds for divorce, alimony, division of marital property, child custody and child support.

Depositions

Tenn. R. Civ. P., Rule 30 allows a party to take the sworn testimony of any person, including a nonparty, upon oral examination and to compel attendance by way of subpoena. Depositions can be an extremely effective way to develop facts and size up witnesses because they involve face-to-face encounters and the opportunity to doggedly pursue lines of questioning. Unlike written interrogatories, it is much more difficult for an oral deponent to evade answering questions about key issues.

Depositions work to pin down a witness's story and are a vital tool for impeaching witness testimony at trial. When witnesses say something different (or say it differently) on the witness stand from what they said (or how they said it) in their depositions, opposing lawyers are permitted to use the witnesses' depositions to impeach their testimony.

Unfortunately, oral depositions, while effective, are costly. They not only consume many hours of attorney time, but require substantial out-of-pocket costs for court reporter and transcription fees (which can run several dollars per page), as well as travel costs for attorneys and witnesses. The costs of a single day of deposition-taking can run into thousands of dollars. In Tennessee, depositions may also be taken by phone upon stipulation of counsel or court order.

Requests for Production of Documents

Tenn. R. Civ. P., Rule 34 allows any party to request the production of relevant documents from any party or nonparty. The Tennessee rule is based on its federal counterpart in the Federal Rules of Civil Procedure. Each state has similar rules. The request must specify the type of documents sought, but it does not have to identify the precise documents. Both Lily and Mario would request production of documents from each other pertaining to all the matters described in the interrogatory discussion above.

Document requests under U.S. discovery rules are a good example highlighting the alternative universes of fact gathering in U.S. litigation as compared to China, Italy, and other civil law countries. U.S. plaintiffs routinely file broad document requests with the hope, not infrequently realized, of finding evidence that will help their case. For example, both Lily's and Mario's attorneys would probably have form requests concerning discovery of assets that would require the other party to produce tax returns and bank statements for all of their accounts, hoping to discover hidden assets of which the other spouse is unaware.

"Fishing expeditions" for incriminating documents do not exist in China and Italy. Other structural mechanisms can work to help offset these limitations. For example, in China, (mainland), evidence is usually produced by the parties concerned, but in certain cases it may be investigated upon and collected by the people's court on its own initiative or at the request of the parties. *See* Article 65 of CIVIL PROCEDURE LAW OF THE PEOPLE'S REPUBLIC OF CHINA and Articles 15, 16 and 17 of SOME PROVISIONS OF THE SUPREME PEOPLE'S COURT ON EVIDENCE IN CIVIL PROCEDURES (2002). In addition, the parties concerned and the law agent (attorney) may plead the people's court to organize and preside over an exchange of evidence in court prior to the courtroom trial (also called retrial discovery, which is similar to the open discovery rules in the U.S. *See* Article 37 of SOME PROVISIONS OF THE SUPREME PEOPLE'S COURT ON EVIDENCE IN CIVIL PROCEDURES, (2002), available in Chinese text at: http://www.dffy.com/faguixiazai/ssf/200311/20031109201210-3. htm, (last visited July 10, 2008). Further, if a witness makes a false statement in court he shall be subjected to the penalties of perjury (such as fine, imprisonment etc.) according to law. In Italy, the spouses are required to proffer their personal income tax returns, and the judge can use the Fiscal Police to locate fiscal information (discussed further under The Preparation Phase (*Istuttoria*), below).

Requests for Physical Examination

Rule 35 authorizes the court, upon request by a party, to order a physical or mental examination of a party when the party's condition is in issue. TENN. R. CIV. P. 35. Sometimes the divorce court will order psychological evaluations of the parties and/or the children in contested custody proceedings, where appropriate. The person examined may request and obtain a copy of the report of the findings of the examination.

Requests for Admissions

Rule 36 authorizes a party to serve on another party written requests to admit facts, including the authenticity of documents. Tenn. R. Civ. P. 36. The matter will be deemed admitted unless the recipient responds to the request within thirty days. The response must admit the fact, object to the request on a lawful ground, specifically deny the matter, or detail the reasons why the party cannot truthfully admit or deny the matter. Any matter admitted within the rule is deemed to be conclusively established in the proceedings.

Not surprisingly, parties resist admitting critical facts, even when they're true, and strain to find ways to avoid doing so. But the procedure can be helpful in nailing down certain matters. Mario's lawyer might, for example, serve requests for admission seeking to establish that Lily has resisted the idea of teaching Dino to read lips and also resisted consideration of medical treatment for Dino's hearing loss.

Fact Presentation (*i.e.*, "The Trial")

Most divorce cases are resolved by settlement and those that go to trial are usually bench trials, (where there is no jury).

At U.S. trials, as during pretrial, lawyers run the show. The lawyers, in consultation with the client, decide on the overall trial strategy and on the particulars for implementing it, which witnesses to call, in what order to call them, what questions to ask them, which documents to admit into evidence, and when to object to the other side's evidence. The judge sits more or less as a neutral referee regarding the introduction of evidence, but also sits as the "judge and jury" regarding the final resolution of all contested factual and legal issues. Here are the basic steps in the trial process:

Jury Selection, If Applicable

Tennessee is one of a few states where juries are available in divorce cases. Tenn. Code Ann. § 36-4-113. Parties rarely request a jury, however, because of the uncertainty of outcome (more is known about the particular tendencies of the various divorce judges) and the interest in privacy (having the parties' intimate private matters told to one judge, rather than to a judge and a jury). If a jury is requested, the first step in a jury trial, not surprisingly, is selecting a jury. Most judges allow lawyers to participate in jury selection through a process known as *voir dire*, in which the lawyers are permitted to question potential jurors (or submit requested questions to the judge who will then pose them to the potential jurors) with the goal of identifying jurors favorably or unfavorably disposed to their client's case.

Any party can move to strike a juror "for cause" (*e.g.*, the juror is related to a party, lawyer, or witness in the case), but each party also gets a certain number of what are called "peremptory challenges" that can be used to strike a juror for any non-discriminatory reason. In fact, no reason need be given. The lawyer would simply tell the court, "The [plaintiff or defendant] strikes Juror No. 4." Although it wouldn't happen in a typical divorce case, in big money cases, lawyers sometimes hire expert psychological jury consultants to help them make these choices.

Opening Statements

The lawyers for each party make an opening statement laying out their respective cases for the court or the jury, if applicable; that is, the lawyers tell the court or the jury what they think the evidence will show. Lawyers use this opportunity to introduce the theory of their case and to try to persuade the judge or jury to begin leaning in their favor.

The Plaintiff's Case

After the opening statements, Lily's lawyer would present all of her evidence, both oral and documentary. Mario's lawyer would have the opportunity to cross-examine each witness called by Lily. When Lily finished presenting her evidence, her lawyer would inform the court that "the plaintiff rests."

Motion for Judgment as a Matter of Law

It is standard practice after the plaintiff has finished presenting her evidence for the defendant to make a "motion for a directed verdict," as it is most commonly referred to, on the basis that the evidence is insufficient to support the plaintiff's case. *See* TENN. R. CIV. PRO 50. To grant such a motion, the judge must believe that, viewing the evidence in the light most favorable to the plaintiff, no reasonable juror could find that the plaintiff has proved the facts supporting her claims by a preponderance of the evidence standard. Such motion would be appropriate in a divorce case, for instance, where the plaintiff failed to present sufficient grounds for divorce.

The Defendant's Case

Assuming the judge denied or reserved ruling on the defendant's motion for a directed verdict, which would usually be the case, Mario's attorney would present his evidence. Lily's lawyer would have the opportunity to cross-examine each defense witness. When the defendant finished, he too would "rest."

Rebuttal

After the defendant rests, Lily would have the opportunity to present rebuttal evidence, generally limited to issues raised by the defendant's evidence. This right of rebuttal is exercised sparingly and, when used, sparsely. Mario's attorney would be able to cross-examine any witnesses presented by Lily's attorney in this rebuttal stage. If Lily's rebuttal witnesses opened new doors of inquiry, Mario would be permitted to present additional testimony as "surrebuttal."

Renewed Motion for Judgment as a Matter of Law

After Mario finished presenting his case, he would renew his motion for a directed verdict. In all but the clearest cases, such motions are denied because judges face a higher risk of getting overturned on appeal when they usurp the role of the jury.

Closing Arguments

At the close of all the evidence, each side presents a closing argument to the court or jury, if applicable. Because the plaintiff bears the burden of proof, the plaintiff gets two bites at the apple. The plaintiff argues first, followed by the defendant, after which the plaintiff gets one more shot to rebut the defendant's arguments. Unlike in the opening statements, in which lawyers are restricted to stating what they believe the evidence will show, the closing argument is just that: an attempt to assemble a persuasive *argument*, using just about any rhetorical method the lawyer thinks will be most effective.

In Tennessee, the statutory right to a jury in a divorce case is limited to contested matters of fact. The jury is presented with special interrogatories to answer the factual disputes. The court will then apply the law to the facts as found by the jury.

Jury Deliberations

After the closing arguments and jury instructions, the jurors retire to select a foreperson and deliberate concerning the contested facts at issue in the divorce.

Verdict

The jury in a divorce case does not render a verdict by finding the facts and applying them to the law as instructed by the court in the ordinary U.S. jury trial. Instead the jury will answer specific factual questions presented to them by the court and usually drafted by the attorneys.

All trial testimony is recorded verbatim by a court reporter.

In China, trial testimony (oral) is usually recorded verbatim by a clerk of the court, but where it is truly too difficult for a witness to appear in court, he may, with the approval of the people's court, submit a written testimony signed by himself. On the other hand, in Italy, evidence is not recorded verbatim, but is summarized by various court employees.

It is not uncommon for U.S. appellate courts to seize on particular statements made by parties or other witnesses as support for affirming or reversing a decision.

China*

Divorce Rates and Factors Influencing the Decision to Divorce

In the last thirty years, China has witnessed a divorce peak. The main reason for the high divorce rate during this time was the development of the economy and society, the improvement of people's living standards, the changes in the attitude towards marriage and family, and the reduction of statutory limitations on divorce. Since 2003, the divorce rate in China's mainland shows an upward trend year after year. According to the statistics of Chinese Ministry of Civil Affairs, in 2003, the national divorce rate was 1.05‰, (1.05 per thousand) 0.15‰ more than 2002, and surpassed 1‰ once again. *See The Statistical Reports on the Development of Civil Affairs 2003,* issued by the Ministry of Civil Affairs, *at:* http://cws.mca.gov.cn/article/tjbg/200801/20080100009381.shtml (last visited Jan.18, 2008). In 2004, there were 1.665 million couples divorced, an increase of 334,000 pairs over the previous year; the national divorce rate was 1.28‰, an increase of 0.25‰, compared with that in 2003. *See The Statistical Reports on the Development of Civil Affairs 2004,* issued by the Ministry of Civil Affairs, *at* http://cws.mca.gov. cn/article/tjbg/200801/20080100009393.shtml (last visited Jan.18, 2008). In

---

* This part is written by Chen Wei, Pi Xijun, and Lai Wenbin.

2005, the number of divorced couples in China's mainland amounted to 1.785 million, with an increment of 120,000 pairs; the national divorce rate was 1.37‰, growing by 0.09‰ over the last year. *See The Statistical Reports on the Development of Civil Affairs 2005* issued by the MINISTRY OF CIVIL AFFAIRS, *at*: http://cws.mca.gov.cn/article/tjbg/200801/ 20080100009380.shtml (last visited Jan.18, 2008). In 2006, 1,913,000 couples got divorced in China's mainland, increasing by 128,000 pairs, compared with those in the previous year; the national crude divorce rate was 1.46‰, a rise of 0.09‰ over the previous year. *See The Statistical Reports on the Development of Civil Affairs 2006*, issued by the MINISTRY OF CIVIL AFFAIRS, *at*: http://cws.mca.gov.cn/article/gzdt/ 200711/20071100003846.shtml (last visited Jan.18, 2008).

Scholars searching to explain the rising divorce rate found that differences in personality and interest, hasty marriages, emotional interposition of the third party, family violence and migrant work (meaning that someone migrates from a rural village to a city or a town to work) are the main reasons that parties seek divorces, resulting in this divorce peak. *See* ZENG YI, RESEARCH ON DIVORCE IN 1980s CHINA, 92–95 (Beijing: Peking University Press) (1995); LIU SHIJIE & LIU YALIN, RESEARCH ON DIVORCE TRIAL, 50 (Chongqing: Chongqing University Press) (1998); CHEN WEI, LEGAL SCIENCE OF MARRIAGE, FAMILY AND SUCCESSION 119 (Beijing: the Masses Press) (2005); DU JUN, ON DIVORCE 121–22 (Beijing: the Masses Press) (2000); HU KANGSHENG, INTERPRETATION OF THE MARRIAGE LAW OF THE PRC 7 (Legislative Affairs Commission of the NPC Standing Committee ed. Beijing: Law Press) (2001); RONG YIYI & SONG MEIYA, NO FAMILY VIOLENCE AGAINST WOMEN—THE THEORY AND PRACTICE OF CHINA 1 (Beijing: China Social Sciences Press) (2003); Wang Jing, *Family Violence Shall not Be Ignored—from Zhao's Case*, in FAMILY VIOLENCE AND LEGAL AID 132–143 (Research Center for Women's Law and Legal Service of Peking University ed., Beijing: China Social Sciences Press) (2003). Several studies indicate the large numbers of migrant workers who obtain divorces. For instance, according to the survey of the People's Court of Xinzheng City, Zhengzhou, Henan Province at the end of 2005, among sixty-eight divorce cases received by this Court, thirty-two divorce cases concerned rural migrant workers, accounting for 48%. (available at: http://zzfy.chinacourt.org/public/detail.php?id=7338 (last visited April 12, 2007) Another example, the statistics of the People's Court of Ningshan County, Shanxi Provincial in 2005 reveal that sixty-one divorce cases concern rural migrant workers from 2003 to 2005, accounting for 31% of the total. (*See* http://www.akfy.org.cn/nsfy/xx.asp?bh=191 (last visited July 26, 2006); Ye Wenzhen, Lin Qingguo, *Analysis of the Divorce Trend and the Reasons in Contemporary China*, *at* website:http://www.hunyu.net/3/detaindex.asp?page=1&id =15554 (last visited Jan.12, 2008).

In addition, Article 13 of the existing REGULATIONS ON MARRIAGE REGIS-
TRATION (2003) stipulates that, where a divorce application of the parties
meets the statutory requirements of divorce, a divorce shall be registered on
the spot and the divorce certificates will be issued. The regulation simplifies
divorce procedures, but it may also open the door to hasty divorces. As early
as the twenty-first century, some Chinese scholars pointed out that, the failure of China's law to provide for a period of consideration for the parties in
divorce proceedings, is not conducive to the prevention of hasty divorces. *See*
CHEN WEI, RESEARCH ON LEGISLATION OF CHINA'S MARRIAGE AND FAMILY
LAW 246–48 (Beijing: the Masses Press) (2000).

Where to File for Divorce

Under Article 31 and 32 of the current Marriage Law, a "divorce shall be
granted if husband and wife both desire it. Both parties shall apply to the marriage registration office for divorce. The marriage registration office, after
clearly establishing that divorce is desired by both parties and that appropriate arrangements have been made for the care of any children and the disposition of property, shall issue the divorce certificate." "If either party alone desires a divorce, the organization concerned may carry out mediation or the
party may appeal directly to a people's court to start divorce proceedings."
Thus, in China, there are two approaches for the parties to divorce, divorce
at a registry and divorce through action.

Divorce at a Registry

Under Articles 10 and 11 of REGULATIONS ON DIVORCE REGISTRATION
(2003), where Chinese residents desire divorce on a voluntary basis, both the
man and the woman shall go together and undergo divorce registration formalities with the marriage registration office at the place where the permanent residence of either party is registered.

Why choose divorce at a registry? If both parties consent to divorce, and meet
the statutory requirements of divorce registration, divorce at a registry will be
the best choice. Compared with divorce through action, divorce at a registry
has the following advantages: it saves time and money; it reduces the harm to
both the parties and their children; and it facilitates the enforcement of the
divorce. *See* WU CHANGZHEN &YANG DAWEN &WANG DEYI, INTERPRETATIONS
AND AN EMPIRICAL STUDY OF THE MARRIAGE LAW OF PRC 144 (Beijing: the
Press of China's Legal System) (2001).

What is required to prepare for a divorce at a registry? The most important
preparation for a divorce at a registry is the signing of a written divorce agree-

ment by both parties. This agreement is triplicate, with a copy for each party, and a third copy for the marriage registration office. The divorce shall come into force after the agreement is signed by both parties and filed at the marriage registration office.

Are attorneys needed for divorce registration? The procedure of divorce registration is not complicated. Typically, the parties can have a divorce registration without attorneys involved. However, in the case of *Lily v. Mario*, in one of the following situations, attorneys may be required to better protect rights and interests of both parties: where the property relationship between the husband and wife is very complex; where either party is at fault, which causes the divorce; or where either party is in need of financial assistance after the divorce.

How shall the registration office deal with applications for divorce? Under Article 49 of the Temporary Regulations on Marriage Registration (2003), where the divorce agreement is signed by Lily and Mario, they shall go together and undergo divorce registration formalities at the relevant marriage registration office. The marriage office shall examine the certificates and certifying materials presented by them and inquire about the relevant information. Where the application meets the requirements of divorce registration, the divorce shall be registered and the certificates shall be issued on the spot.

Divorce through Action

Mediation out of action. Under Article 32 (1) of the current Marriage Law, if only one party desires a divorce, the mediation committee will carry out mediation before the party files for divorce in court. Here, the mediation is usually regarded as pretrial mediation or mediation outside the court. The mediation committees are non-governmental organizations composed of parties' working units, the neighborhood or village committee, or the legal service offices in towns or villages, and so on. It is worth noting that mediation outside the court is not a necessary procedure of the divorce case. The parties who desire to divorce may request and accept the relevant organization's mediation, or refuse the mediation of relevant organizations and file directly to the people's court for divorce.

As to the divorce case of *Lily v. Mario*, if one party, Lily, desires a divorce but the other party, Mario, disagrees, he or she may require the relevant organization to carry out mediation. After mediation by the relevant organization, there may be one of three results. The first is an amicable settlement, with the parties becoming reconciled through mediation and abandoning the request for divorce. A second result may be that both parties will agree to divorce following mediation and will reach a consensus agreement on child rearing, property disposition, and paying off the debts. Under such circumstances, both parties should go to the marriage registration office and apply for divorce registration. After examination and ratification by the marriage registration office, divorce certificates shall be issued, which means their husband-wife relationship no longer exists. The third result is that mediation may fail. That is, after mediation, Lily may still insist on a divorce, and Mario may still insist on staying married. Under such circumstances, the party who desires a divorce may apply directly to the people's courts to start divorce proceedings.

Preparation for divorce proceedings. When both parties desire to divorce through action, the first requirement is that the bill of complaint as well as copies shall be submitted to the people's court. For the purposes of Article 110 of CIVIL PROCEDURE LAW OF THE PEOPLE'S REPUBLIC OF CHINA, a bill of complaint shall clearly state the following items: the claims of the lawsuit and the facts and grounds on which the lawsuit is based; evidence and the sources; and the names and addresses of witnesses. Therefore, the parties should collect the relevant evidence completely.

Collection of evidence. In divorce proceedings, there are usually five main types of evidence required to be collected, including:

(1) Evidence concerning the breakdown of affection between husband and wife;
(2) Evidence concerning the jointly possessed property, creditor's rights and debts;
(3) Evidence concerning child custody and the right of visitation;
(4) Evidence concerning compensation on divorce; (Subject to Article 46 of the current Marriage Law, only under the following four circumstances which lead to divorce, shall the innocent party have the right to claim compensation: 1) bigamy is committed; 2) one party cohabits with another person of the opposite sex; 3) domestic violence is committed; or 4) a family member is maltreated or abandoned. Accordingly, the acts such as extramarital love and adultery without cohabitations are not included. *See* Chen Wei: *Research on Some Issues in the Application of Divorce Compensation,* 2 RESEARCH ON LAW AND BUSINESS 83 (2002). Therefore, each party should collect evidence concerning the main aspects above. It is not necessary to spend a lot of money and effort in investigating the other party's acts of extramarital love and adultery.
(5) Other evidence. For instance, evidence supporting a claim for financial assistance, compensation on divorce, the economical compensation for the value of housework, a claim for consideration in property disposition, or a claim for protection of rights on contractual

land, etc., shall be collected in accordance with the legal requirements of the current Marriage Law.

As to the divorce case of *Lily v. Mario*, the plaintiff and the defendant both should collect relevant evidence concerning the above issues, to support their claims. If the parties can not collect evidence by themselves, they may also apply to the court for the investigation and collection of evidence by the court, or the lawyers commissioned by the parties to collect evidence under an order issued by the court.

In addition, it is noteworthy that the parties should take legal means to collect evidence, but not resort to illegal means, if so, the evidence collected thereby can not be used as the basis to clarify the facts of the case.

Interim relief. In divorce proceedings, there are two main interim relief measures as follows:

> **Property preservation.** For the purposes of articles 92 and 93 of the CIVIL PROCEDURE LAW, property preservation can be classified into two categories: property preservation before filing the lawsuit and property preservation during the proceedings. The former means that, due to urgent circumstances, the interested party whose lawful rights and interests would suffer from un-remediable harms if he fails to petition for property preservation immediately, may, before filing the lawsuit, petition to the people's court for the adoption of property preservation measures. The latter refers to a type of interim relief by which the people's court restrains the party from disposing of property, or the object in dispute, or from carrying out certain acts. *See* JIANG WEI, LAW OF CIVIL PROCEDURE, 3rd ed. 275 (Beijing: the Press of China Renmin University) (2007).

> Either party who believes that the other party may dispose property without authorization, transfer, or conceal the property in the joint possession of the couple; or who would suffer from un-remediable harms if he fails to petition for property preservation immediately; may, before filing the lawsuit or during the proceedings, petition to the people's court for the adoption of property preservation measures. It is noteworthy that where a petition is wrongfully made, the petitioner shall compensate the defending party for any loss incurred from the property preservation.

> **Advance enforcement.** Advance enforcement refers to a type of interim relief by which the people's court in the proceedings, at the request of one party, may order the other party to pay a certain amount of money or other property, or carry out, or stop certain acts, in ad-

vance. *See* JIANG WEI, LAW OF CIVIL PROCEDURE 3rd ed. 282–83 (Beijing: the Press of China Renmin University) (2007). Under Articles 97 and 98 of the CIVIL PROCEDURE LAW, the people's court may, at the request of a party, order the advance enforcement measures in cases involving claims for alimony, support for children or elders, pensions for the disabled or the family of a decedent, or expenses for medical care to be enforced in advance.

In the case *Lily v. Mario*, after filing a lawsuit for divorce, if Lily has economic difficulty in life owing to living expenses and child support unpaid by Mario, she may petition to the people's court for advance enforcement measures. After receiving the petition and making sure the relevant conditions are met, the people's court shall order the petitioner Lily to provide security, and accordingly make a ruling to force Mario to pay Lily a certain amount of spousal maintenance and child support in advance.

The cost of divorce through action. Divorce through action often costs a great deal of money, requires a lot of time and manpower, and results in much sadness. Under Article 107 of the CIVIL PROCEDURE LAW, the parties to the civil litigation must pay litigation costs and other expenses discussed below.

Litigation costs. The litigation costs include: 1) case acceptance fee; 2) application fee; and 3) the traffic expenses, accommodation expenses, living expenses, and subsidies for missed work, incurred by witnesses, authenticators, interpreters, and adjustment makers for their appearance in the people's court at designated dates.

Attorney fees. In China, as the economic level differs in different regions, there are no national uniform criteria for attorney's fees, at this time. Competent lawyers' authorities in some provinces and municipalities have promulgated local regulations on the standard for attorney's fees, which are not uniform. For example, the fees for an attorney's legal services charged by the hour, is 3,000 Yuan per hour in Shanghai and Guangdong, while in Chongqing, it is 2,000 per hour. *See* Article 2 of the GOVERNMENT-GUIDED PRICE FOR ATTORNEY'S LEGAL SERVICES OF SHANGHAI *(temporary)* (2001); Article 1 of THE GOVERNMENT-GUIDED PRICE FOR ATTORNEY'S LEGAL SERVICES OF GUANGDONG PROVINCE (2006); Article 4 of the STANDARD ON ATTORNEY'S FEES OF CHONGQING (2006).

Assessment expenses. If both the husband and the wife strongly disagree on the value of jointly possessed housing, the court will generally advise the plaintiff to apply for a property assessment appraisal. The assessment expense is charged according to the value of housing, and typically no less than 2000 Yuan.

Time of litigation. In China, the time of divorce proceedings varies with the complexity of the case. After mediation, if both husband and wife have reached a divorce agreement; appropriate arrangements have been made for property disposal, child custody, and other issues; and there are no joint claim rights or debts, judges can often handle the case quickly through a mediation agreement. However, if one party fails to reach a divorce agreement with the other party, the proceedings will take longer. For the ordinary (clear) divorce case, judges typically apply the summary procedure and hear the case within three months after the case is accepted. In the case where marriage is related with foreigners or where the facts are complex, the people's court may apply the ordinary procedure to hear the case within six months after the case is accepted.

In summary, as to the divorce case of *Lily v. Mario*, if Lily desires a divorce through action, the costs spent in divorce proceedings include litigation costs, attorney's fees, assessment expenses, and the time of lawsuit. For the litigation costs, as Lily has no job or income, if she really has difficulty in paying litigation costs, she may, according to relevant regulations, petition the people's court to postpone, reduce, or waive the costs. As to the attorney's fees, in the case of claiming child support or maintenance, where she needs an attorney and fails to entrust one due to economic difficulty, Lily may apply for legal aid to the legal aid institutions at the place where the person obliged to pay for the child support or maintenance is situated, and obtain free legal services including legal consultation, agency, etc.

Divorce Proceedings

Divorce proceedings are mainly regulated by the Civil Procedure Law. Generally speaking, the divorce proceedings do not differ greatly from other general civil proceedings. However, there are some special provisions on divorce proceedings in the Civil Procedure Law (discussed below).

When hearing divorce cases, judges generally apply ordinary procedures. The ordinary procedure of first instance includes filing and accepting lawsuits, pretrial preparation, courtroom trial (including litigation mediation), judgments and rulings, enforcement procedure, etc., which are discussed below.

Filing and Accepting Lawsuits

Typically, a divorce lawsuit shall be under the jurisdiction of the people's court located at the place where the defendant has his domicile. The defendant's domicile is usually the place where the defendant's residence is registered. If the defendant's domicile is different from his habitual residence, the lawsuit shall be under the jurisdiction of the people's court located in the place of his habitual residence.

The plaintiff shall submit the bill of complaint for divorce along with one copy of the marriage certificate, one copy of an identification card, and a property list when he/she brings an action.

Under Article 112 of CIVIL PROCEDURE LAW OF THE PEOPLE's REPUBLIC OF CHINA, when a people's court receives a statement of complaint or an oral complaint and finds, after examination, that it meets the requirements for acceptance, the court shall place the case on the docket within seven days and notify the parties concerned; if the complaint does not meet the requirements for acceptance, the court shall make an order within seven days to reject it. The plaintiff, if not satisfied with the order, may file an appeal.

Preparations before Trial

Preparations before trial include submitting the statement of defense to the complaint and evidence materials.

The people's court shall send a copy of the statement of complaint to the defendant within five days after docketing the case, and the defendant shall file a defense within fifteen days from receipt of the copy of the statement of complaint. When the defendant files a defense, the people's court shall send a copy of it to the plaintiff within five days from its receipt. Failure by the defendant to file a defense shall not prevent the case from being tried by the people's court. As to the divorce case of *Lily v. Mario*, Mario shall file a defense within fifteen days from receipt of the copy of the divorce complaint.

As to submitting evidential materials, it should be noted that Article 34 of SOME PROVISIONS OF THE SUPREME PEOPLE's COURT ON EVIDENCES IN CIVIL PROCEDURES, (2001), stipulates that the parties concerned shall submit evidential materials to the people's court within the time period for producing evidence; in case any party fails to submit evidence during this period he shall be deemed as giving up the right to produce evidence. The evidential materials submitted by the parties concerned beyond the time period allowed shall not be cross-examined during the court hearing of the people's court, unless both parties agree to have the evidence cross-examined. In case any party adds or changes allegations or lodges a counterclaim, he shall do so prior to the expiration of the time period for producing evidence.

As to the divorce case of *Lily v. Mario*, both parties shall submit evidential materials to the people's court within the time period for producing evidence. If either party fails to submit evidence during this time period, that party shall bear the adverse consequences for failure to produce evidence during the prescribed time period.

Courtroom Trial (Including Litigation Mediation)

The courtroom trial includes the following procedures: notifying the parties and other participants and, when necessary, announcing the case publicly; beginning trial; proceeding with the courtroom investigation, courtroom debates, and litigation mediation; making a judgment; and recording the entire court proceedings into a transcript. Owing to the length of this book, only mediation in the proceedings of divorce cases will be discussed below.

As to mediation in action, Article 32 of the current Marriage Law provides that the people's court shall carry out mediation in the process of hearing a divorce suit; that is, litigation mediation is one of the necessary procedures when hearing a divorce suit. Furthermore, under Article 88 of the Civil Procedure Law, a mediation agreement must be based on the free will of both parties, and shall not be reached upon through compulsion. The content of the mediation agreement may not contravene the law.

As to the divorce case of *Lily v. Mario*, after mediation by the judge, there may be three results. The first possible result is amicable settlement, that is, Lily and Mario become conciliated through mediation and Lily withdraws the suit. The people's court need not draw up a mediation agreement for a divorce case in which both parties have become reconciled after mediation. Any agreement that does not require a mediation agreement shall be entered into the transcript and litigation shall be ended after the transcript is signed or sealed by the parties, the judge, and the court clerk. The second possible result is that both parties may agree to divorce. That is, after mediation, Lily and Mario may consent to divorce and reach a consensus agreement on child rearing, property disposition, and the discharge of debts. Under such circumstances, both parties shall go together to the marriage registration office and apply for divorce registration. After examination and ratification by the marriage registration office, divorce certificates shall be issued, which means the husband-wife relationship no longer exists. Here, the mediation agreement is of the same effect as a judgment and divorce certificate. The third possible result would be that mediation fails. That is, after mediation, Lily still insists on a divorce, and Mario still insists on not divorcing. Under such circumstances, the judge will make a judgment as soon as possible.

Judgments (Including Rulings) and Enforcement Procedure

If no agreement is reached through mediation or if both parties can not become reconciled, the people's court shall render a judgment without delay.

A divorce shall be granted, if mutual affection no longer exists, or a divorce shall not be granted.

As to the divorce case of *Lily v. Mario*, if either or both parties disagree with a judgment rendered by a local people's court of first instance, he shall have the right to file an appeal with the people's court at the next higher level within fifteen days from the date when the written judgment is served. If no appeal is filed within the prescribed time limit, the divorce judgment shall enter into force and the marital relationship shall be dissolved.

Italy

Factors Influencing the Decision to Divorce

Divorce rates in Italy are significantly lower as compared to the U.S. and many industrialized nations, including neighboring European countries. This generalization holds true even after decades of social, political, and institutional evolution have brought about further transformation of Italian civil society after the introduction of the controversial Law of Divorce. Current statistics, while recording relatively dramatic increases in absolute numbers of separations and divorces during the last decade SEPRAZIONI E DIVORZI IN ITALIA ANNO 2005 [SEPARATIONS AND DIVORCES IN ITALY 2005], 1 (ISTAT, Giustizia 2007 *available at*: http://www.istat.it/salastampa/comunicati/non_calendario/20070626_01/testointegrale.pdf (last visited Dec.16, 2007), support the conclusion that the much delayed and opposed introduction of divorce failed to produce the doomsday results of a flood of divorce petitions predicted by the opposition.

Many factors contribute to explain low divorce rates. First and foremost, divorce is available in a relatively limited number of cases, the most common of which is a three-year predicate separation period after multiple attempts at reconciliation have failed. In 2005, 99.3% of divorces were based on the predicate legal separation. *Id.* at 3. Whether by petition of both spouses or at the initiative of one, legal separation is a full blown legal proceeding the couple has to go through together marking the beginning of a period during which married life continues in a sort of suspended animation. This mandatory cooling off and reflection period retains the obvious purpose of confining divorce to a remedy of last resort. A mandatory separation of three years, reduced from the original seven, may cause people to think twice about their commitments to spouse and children, while simultaneously, through its mechanisms, may dispel any misconceptions that the substantial obligations incurred by marriage can be shed lightly, especially when children are involved. On the other hand, a separation which provides a consensual or mandated solution to the challenges of untangling a failed marriage may become the permanent solution even though it does not change the status of the couple, and does not permit remarrying. Indeed, the total number of legal separation proceedings started every year is consistently almost double the number of divorce proceedings. *Id.* at 1. The number of divorces does not catch up with the filings for separation: only about 50% of the separations end in divorce. *Id.* at 3. Where separation ends up becoming the final solution to a failed marriage the outcome is the same as pre-divorce law, except for the modern day shared responsibilities with respect to property, mutual support between the spouses, and shared responsibilities towards the children.

The historical unavailability of divorce may in fact be one of the factors explaining low marriage rates in Italy in modern times. Marriage is a choice many couples undertake later in life. There has been persistent negative population growth in Italy for decades. Social and cultural mores tend to cradle the new generations within the safety net of their parents' homes diminishing the economic and social pressures to form a separate family. Indeed, many couples choose long courtships, while still living with their respective families, and trial periods of cohabitation that can be broken informally before tying the proverbial knot, and, therefore, never translating into divorce statistics, if the relationship fails.

For those who marry, the spouses' families may influence the decision to forego divorce, especially when family businesses are involved, and the presence of children mandates that the couple, even though failing to live up to the promises to each other, continue to share in the responsibility of raising their children. Indeed, Italian law regarding separation is clear in its paramount concern for the spouses' continued obligations towards their children, and its attempt to discourage a cavalier approach to the challenges of raising children from multiple marriages.

Another factor, albeit not peculiar to Italy, is that even though divorce is available in the secular sphere, couples raised in observance of stricter religious beliefs may prefer to delay marriage, and once married, forgo the divorce remedy even in failed relationships. Older couples who somehow managed to share a life together may be less likely to resort to divorce, and will maintain the formalities of marriage out of a deeply rooted need to abide by their religious value system.

In other words, social and legal tradition, and, at least until recently, a relatively homogeneous religious landscape work together as an overall restraining force, counterbalancing the pull offered by the relative ease with which one can break the secular matrimonial bond. This said, although Italy has lower divorce rates than any other European country as a percentage of marriages, a mere 3.2/1000, there has been a steady increase in the total numbers of separations and divorces during the last decades. *Id.* at 1. Between 1995 and 2005 the total number of separations rose from 52,323 to 82,291 or 57.3%, and the total number of divorces rose from 27,028 to 47,037 or 74%. *Id.*

Where to File for Separation and Divorce

The choice of tribunal is a matter more akin to venue (*competenza territoriale*), and is based on the last marital residence. Both at the stage of separation and at the stage of divorce, there are in Italy short form proceedings mirroring what is found in many jurisdictions with respect to divorce where there are no contested matters. At the stage of separation, the short form is called the consensual. Later, after the predicate three years of separation, the short form proceeding for divorce is called the joint petition. The alternative full blown judicial proceedings are the judicial separation and the individual petition for divorce. A full blown ordinary proceeding is also started when, following a joint petition for divorce, the Tribunal, in chambers as a panel of three, [*camera di consiglio*], finds that the conditions relative to the children do not correspond to their interests, thus denying the petition for divorce, based on the best interests of the children.

The outcome of a legal separation proceeding is only a separation decree with no permanent effect on the spouses' status, other than the fact that the parties are authorized (some would say required) to live apart, especially if they eventually intend to petition the court for a divorce. It is only at the end of the divorce proceeding that the end of the status of marriage is attained. Due to this stepping stone process, it is possible that the tribunal that granted the separation may in fact not maintain territorial competence (jurisdiction) on the subsequent divorce proceeding. Either on consensual or judicial, to start with, Mario and Lily will petition the Ordinary Tribunal of Bologna by depositing a *ricorso (a style of pleading)* in its *cancelleria* (clerk's office), which will list the civil action in its registry of civil actions.

Obtaining Legal Representation

Lily and Mario need to obtain counsel even if they are in agreement on all relevant issues and are seeking a consensual separation. In fact, even if they could resolve their multiple differences with respect to custody, marital residence, the maintenance check, and child support, at least provisionally, their agreement to be presented to the court should be prepared by an attorney to make sure it does not run afoul of a few basic substantive rules that would make it void and therefore not susceptible of homologation (official recognition).

In family law matters, normally an attorney's advice is sought long before the spouse (or spouses) have actually made a definitive decision on what to do. The attorney, who may be providing a first consultation free of charge as a matter of course, is likely to act as a family counselor, or as an authority figure, in his role as officer of the court, or as part of his public relations and goodwill building effort, to help the spouses in distress focus on the issues that need to be resolved with the help of the legal system as opposed to those that may be best addressed by multiple social services, family counseling, or with the support of extended family and friends.

Attorneys in Italy generally do not advertise. Clients seek a specific attorney based on word of mouth, and referrals. However, information posting on the equivalent of the Yellow Pages is common, and maintaining a website is gaining momentum as well. Legal practice in many cases still tends to be general in nature, even though each attorney after a few years will gravitate to—and focus their work towards—the area of law that most suits the attorney's individual preference and local demand. In the last few decades, especially in large metropolitan areas, it has become more common for successful groups to specialize. However, very large firms in the style of the U.S. do not exist.

Generally, attorney's fees tend to be lower, relative to U.S. attorney's fees, even though any historical difference may by now be closing in because of the depreciation of the U.S. dollar as compared to the currently strong Euro. There are professional fees guidelines that attorneys tend to fall within, based on the locality, the type of service rendered, and the time devoted to each activity. For a consensual separation, fees may vary between $1,000 and $5,000, depending on the firm and the complexities of the agreement between the spouses. For a judicial separation, fees may compound to much more substantial figures, especially if there is an appeal and a petition to the Supreme Court of Cassation. Contingency fees, generally disallowed in the U.S. for the vast majority of family matters, are flat out prohibited in Italy with respect to all legal matters. Unlike in the U.S., the client tends to keep the same attorney throughout a legal matter once the initial choice has been made, unless forced to change by a change of territorial competence (venue).

Initial Client Interview

Like in the U.S., lawyers in Italy have an obligation to represent their clients zealously. However, there is both in theory and in practice just as much emphasis on their obligation to counsel and advise. The client's expectation, especially in matters where emotions tend to cloud sound judgment, or when the client is less sophisticated, often is that the lawyer, acting as counselor, will suggest or even spell out what the client should do. Although this generalization varies depending on the area of practice, traditionally the approach in the relationship between client and lawyer tends to be more paternalistic as compared to the U.S.

In divorce cases, the lawyer will spend time with his client in informal sessions, getting background information, accumulating factual data, likely making interim recommendations relative to the management of family life pending a decision of how and where to file, and perhaps recommending medical and psychological help for the client's spouse and children. However, unlike in the U.S., it is not the role of the lawyer to fully develop the facts of the case by pre-trial investigation, and there is no discovery. At this point, the only factual investigation is carried out by interviewing the client and obtaining and examining relevant documents in the possession of the client. The attorney's role is not to collect all the relevant information but only as much as is available from the client for presentation to the court of the basic legal and factual premises for the cause of action and foundation for the relief sought.

In a separation and following divorce, a settlement could mean that the parties reconciled. As unlikely as it may be at most any stage, a ritual reconciliation attempt is carried out by the President of the Tribunal with the spouses personally, both at the time of separation and again at the time of divorce. Most likely, a settlement means that the parties are successful in reaching a workable agreement and therefore will first petition the court on a consensual separation, then follow it up with a joint divorce petition. This is where the animosities likely to have escalated between spouses and vindication of moral and personal attacks are confronted, along with the realities of procedural and practical obstacles of unmanageable proportions: the attorney has the unenviable task of making his client understand the alternatives and choose what is logical and practical.

Accordingly, the attorney's biggest challenge in the early stages of a divorce action is to determine whether to seek a consensual or a judicial separation. The issue is not whether to go to trial, but whether the matters in dispute, although rarely simple, can be negotiated beforehand to present to the judge for homologation (official recognition) in a non-contentious consensual proceeding, or whether the situation is out of the reach of the attorneys, and has no other outlet than a judicial separation, a full blown contentious civil suit with its economic and emotional costs. By happenstance or by design, the Italian legal system has built in incentives to facilitate a mediated solution reached out of court that is in line with legal requirements, is an agreement that the parties can live with, and is one that the court can approve.

Roles of Lawyers and Judges

The most striking differences between the Italian and the U.S. common law systems relative to the roles of lawyers and judges stem from one pivotal legal institution: the jury. Because of the institution of trial by jury, the U.S. common law system has developed concentrated trials, and a full blown discovery phase where all factual issues are investigated and developed by each party's lawyer before trial, researched, and rehearsed in preparation for the day in court, a day, or many days of performance or unfolding of the legal plot before a jury of one's peers.

By contrast, in the Italian system there is no jury, the legal proceeding does not culminate in a trial per se, rather it unfolds over time through a series of hearings where the formal distinctions between fact finding and decision phases have completely different significance for the parties, the lawyers, and the judges. In general, in Italy the lawyers on each side prepare each segment of the case as needed, and the judge (more precisely, the examining judge appointed by the President of the Tribunal to be in charge of the initial phase of the proceeding, receive and assemble the evidence, and later summarize it in his report to the panel of three judges in preparation for discussion and decision) maintains a more active role in the development and compiling of the evidence on the record. In general, Italian judges also maintain a more active role in directing the clarification or narrowing of issues and evidence taking throughout the proceeding. To be sure, the presentation of all relevant issues and of the legal bases for a decision is the responsibility of each party's attorney, much like in common law systems, but the judge can and does request explanations and offer suggestions as to what he would need to see developed by each party to help in reaching a decision. In Italy therefore, unlike the U.S., the overwhelming majority of a lawyer's work before the court is in written form, punctuated by brief interludes of oral advocacy, both in chambers and at public hearings.

A corollary important difference between the Italian civil law system and the U.S. common law system that affects the role of the judge stems from the different import in the two systems of evidence admission or exclusion. The role of the judge in dealing with evidence taking in both systems is similar in labels only. On one hand, the overarching principles in U.S. rules of evidence tend to avoid exposing the jury to evidence that is inflammatory, unduly prejudicial, repetitive, or irrelevant. See FED. R. EVID. 403. On the other hand, the Italian judge need not worry about these aspects in evidence taking because there is no jury to influence, but is mainly interested in complying with the rules relative to admissibility, in achieving judicial economy, and avoiding delay. In fact, the whole subject area of evidence is dealt with by sparse provisions of the CODE OF CIVIL PROCEDURE and, for our purposes, several CIVIL CODE provisions relative to the substance of evidence and its form. *See, e.g.,* C.p.c. Arts 202 *et seq.*; C.c. Arts. 2697 *et seq.*

This difference in evidence presentation and exclusion also affects the role of the lawyer: he will not spend much time in disputing evidence admissibility. If there should be a challenge it would be in writing, and not orally under the fire of the counterpart sneaking in potentially inadmissible bits of damaging evidence through cleverly phrased oral and public witness questioning. Another corollary distinction is the emphasis placed in Italian law in the creation and maintenance of the record, which is the responsibility of the examining judge. The record is not a verbatim reproduction of all that was presented, but rather a summary of the evidence taken which constitutes the factual basis in the possession of the court to use when the three judge panel deliberates and decides the case.

Phases of the Judicial Proceeding

Separation and divorce proceedings, unravel through a series of phases common to all civil proceedings: "*istruttoria*" (preparation), discussion, and decision. These phases bear a very loose resemblance to the corresponding stages in a U.S. civil proceeding of discovery and trial. Indeed, unlike in common law countries, there is never a time where the whole case is presented in open court. Instead, evidence taking and preliminary and interim decisions are made at sequential hearings which are not open to the public. In separation and divorce there is an additional preliminary phase before the President of the Tribunal, who will make a formal attempt at reconciliation.

In family matters, the process is complicated by the fact that there are two distinct proceedings, separation and, afterwards, divorce, and each must go through its phases before a final decision of divorce can be reached. In addition, both separation and divorce have abbreviated forms, consensual separation and joint divorce, predicated on a measure of agreement between the parties. However, while consensual separation falls into the category of voluntary jurisdiction, joint divorce is a contentious proceeding, even though recent legislative efforts have endeavored to equalize the practical aspects of the short form proceedings of separation and divorce.

To be sure, voluntary jurisdiction, [*giursdizione volontaria*] is a rather elusive concept defined somewhat tautologically as comprising all proceedings necessary to effectuate private law relationships which would otherwise be ineffective. *See e.g.,* Leroy G. Certoma, The Italian Legal System, 213 (London Butterworth) (1985). These proceedings provide a safety valve for private agreements that dispose of rights, by requiring the parties' agreement to be sanctioned by formal legal system oversight. In 2005, 85.5% of the separation proceedings were consensual with an average length of 150 days as compared to 886 days for a judicial separation. Separazioni, at 3.

On the other hand, there is emphatically no consensual divorce, as even a joint divorce petition, albeit shortening the time frame of the proceeding, ends in a decision by the Tribunal that, unlike in the somewhat parallel case of a consensual separation, has the function of ascertaining the "impossibility to maintain or rebuild the material and spiritual communion between the spouses" based on one of the enumerated cases identified in Art. 3 L. 898/70, with the most common being the fact that the predicate separation of three years has occurred.

In contentious judicial separation proceedings, like any other civil proceeding, as indicated above, the formal process is divided into the preparation phase, discussion, and decision making phase. The preparation phase could be likened to the common law discovery phase: only it is directed by the tribunal, through one of the judges of the panel of three, the examining judge, (the G.I.). Like in the common law discovery phase, all the material the panel will later consider in making its decision is collected. However, this phase of the proceeding is under the authority of the examining judge who sets all the sequential hearings for receiving the evidence, sets deadlines for the parties to abide by, and makes interim decisions on any matter by revocable ordinance. *See* C.p.c. Arts. 183–186. At the conclusion of the "*istruttoria*," the examining judge will forward the matter to a tripartite panel of judges, of which he is part, for the decision phase. C.p.c. Art. 187. Hence, the "*istruttoria*," through the efforts of the parties and the examining judge, is devoted to the creation of the record and the preparation and narrowing of the issues that the panel of judges will later use to formulate its decision.

In addition, in separation and divorce the law prescribes the mandatory intervention of the *Pubblico Ministero* (PM) a representative of the state whose primary function is to oversee that the law is observed and that justice is administered promptly and effectively. C.p.c. Arts. 69–73. The discussion and decision phases are normally short and uneventful, relying on the record developed earlier. The discussion is public and oral. However, since there is nobody to impress, the parties by their attorneys forego the reading of the summary of the evidence and limit their oral presentations to a few highlights or conclusions. Deliberation and decision is in secret and the decision is rendered within a time limit of sixty days.

Preliminary Phase before the President of the Tribunal

The right to petition by "*ricorso*" (a style of pleading) for judicial separation or for the homologation (official recognition) of the consensual is an absolute and personal right that belongs exclusively to the spouses. C.c. Art. 150. The petitioner (*ricorrente*) gives notice to the other spouse of the *ricorso* and the relative decree setting the hearing before the President of the Tribunal, inviting the other spouse to appear. This part of the process is very similar to the delivery of a complaint and summons in the U.S. In the consensual, most commonly the petition is presented by both spouses jointly. The President of the Tribunal attempts reconciliation: if successful, the conciliation is memorialized. C.p.c. Art. 708.

If the attempt at reconciliation is not successful, in the consensual, the Tribunal proceeds to note the agreement of the parties to the separation, and the agreed conditions relative to the children and the financial arrangements during separation. C.p.c. Art. 711. Then in chambers (*camera di consiglio*) the Tribunal, based on the referral of the President, proceeds to homologation (official recognition) of the spouse's agreement. *Id.* The conditions of separation remain modifiable. C.p.c. Art. 710. The agreement regarding separation, although originating from the agreement of the parties, acquires juridical effect based on homologation which has the function of ascertaining that the pacts between the spouses conform to the interests of the family. *See* Cass. Civ. sez. I, 18 settembre 1997 n. 9287. The consensual, therefore, skips the *istruttoria* (the preparation phase) altogether, and ends in an expedited decision phase, a mere check on the legality of the agreement.

On the other hand, in the judicial separation, if the attempt at reconciliation is not successful, the President of the Tribunal rules on any urgent and necessary matters, determines the amount of the maintenance check due, and indicates the parent who gets provisional custody of the children. C.p.c. Art. 708. The President of the Tribunal also appoints the examining judge (the G.I.) and sets the hearing for the parties to appear before the G.I. and for the development [*trattazione*] of the case C.p.c. Art. 708 (2). The *istruttoria* (preparation phase) is thus opened.

In a divorce proceeding, either individual or joint, the Tribunal will again attempt reconciliation. In the joint petition, after the failed attempt at reconciliation, the Tribunal proceeds to a decision based on the existence of the legal conditions for dissolution of marriage or cessation of the civil effects of a Concordat marriage. The Tribunal will however, transmit the file to the G.I and thereby initiate an ordinary proceeding starting with the *istruttoria*, if the conditions identified by the spouses do not conform to the interest of their children. In a divorce started by individual petition, the failed attempt at reconciliation leads to the *istruttoria*, discussed below.

The Preparation Phase (istruttoria)

The President of the Tribunal fixes, by order, a time limit for the proponent to deposit with the clerk of the court a supplemental brief (*memoria integrativa*) which perfects the proponent's complaint as in an ordinary civil suit, and affords him the opportunity to add and modify the requests he had introduced with his original petition, and to propose additional requests (*riconvenzionali*), such as a request of "*addebito*" (charging one spouse with responsibility for the separation), in other words a request that that the separation be charged to the other spouse, which is the only vestige of fault in the system. C.p.c. Arts. 709 and 183. The same order contains a time limit for the opponent to file an answer. C.p.c. Art. 183. If the opponent fails to answer he loses the ability to propose exceptions, and *riconvenzionali* and he remains *in absentia* (*contumace*). *Id.* Once before the G.I. (examining judge), the proceeding unfolds as any ordinary civil suit. In fact, the special rules of procedure for separation make reference to the procedural rules for the *istruttoria*, in ordinary civil proceedings. The hearings are generally informal, closed to the public, other than the parties and their counsel, and oral. C.p.c. Art. 180. The clerk of the court memorializes the content of the hearings, annexing the conclusions of the parties, and including the orders pronounced by the judge during the hearing. *Id.* Although the time limits to modify the complaint and to respond are peremptory to move the case along as expediently as possible, dilatory tactics by the parties are possible, and justifiable delays are a common occurrence in a system plagued by scarce resources and large dockets.

Temporally, the preparation phase consists of a number of separate hearings which may stretch over a long period of time: a judicial separation proceeding can last over three years; a divorce proceeding, even though benefiting from several shortcuts can last two years or more. Most of the time is taken up by the *istruttoria*. In an effort to reduce the length of all civil proceedings, recent changes to the CODE OF CIVIL PROCEDURE focused on eliminating unnecessary delays by mandating shorter time limits and redacting language admitting automatic continuances. *See e.g.,* new text of C.p.c. Arts. 183–184 after changes by special law which became effective in 2006. Even so, the *istruttoria* can still take a long time because of the necessary participation of many actors in the process, and because of the very fact that evidence taking is before a judge.

During the course of the *istruttoria*, the examining judge may remit to the three judge panel *(collegio)* for separate decision of preliminary issues, or postpone the decision until the case passes to the panel for final decision. C.p.c.

Art. 187. At the behest of the parties, the panel has the right to immediately decide evidentiary issues that the examining judge chose to postpone. By the same token, the panel maintains control over the examining judge's orders, and once the case passes to the panel, it will re-examine all the orders and even reach different conclusions. C.p.c. Art. 178.

The most important aspect of the preparation phase (*istruttoria*) is the collection of evidence. Evidence is rarely gathered later during the decision making phase, even though the panel has the right to re-hear the evidence presented orally to the examining judge. C.p.c. Art. 281. Documentary evidence is usually produced by the parties as attachments to pleadings, but other evidence is taken pursuant to orders of the court made after the parties' motion. Courts place greater emphasis on documentary evidence and court appointed experts than on testimonial evidence, the object of a generalized distrust.

As a general rule, the burden of proof of a claim or defense lies with the party asserting it. C.c. Art. 2697. Procedurally, the court must base its ruling on evidence introduced by the parties or by the *Pubblico Ministero* (PM), the representative of the interests of the state in that justice be done in the case. C.p.c. Art 115. Therefore, as a general rule, the court cannot, and would not, for lack of time or resources, investigate facts that, even though important to reach a decision, were not adduced by the parties, but may seek clarification and explanation from the parties. However, both in separation and divorce proceedings, the examining judge exercises powers *ex officio* in evidence gathering as it pertains particularly to custody and maintenance of the children, which is considered a function with public connotations, similar to the parens patriae power of U.S. courts. C.c. Arts. 155 *et seq.* To facilitate the task, Art. 5 L. 898/70 states that the parties to the hearing before the President of the Tribunal are required to produce their Income Tax Reports and all other documents relevant to the determination of their respective financial condition. If issues arise, the examining judge *ex officio* can order an investigation on the spouses' financial condition and lifestyle, relying on the Tax Police if necessary. SESTA, 3264. The examining judge can also avail himself of the support and expertise of social services or experts to help identify the true interest and the true desires of minor children. *Id.* at 3265.

Undisputed facts and notorious facts need not be proven, and rules of law may only be ascertained and applied by the court. C.p.c. Art. 115(2). The control of the court over the admissibility of evidence deals primarily with its relevance. As a general rule, the judge may freely evaluate the evidence based on his prudent judgment, but must provide an explanation of his use of evidence in his judgment and its insufficiency or contradiction is grounds for review. C.p.c. Art. 116(1). In Italian law, there are certain forms of evidence to which the legal order continues to attribute a definitive (dispositive) value, and in those cases the judge has no evaluative power, but can only assign a definitive effect to the evidence presented. Also it should be noted that inadmissible evidence may indeed come before the court and not be challenged: in that case, the judge may not place formal reliance on it in his decision.

The tools of evidence gathering are somewhat similar to the tools available in common law discovery, but the key difference is that these tools are used within the proceeding, for the most part take place before the G.I., and right then become, in their entirety or in summary form, part of the record of the case.

Formal interrogatories represent the means by which a party provokes an admission by his opponent. In ordinary civil proceedings (unlike in separation and divorce) a party is not a competent witness, and therefore his information on the facts of the case can only be obtained through formal interrogatories, informal interrogatories, party oaths, and spontaneous admissions. Formal interrogatories seldom produce the desired result of causing the opposing party to admit relevant facts because the opponent is informed ahead of time of the questions and is not answering under oath. The party who wants to have the opponent interrogated has to formulate the specific questions to be asked by the examining judge, who cannot go beyond the questions thus prepared unless by agreement of the parties or in order to seek clarification of an answer given. C.p.c. Art. 230. The party subject to interrogatory must answer personally and not through prewritten answers, although he is allowed to avail himself of notes. C.p.c. Art. 231. Failure to appear by the party subject to interrogatory without just cause may result in the panel, taking into consideration the rest of the evidence, to regard the facts that were to be deduced from the interrogatory as admitted. C.p.c. Art. 232. Although the attorneys prepare the questions, they are posed by the judge. In the case of Mario and Lily, in a judicial separation or in a full blown divorce their respective attorneys would likely formulate questions relevant to the determination of the maintenance check, child support, child custody, and the division of marital property.

Informal Interrogatories are the tools by which the court, at any stage or grade of the proceeding, can order the personal appearance of both parties to confront and interrogate them freely at the same time on the facts of the case. C.p.c. Art. 117. The parties may request the presence of their attorneys. *Id.* The court is allowed to draw inferences from the answers given and the behavior of the parties during the interrogation. C.p.c. Art. 116. Admissions against interests given during informal interrogatories do not constitute conclusive evidence but may be freely evaluated by the court. However, all answers given constitute evidence, not only admissions against interest as in formal interrogatories. Both during separation and divorce, the examining judge (G.I.) avails himself of this tool to clarify issues of fact that remain unclear, since during formal interrogatories there is no probing beyond the pre-formulated questions. The examining judge can start using informal interrogatories in the first hearing before him, to get a better understanding of the case first hand, and will continue to use them as necessary in the course of the proceeding.

Testimony is the oral narration of evidence by a third person. Italian law distrusts testimony as a form of evidence and places limitations on its admissibility. But once admitted, the content and the credibility of the witness can be freely evaluated by the court. All people with an interest in the controversy are incompetent to give testimony, with the exception of the spouse and relatives in controversies concerning status, personal separation or family relations. C.p.c. Arts. 246 and 247. Other limitations are that the taking of testimony by the court is limited to the list of persons who are to be called as witnesses submitted by each party, and the facts on which each is to be examined. C.p.c. Art. 244. As in the U.S., the court generally has no power to call additional witnesses on its own motion. The court may also refuse to hear witnesses it considers superfluous. C.p.c. Art. 245. Unlike the U.S., witnesses are questioned by the judge who cannot depart from the matters specified by the parties unless to ask clarification and explanation of an answer given, while the parties and their attorney cannot independently conduct examination or cross examination of witnesses. C.p.c. Art. 253. Witnesses are heard separately and under oath. C.p.c. Art. 251. There is none of the probing and precision that characterizes U.S. depositions, and the information is not taken down verbatim, as in the U.S., but is summarized by the clerk of the court in a written statement that the witness then subscribes to. The court then has powers *ex officio* relative to witness testimony: 1) if a witness refers to another person during his account, the other person may be also called in by the court; 2) the court can call in as a witness a person it had earlier disallowed or considered superfluous; and 3) the court may require a witness to be heard again or confronted with other witnesses. C.p.c. Art. 257 and 254. Failure to appear before the court to be heard as a witness may result in the person being forcibly brought before the court, or, unlike the U.S., a pecuniary penalty being assessed against him for the cost of the adjournment. C.p.c. Art. 255. Unlike the U.S., witnesses cannot be prepared by the party who offers their testimony. Questions tend to be general and open ended to uncover as much information as possible. Answers tend to be narrative in form. There is no cross examination and there is no discovery deposition, recorded verbatim and followed by oral witness testimony at trial. Testimony is taken once, with the advantage that it is not rehearsed; the judge can evaluate the truthfulness of the witness and theoretically gain a lot of information by the witness's own rendition of the answer. However, since the testimony is never memorialized verbatim, but only summarized, the three judge panel, during discussion and decision, loses the immediacy of the witness's demeanor, the precision of a verbatim record, and the narrowing and probing of cross examination, both as a fact finding tool and a way of probing the truthfulness of the witness. Unlike the U.S., there is no impeachment of the testimony. A similar result can be achieved, however, by witness confrontation.

A *party oath* is a solemn declaration of the truth of a fact favorable to the declarant. The fact sworn is considered conclusively proven. If he has perjured himself the declarant is liable criminally under C.p. Art. 371, and once convicted he is liable for damages to the opponent, but the original judgment cannot be set aside. There are two types of party oath: 1) the decisionary oath is the oath that one party defers to the other so that the decision of the case will depend on it totally or partially; and 2) the supplementary oath is deferred *sua sponte* by the court to one of the parties when the evidence is in equipoise, or to establish the value of the object in dispute if it cannot otherwise be established. C.c. Art. 2376(1) and (2). Party oaths can be used to establish the ownership of personality, or the presence of people in relevant places, or to establish facts that only a party could testify to. To elicit the truth, party oaths rely on the moral, civil, and criminal consequences that may befall the individual who perjures himself.

Admissions, also called confessions, are statements made by a party as to the truth of facts unfavorable to him and favorable to his adversary. C.c. Art. 2730. When confronted with this form of evidence, the judge is not at liberty to evaluate it but must accept the facts confessed as true. The person admitting the fact must have the ability to dispose of the rights to which the admission refers, and the admission must concern immediate and certain facts which create, impede, or extinguish the disputed relationship and eliminate the need for further evidence in the matter. C.c. Art. 2731. An admission can either be spontaneous, made in the course of the proceeding in any document signed by the party, or provoked, that is through the use of formal interrogatories.

Documentary Evidence

There is a very important distinction in Italian law between a private writing and public writing (*atto pubblico*). A *atto pubblico* is a document drawn based on predetermined formalities by a notary or other public official who confers public faith upon it. C.c. Art. 2699. A *atto pubblico* constitutes conclusive evidence of its source, that the public official who prepared it was its author, and of the declarations and events that the public official declares were made or performed either in his presence or by him. C.c. Art. 2700. On the other hand, a private writing is a document drawn by the party and subscribed by him which constitutes conclusive evidence only that the person subscribing it was the author if either that person acknowledges his subscription, or the subscription is authenticated by a notary. C.c. Art. 2303. Neither constitutes conclusive evidence of the truth of the statement contained in them. Telegrams and books and records kept by enterprises exceptionally receive the same treatment as private writings, although they are not signed. Writings of third persons can be introduced as evidence, although they are treated as circumstantial evidence.

If a document or other tangible evidence necessary for the decision is in the possession of a third person or the public administration, the court may order its production if it does not seriously damage the party or the third person, does not give rise to a violation of professional privilege or official secrecy, and the proponent advances the cost of production. C.p.c. Art. 118. The party subject to the order may move to set it aside, but the court is free to draw conclusions from an unjustified refusal. C.p.c. Art. 116. The order of the court may be on motion of the party or by the court *sua sponte.*

Inspections

Inspections include physical and psychological examinations that in separation and divorce proceedings may be ordered by the examining judge (the G. I.), especially with respect to custody determinations. Inspections may be of persons or things movable or immovable, and are ordered by the examining judge, who may proceed to carry it out personally even if it is to be performed outside of the territorial area of the court, or through an expert appointed by the court, who will either carry out the inspection personally or along with the judge. C.p.c. Art. 258–262. In the case of Lily and Mario, a physical and psychological examination of Dino would probably be ordered to help determine how his best interests can be served in deciding custody, as well as what approach may be better suited for his cognitive and social development to help resolve the dispute between Lily and Mario.

Expert Evidence

Unlike the U.S., experts are auxiliary court officials rather than witnesses in the eyes of Italian law. Yet, like the U.S., the court is free to evaluate expert evidence or even reject it completely. The court can appoint a technical consultant, either at the instance of a party or *sua sponte* from a list of relevant experts kept by the court. The parties have the opportunity to simultaneously appoint a party expert to assist the court expert who may then present his own written report. Like the U.S., the expert usually conducts his own inquiry without court intervention, but, unlike the U.S., the expert may also request clarification for the parties' information from third parties and be called upon by the President of the Tribunal to assist *in camera* when the three judge panel is considering its decision.

Fact presentation is mostly accomplished in writing by way of summary of the evidence taken orally. Lawyers have less of an opportunity to control the information that reaches the court once the tool of a party or a witness testimony is offered to the court. Strategy, especially in civil cases, has more to do with evidence selection, question formulation, document presentation, and with the written communication that the attorneys prepare for the examining judge first, and for the three judge panel last, to help frame the issues and suggest the applicable legal standard, and later to help summarize the facts as supported by the evidence and suggest how each issue should be decided based on the applicable law.

Trial strategy in civil law systems should be thought of as a prolonged and diluted effort that starts the day the case is referred to the examining judge (the G.I.) and ends with the equivalent of a brief summary of the facts, the law, and the conclusions in favor of the position of the client that the panel will ultimately consider. The three judge panel will also conduct independent review of all the evidence, the summation of the examining judge, and his recommendation before they render their decision.

Oral advocacy has limited application during the preparation phase, culminating in the last hearing of this phase (*udinza di trattazione*) where lawyers can present their theory of the case and argue their conclusions before the examining judge. Normally, a more elaborate theory of the case, summary of the facts and law, and arguments favoring the represented party are contained in the *comparsa conclusionale* (concluding brief) presented within sixty days after the case has been referred to the panel for decision. *See* C.p.c. Art. 190.

Like in common law systems, the parties and their lawyers are not beyond abusing the system by way of tactics directed at delaying the course of the proceedings by asking for unnecessary continuances and by requesting evidence production and evidence taking even when redundant and duplicative. The control of the examining judge is not always effective—even after time limits have been made more stringent and continuances less of a routine—in reducing the effect of vexatious practices directed at wearing out the opponent emotionally and financially. In other words, a rather open evidence taking system is prone, much like the open U.S. discovery system, to abuse by those who are determined to mock the letter and the purposes of the rules.

Decision Making Phase

In consensual separation, preparation and discussion are bypassed, as the judicial intervention consists of a mere check of the legality of the conditions of separation as established by the spouses by agreement. The homologation (official recognition) can and will be denied by the President of the Tribunal if the agreement is in contrast with the interest of the children. C.c. Art. 158. Other reasons that would cause a denial of the homologation (official recognition) are the purported disposition by agreement of non-disposable rights of the spouses. Examples include a clause that renounces the right to modify the conditions of separation based on a change of circumstances, or a clause whereby the non custodial parent renounces the right/duty to oversee the education and upbringing of his children. C.c. Art. 155. Both clauses are contrary to substantive law and void. *Id.* The President of the Tribunal does not redact the consensual agreement, and can deny homologation if the agreement is not modified by the spouses. C.c. Art. 158.

In judicial separation, after all the evidence has been taken, the examining judge remits the case to the three judge panel for decision. C.p.c. Arts. 188–189 and 275. Unlike in the instruction phase, in the discussion/decision phase, the hearings are public, although the deliberation of the panel is held *in camera* and in secret. C.p.c. Arts. 275–276. If the parties ask that the case be discussed before the panel, the examining judge reads the reports (*rapporteur*) relating the undisputed facts, and then the issues of fact and law in dispute. C.p.c. Art. 275. The parties may read their written submissions and address the court. Generally though, the parties waive this right and ask for the case to go to decision. *Id.* The fact is that, although the hearing is public, there is really no one to impress with the unfolding of the events, the issues of fact and law, and the respective arguments. Therefore, once more, oral advocacy, although possible is seldom used. The parties are normally not present, there is no jury, and the judges of the panel receive the whole record for deliberation. Hence, sadly for those naïve students who are enticed to join the legal profession based on the reruns of Perry Mason dubbed in Italian, there is not much drama in Italian civil court.

The decision of the panel is made *in camera di consiglio*, evaluating first prejudicial issues and then the merits. C.p.c. Arts. 276 and 277. The decision is reached by majority: the *rapporteur* votes first, and the President of the Tribunal writes the decision and signs it leaving the *rapporteur* to write the opinion, unless the President of the Tribunal chooses to write it personally or delegates it to another judge. C.p.c. Art. 276. The decision is then deposited in the court registry within sixty days. C.p.c. Art. 275. The decision is subject to appeal before the Court of Appeal, and recourse before the Supreme Court of Cassation. A judgment may not be enforced during the time allowed by law to appeal or during the pendency of an appeal.

After the divorce decision becomes final (no longer subject to appeal as to the status of the ex spouses), the decision has to be transmitted in authenticated copy to the official of the Registry of Vital Statistics to be annotated to the act of marriage and other formalities. A divorce decision becomes effective *erga omnes* (for everybody, *i.e.*, notice to the world) from the time of annotation, while between the ex spouses the divorce decision takes effect from the day it becomes final, leaving them eligible to marry again.

Summary Chart—Whether to Divorce: The Divorce Process

	U.S. (Tennessee)	China	Italy
Core principles of divorce litigation are adversarial in nature.	Yes	Yes (litigation mediation exception)	Yes
Parties have primary control over fact development.	Yes	Yes	Yes
Judges play a significant role in developing facts.	No	Generally not, but sometimes some judges may do so in certain cases.	No, but in judicial separation and divorce, the examining judge is in charge of evidence presentation and record development.
Pretrial discovery is available.	Yes	Yes (evidence exchange in court, etc.).	Yes, but discovery is part of the proceeding under the examining judge.
Juries serve as fact-finders.	Juries are usually not available in divorce trials, but to the extent that they are available, they are usually limited to fact finding.	In China, there are no juries, but there are people assessors. The assessors usually serve as fact-finders with judges except for the summary procedure handled by one judge only.	There are no juries for the panel. Limited Exception: in criminal cases, for heinous crimes, the special court has its own permanent technical jury.
Fact presentation is governed by extensive rules of evidence.	Yes	Yes	No. The rules of evidence taking and presentation exist but they are part of substantive and procedural law.
Testimony is almost always received orally in open court.	Yes	Most	No, testimony is received orally *in camera* and summarized in the record. Most evidence is documentary.

continued	U.S. (Tennessee)	China	Italy
Lawyers conduct examination of witnesses.	Yes	Yes	No, the examining judge does, while the parties' lawyers offer the questions for the judge to ask.
Parties are permitted to testify as "witnesses."	Yes	No (but statements of involved parties are one kind of evidences).	Generally no, but yes in separation and divorce.
All witness testimony is recorded verbatim.	Yes	Yes	No, it is summarized.
Court gives hints and feedback to parties as case progresses.	Generally not, but some judges may do so in certain cases, in order to encourage the parties to settle the case.	Generally not, but some judges may do so in certain cases, in order to encourage the parties to settle the case with negotiation.	There is an interchange between the court and the parties.
Judges have the power to summon witnesses who have not been named as witnesses by the parties.	No	No	Yes, in limited cases, but rarely used due to time and resource constraints.
Use of Alternative Dispute Resolution.	ADR, especially mediation is widely used and, in Tennessee, is mandated in all cases, except those involving domestic violence.	Mediation (mediation out of court and litigation mediation) is widely used in most cases except where the party (or the parties) does (do) not want to accept mediation.	Trend in that direction, regarding mediation.
Average cost of divorce.	Varies from state to state: court costs are usually less than $300, but expert fees and attorney's fees can range from several hundred to many thousands of dollars.	Varies based on different factors such as regions and the subject matter, etc. For each divorce case, 50–300 Yuan shall be paid usually. If property partition is involved, and the total amount of	Court costs are low, but because it is a two step process, the minimum attorney fees are several thousand dollars, and increase dramatically in contested cases.

continued	U.S. (Tennessee)	China	Italy
		property does not exceed 200,000 Yuan, no additional fee shall be paid; for property in excess of 200,000 Yuan, the fee shall be paid at the rate of 0.5%. Where a case is heard through mediation, or the party concerned withdraws the lawsuit, or summary procedures are applied, the case acceptance fee shall be paid at half the rate.	
Who pays the costs?	Costs are allocated by the court, unless the parties reach an agreement. Each party usually pays his attorney and expert fees, but courts can generally order the monied party to pay some or all of these fees.	Each party usually pays his/her attorney and expert fees. The parties may seek an agreement about the costs of the case. If no agreement is reached, the people's court shall make a judgment. In that case, the costs are paid by the loser, monied party, or both parties.	Each party usually bears his/her attorney expert fees. Attorney fees can also be allocated by the court. There are no expert fees for the experts named by the court. Rarely are experts hired by the parties.
Average length of time from filing to final divorce, if contested.	Varies from state to state, but usually several months for uncontested matters to several years for contested matters. Appeals can add more years to the process.	Varies from district to district, but usually three months for the ordinary divorce case to six months for the case involving foreigners or complex facts. Appeals can add more months to the process.	After the three-year separation, from a minimum of several months for joint divorces to years for contested cases. Appeals can add more years to the process.

continued	U.S. (Tennessee)	China	Italy
Minimum waiting time for divorce, if by consent of both parties.	Sixty days if there are no minor children, and ninety days if there are minor children.	None	Three years of legal separation before the parties can seek a divorce by consent.

CHAPTER 6

GROUNDS FOR DIVORCE

Marriage is sometimes described as a three party contract between the wife, the husband, and the state. The state regulates entry into marriage (restrictions on age, capacity, gender, incest, polygamy, etc.) and also controls marital dissolution. In this chapter we will consider the similarities and differences between our three countries regarding grounds for divorce.

United States

Historically, in the United States, grounds for divorce varied greatly from state to state. Originally, a divorce could be obtained only from the state legislature through private divorce laws. Later, private divorce laws were eliminated and all divorces became judicially obtained by court decree, based on state laws setting forth grounds for divorce.

Legal Separation was available to the injured spouse as an alternative to divorce and is still sought in some cases. The injured spouse can prove fault grounds (based on statutory divorce fault grounds) and obtain a legal separation over the objection of the other spouse. If neither party objects to the request for a legal separation, however, it can be granted by the court without proof of fault grounds. The court will simply declare the parties to be legally separated. Legal separation does not affect the bonds of matrimony, but does permit the parties to discontinue sexual cohabitation. While legally separated, neither party is free to remarry, and sexual intercourse with someone other than one's spouse while legally separated constitutes adultery. Any property acquired while legally separated is considered marital property unless the court divides the marital property at the time of the legal separation, in which case property acquired thereafter is the separate property of the acquiring spouse. If one spouse dies during the legal separation, the other is the surviving spouse for purposes of dissent and distribution of the decedent's estate.

Divorce, unlike legal separation, does affect the bonds of matrimony by dissolving the marriage absolutely. Historically, divorce was seen as a remedy for an innocent spouse who could prove fault on the part of the other spouse. If each party could prove fault of the other, called recrimination, the court would not grant a divorce. The parties didn't have to live together, but they weren't free to marry anyone else, either. Currently, however, Tennessee allows a court that finds both parties at fault, to award the divorce to the party less at fault or simply to declare the parties divorced.

Typical fault grounds ranged from adultery and abandonment to the catch-all ground, cruel and inhumane treatment, also known as inappropriate marital conduct. Prior to the adoption of no fault divorce grounds, most parties would obtain a divorce upon grounds of inappropriate marital conduct. In many instances, where both parties wanted the divorce, the courts would typically require very little in the way of proof of fault grounds before granting the divorce. Additional Tennessee fault-based divorce grounds currently include the following: impotency, bigamy, adultery, desertion, criminal conviction of a felony, conviction of an infamous crime, attempt upon the life of the spouse, willful refusal to join the plaintiff spouse at the plaintiff's domicile for two years, pregnancy of the wife by another man, habitual drunkenness or abuse of narcotic drugs, indignities that force the plaintiff spouse to withdraw, and abandonment. TENN. CODE ANN. § 36-4-101. Fault grounds must be proved by corroborating evidence. Defenses are also recognized. In Tennessee all divorce defenses, other than insanity, are statutory.

A party may prove justifiable cause as a defense to fault grounds based on inappropriate marital conduct, *i.e.*, that the ill conduct of the plaintiff was the justifiable cause of the defendant's inappropriate marital conduct. Where the grounds are adultery, the defendant has the option of three statutory defenses: connivance, proof that the husband "allowed the wife's prostitutions and received hire for them;" condonation, proof that the plaintiff, with knowledge of the defendant's adultery, voluntarily engaged in sexual relations; or recrimination, proof that the plaintiff was also guilty of adultery. If a defense is proved against an alleged fault ground, that ground no longer exists as a basis for granting the divorce.

In some states, the grounds for divorce were very restrictive, in some cases limited only to adultery, leading the parties to collude regarding proof of fault, in order to obtain a divorce, or to try to obtain a divorce in another state or country. The reform movement to no fault grounds started in California, in the 1960s, and by the mid-1980s had spread to every other state. Some states adopted no fault exclusively while others simply added a no fault ground to existing fault grounds for divorce. Tennessee adopted what could be called "no fault only by consent," meaning that the parties were able to proceed under no fault grounds, called an irreconcilable differences (ID) divorce, only where they could complete a separation agreement, called a marital dissolution agreement (MDA), resolving all of the issues concerning financial matters and child custody, if applicable, making the divorce clearly uncontested. If any of the issues were contested, the parties would have to proceed under a fault ground for divorce. If a party could not prove grounds and the other spouse would not sign the MDA, no divorce could be obtained. Tennessee also imposed a waiting period on ID divorces—sixty days from filing if there were no minor children involved, and ninety days from filing if there were minor children involved. More recently, Tennessee has adopted a true no fault ground for divorce that is available where there are no minor children of the marriage and the parties live in separate residences for two continuous years without cohabitation during that period.

Finally, there is a hybrid divorce ground based on failure to reconcile for two years after entry of a decree of legal separation. This is a hybrid ground because the court will declare the parties to be legally separated upon the filing of a petition unless one party objects. In that case, the party seeking legal separation must prove one of the fault grounds as a basis for the legal separation. Once the parties have been legally separated for two years however, either party may use the two-year separation as a basis to obtain a divorce. Historically, legal separation was a scorned wife's ultimate revenge. She could obtain a legal separation which would relieve her of the obligation of cohabitation but allow her to retain all the financial benefits and status of marriage, while at the same time preventing the husband from remarrying if he could not prove fault grounds against the wife. Under current law, his marital limbo ends after two years.

Typically, parties seek to end a marriage by divorce, but in some cases the parties may want an annulment. If an annulment is granted, the marriage is legally treated as though it never occurred. Annulments are available where there is some serious infirmity in the validity of the marriage. If the infirmity offends the strong public policy of the state, the marriage will be considered *void ab initio.* In such cases, a divorce or annulment is not necessary, but the parties may seek one in order to prove the grounds for the nullity and to clarify the status of the marriage. In Tennessee, grounds for void marriages include bigamy, incest, same sex marriage, and insanity. Lesser infirmities may result in the marriage being voidable, rather than void. In such cases, the injured party may seek to have the marriage annulled or dissolved on the basis of the grounds making the marriage voidable. Those grounds generally go to the capacity of the parties to the contract: underage, fraud, duress, incompetence, etc. A voidable marriage is considered valid until challenged by a party to the marriage, and generally only the party sought to be protected by the regulation. For instance, in the case of an underage female and an adult male, only the underage wife can challenge the underage marriage, not the adult husband. Suit can also be brought, however, by the parents of the wife on her behalf, without her consent.

Generally, parties will be living separately at the time they file for divorce, as are Lily and Mario. It is not an impediment to obtaining a divorce that the parties continue to reside in the marital home while the divorce is pending. Nor can failure of the offended spouse to leave the marital home be raised as a defense to the alleged wrongful conduct of the other spouse. TENN. CODE ANN. §36-4-111.

In our case, if Lily files for divorce, she will probably allege both irreconcilable differences and inappropriate marital conduct. If the parties are able to resolve all their legal issues and sign an MDA, they can proceed with the ID divorce. If not, she will have the inappropriate marital conduct to fall back on as a fault ground for a contested divorce. As we mentioned earlier, most cases do settle prior to trial, but most attorneys will include a fault ground in the pleading as a precaution to prevent having to amend the divorce complaint in the event that the matter goes to trial. Mediation is mandated in most cases.

After Mario is served with the complaint for divorce, he will have to answer the allegations of the complaint and may choose to file a counter-complaint in which he also asks for a divorce. He will probably allege the same grounds that Lily alleged because at this point he is unaware of Lily's adultery. After Lily's adultery is revealed during discovery, Mario can amend his counter-complaint to allege adultery as an additional divorce ground.

In Tennessee, the complaint for divorce, the counter-complaint, and the answer must be verified, meaning that the parties have to swear that the allegations in the pleadings are true, to the best of their knowledge. The complaint must also be accompanied by written notice of an automatic temporary injunction imposed on both of the parties preventing them from: 1) dissipating marital assets; 2) changing insurance policies; 3) harassing, threatening, assaulting or abusing the other or making disparaging remarks about the other to, or in the presence, of the children or to either party's employer; 4) destroying electronic evidence (*i.e.*, home computers); or 5) relocating out of state or more than 100 miles away with the children.

China[*]

Unlike in the U.S. and Italy, where both legal separation and divorce are available as remedies for failed marriages, in China, separation is only a fac-

---

[*] This part is written by Chen Wei, Pi Xijun, and Ran Qiyu.

tor for courts to consider in deciding whether to grant a divorce. Article 32 Section 3 of the current Marriage Law provides that where both parties have lived separately due to irreconcilable differences for up to two years, it demonstrates that mutual affection has been broken and the marriage only exists nominally. Under this Article, the court is given flexibility to grant a divorce if mediation fails. However, if parties separate for other reasons such as working, studying, being in the hospital, or going abroad, etc., it will not fall into the type of separation needed for granting a divorce because neither party had a subjective desire to separate. Accordingly, a divorce will not be granted in such a case.

As previously mentioned, in China, a divorce can be achieved in two ways. The first is divorce at registry, by mutual consent. Similar to Tennessee's "no fault, only by consent" divorce, parties will receive divorce certificates if they both agree to get divorced and settle amicably their property, any debts, and care of children. In this approach, both parties should first desire to dissolve the bonds of matrimony and reach an agreement. Both parties must then go to the registration office in person and fill in the divorce application together. Upon examination and ratification by the registry office, a divorce can be granted and a divorce certificate can be issued. Unlike Tennessee, where ID divorces require a sixty-day or ninety-day waiting period, no waiting period is required in China.

Until recently, a divorce was rare in China. Parties needed to get permission from their work units before they could go to the divorce registration office. The permission, however, was rarely given. The rules changed at the end of 2003. Now unhappy couples, upon reaching consent, can directly go to their local divorce registration office. The divorce certificate will be issued in only a few minutes, for as little as 9 Yuan. The ease and speed with which the parties can now divorce has lead to the use of a new term, "flash divorce."

The second way to get a divorce is to file a petition. Under the current Marriage Law, when a divorce is initiated by one party by filing for divorce in court, a procedure of mediation is required. Unlike in the U.S., where mediation is usually an optional alternative way to solve divorce issues, mediation in China is mandatory in the divorce process. After filing for a divorce, the courts require both parties to go through the mediation process with the intent to preserve the marriage. Here, the mediation is really a reconciliation process, similar to that imposed in Italy. In the U.S., it would be similar to the court ordering the parties to attend marriage counseling for the purpose of trying to save the marriage, which is rarely done. In the U.S., if the parties get to point of being in court, it is generally assumed that the marriage is beyond repair. If this mediation process fails, then the court will proceed to another mediation process attempting to help couples to reach agreements on all divorce issues such as child custody, child support, property division, etc. The courts arrange this mediation process and appoint the mediators. If this mediation process also fails, then the divorce action will go to trial.

Article 32(2) of the current Marriage Law provides that a divorce should be granted if mediation fails and mutual affection has completely broken down. At first glance, the current Marriage Law is quite liberal regarding grounds for divorce because it emphasizes the loss of mutual affection as the only ground for a divorce. As pointed out by the SEVERAL OPINIONS ON THE JUDGMENT OF BREAKDOWN OF MUTUAL AFFECTION IN THE TRIAL OF DIVORCE CASES BY THE SUPREME PEOPLE'S COURT (1989) (Hereinafter referred to as Opinion 1989): "breakdown of mutual affection is the threshold question for the people's court to decide if divorce should be granted." However, it is rather difficult for the courts to assess the actual mutual affection between parties.

The Opinion 1989 gives courts a "four assessment" guideline in determining the breakdown of mutual affection under Article 32(2) of the current Marriage Law. Courts will comprehensively analyze the marriage foundation, the mutual affection after marriage, the current condition of mutual affection, and the possibility of reconciliation between the parties.

First, the court needs to make an assessment on the marriage foundation. A well-based marriage means the parties married voluntarily after a long-term loving relationship. An ill-based marriage means that the marriage was arranged or coerced by others. The later type of foundation is more likely to cause a breakdown of mutual affection because there was little to begin with.

Second, the court will make an assessment on the mutual affection after marriage. When the parties are still respective and considerate to each other, and still share the responsibility of rearing the young children and looking after their elder parents, the mutual affection most likely is not broken down.

Third, the causes for divorce will be evaluated by the court. The parties are required to list the reasons for divorce. However, some of the reasons are false. A judge is required to assess the credibility of the reasons to decide if the mutual affection has broken down.

Fourth, the court has to assess on the possibility of reconciliation. Based on the three assessments above, the courts make an assessment on the current marriage situation and predict whether reconciliation is possible. If the judge believes that there are prospects for reconciliation, then a divorce will not be granted. In contrast, a divorce will be granted if the judge believes that it is impossible for the parties to reconcile.

Even though the above "Four Assessments" method by the Supreme People's Court has offered a guideline for judicial practice, assessment on the breakdown of mutual affection remains a rather complicated issue. In order to reduce the mistakes in exercising the courts' discretion in deciding divorce cases, the current Marriage Law listed the following five legal grounds for courts to make a definite decision that the mutual affection has broken down. These grounds are clearly similar to "fault grounds" in U.S. divorce law.

The first ground is bigamy and extra-marital relationships. Bigamy refers to the act of anyone, who has a spouse, marrying another person. In China, bigamy can be classified into two kinds. One is legal bigamy, which means anyone conceals the fact of having a spouse and registers another marriage. The other is *de facto* bigamy, which refers to a married person who cohabits with someone of opposite sex, in the name of spouse, without marriage registration. According to Article 32 (3) of the current Marriage Law, where divorce is caused by the fact that either party is a bigamist or a person who has a spouse and cohabits with another person of the opposite sex, a divorce will be granted if mediation fails.

The second ground is abuse and abandonment. In accordance with Article 32 (3) of the current Marriage Law, where a divorce is caused by the acts of family violence or maltreatment or desertion of any family member, a divorce will be granted if mediation fails. Article 1 of Judicial Interpretation I of the current Marriage Law stipulates that family violence refers to acts causing certain harmful results to family members, regarding physical or mental injury, by battery, seizing, cruel treatment, or limiting personal freedom, forcefully or by other means. Maltreatment refers to the acts of beatings, verbal assaults, deprivation of food or clothes, isolation, forcing over-laboring, refusing to offer medical treatment to sick members, and so on, resulting in the physical and mental harm of family members. Desertion means the act of refusing legal support of the old, the young, the sick members, or other members who can't live independently without just cause.

The third ground is habitual gambling and drug abuse that remain incorrigible after frequent attempts at rehabilitation. Where either party has indulged in gambling, drug-abuse, or has other vicious habits, these activities dissipate community property, cause difficulty in family life, and shake up the material foundation of marriage. Pursuant to Article 32 (3) of the current Marriage Law, where one party indulged in these activities and refuses to correct his or her ways, despite repeated admonitions, a divorce should be granted when mediation fails.

The fourth ground is having lived apart for two years as a result of failure to maintain a loving relationship. Husband and wife have the duty of cohabitation after marriage. When both parties have lived separately due to the lack of mutual affection for up to two years, it demonstrates that mutual affection has died out so that marriage only nominally exists. Article 32 (3) of the current Marriage Law provides that if both parties have lived separately due to the lack of mutual affection for up to two years, a divorce will be granted if mediation fails. But where both parties separate for objective reasons such as working, studying, being in the hospital, and going abroad, etc., it will not constitute separation due to the lack of mutual affection. A divorce will not be granted, even if mediation by people's court fails in such a case.

The fifth ground is the catch-all ground that includes all other circumstances leading to failure to maintain a loving relationship (Article 32(3)). In addition to the four main grounds to judge the breakdown of mutual affection, this provision of Opinion 1989 generalizes other circumstances that have led to the nonexistence of mutual affection between husband and wife:

(1) Where either party suffers from statutorily prohibited diseases, or one is suffering from physical disability, or there exists other circumstances causing the failure of sexual activity, which are difficult to cure;

(2) Where the marriage was entered into hastily, parties lacked mutual understanding before marriage, and mutual affection has not been established after marriage;

(3) Where either party conceals the fact of suffering from mental disease before marriage that is not cured after marriage, or one suffers from mental disease during marriage, which can't be cured after treatment of a long time;

(4) Where both parties don't cohabit after marriage registration, and it is impossible to become reconciled;

(5) Though both parties have cohabited for many years in arranged or mercenary marriages, mutual affection has not been established.

(6) Where either party commits adultery, which harms mutual affection severely; or

(7) Where either party was sentenced to long-term imprisonment, or her or his illegal conduct or crimes damage mutual affection seriously.

In addition, unlike in the U.S. where the party at fault cannot, under some conditions, obtain a divorce, without the other party's consent, in China, the party at fault has the right to file for a divorce because the breakdown of mutual affection is the sole legal ground for a divorce action according to Article 32(2) of the current Marriage Law. Furthermore, Article 22 of Judicial Interpretation I of the current Marriage Law states that in dealing with a divorce petition on Article 32(2), the courts should not deny a divorce because the party who filed for a divorce is at fault. That is, the party at fault still has the right to bring an action for divorce, when a claiming breakdown of mutual affection as the only ground for divorce.

The current Marriage Law also recognizes void and voidable marriage. Under the Article 10 of the current Marriage Law, if one of the following four circumstances is found, the marriage will be announced void by courts. The four circumstances are bigamy, consanguineous marriage that is forbidden by law, having a certain illness before the marriage where it is forbidden by law to marry, and having not reached lawful matrimonial age. In addition, Article 11 states that the marriage is voidable where one party was coerced to marriage. The coerced party must apply to annul the marriage within a year of marriage registration. The void and voidable marriages are invalid *ab initio*, and the parties do not have the rights and obligations of husband and wife. The property incurred during the cohabitant period should be disposed of by both parties upon agreement. If no agreement is reached, the court will make a judgment in the light most favorable to the innocent party.

In our case, if the parties cannot go through divorce by the mutual consent process, by reaching an agreement regarding all their legal issues, either Mario or Lily will have to file for a divorce in court. The court will first mediate. If mediation fails, the litigation procedure will begin. If Mario initiated the litigation for divorce, it is quite possible that Shaping Ba District People's Court in China will not support the claim of Mario in the first suit. Mario may argue that the mutual affection has broken down for the following reasons: 1) the views of the plaintiff and the defendant about child-rearing and education of the children diverges so greatly that it has resulted in the breakdown of mutual affection; 2) the defendant's interest in the neighbor has harmed mutual affection severely. Though no evidence has been found by the plaintiff to prove the defendant has a sexual relationship with Alex, many signs show that the defendant has a close relationship with Alex. The plaintiff thinks the disloyalty of the defendant has harmed mutual affection gravely; and 3) the defendant's unwillingness to go to work outside caused complaints of the plaintiff, which strengthens the family conflict.

Mario will allege that the facts and causes above have demonstrated that the mutual affection has completely broken down, so a divorce should be granted according to Article 32 of the current Marriage Law. Therefore, he will plead the court to find out the truth and make a just decision according to law.

However, Lily will argue that the mutual affection has not broken down for the following reasons: 1) although the couple had differences in child-rearing and education, these differences only caused a small crack in their mutual affection, which has not broken down completely; 2) they should be able to resolve their differences and repair the small crack in their mutual affection. Therefore, the requirements to grant a divorce in Article 32 of the current Marriage Law are not satisfied. Therefore, Lily will plead the court to find out the facts and make a fair judgment.

Next, the court will carefully examine the representative opinions given by the respective attorneys of the plaintiff and the defendant. The judge will most likely hold that the grounds for divorce are not sufficient. Therefore, the requirements of the breakdown of mutual affection to grant a divorce in Article 32 of the current Marriage Law are not fulfilled. As a result, if mediation fails, the people's court will not grant a divorce according to law. According to Article 134 of PROCEDURE LAW, the people's court will publicly pronounce its judgment in all cases, even if the case was not publicly tried. If a judgment is pronounced in court, the written judgment shall be issued and delivered within ten days. Upon pronouncement of a judgment, the parties concerned must be informed of their right to file an appeal.

If the plaintiff insists on filing for a divorce again and the defendant agrees, but they still cannot reach an agreement on the child-rearing, the disposal of joint property and the financial assistance, a divorce can be granted and issues concerning the rearing of the child, the disposal of joint property, and the financial assistance can be rendered according to law. If the plaintiff files the divorce suit again and the defendant agrees to a divorce, it shows that they reached agreement that their mutual affection has broken down. Accordingly, the people's court should grant a divorce. It should be pointed out that if the plaintiff insists on a divorce in the second suit, even if the defendant does not agree to a divorce, and the mediation fails, the judge usually grants a divorce. Because if the court denies a divorce the second time, the plaintiff will most likely file for a divorce again, which shows that there is no hope for parties to reconcile, and that the mutual affection has broken down so that the requirements to grant a divorce in Article 32 of the current Marriage Law has been fulfilled.

In addition, in the divorce case of *Mario v. Lily*, if the plaintiff Mario has evidence to prove that the defendant Lily has committed adultery with the neighbor Alex in the trial of the first suit, and Mario had tried to persuade Lily to be loyal to the marriage, but she didn't make an effort to stop seeing Alex, which resulted in hard quarrels between them so that mutual affection has broken down and both parties can not live together, the court may grant a divorce according to Article 32(3)(v) (the "catch-all ground") of the current Marriage Law where the mediation fails under such circumstances. The court can grant a divorce on the ground that the adulterous relationship of the defendant with the neighbor harmed mutual affection severely, which led to the breakdown of affection between husband and wife.

Furthermore, in the divorce case *Mario v. Lily*, where both parties have separated from each other for two full years for lack of mutual affection, even if the plaintiff is asking for a divorce for the first time, the judge may grant a divorce according to Article 32(3)(iv) (the "separation ground") of the current Marriage Law where mediation fails.

Italy

Unlike in the U.S. and in many other countries where divorce is available as a direct remedy to a failed marriage, in Italy legal separation and divorce are combined and connected remedies. As we have seen, historically, separation was the only remedy available in the Italian legal system for a failed marriage until the Law of Divorce in 1970. But even after passage of the Law of Divorce, legal separation still receives thorough, some say excessive, with respect to its current purpose, formal treatment in the Civil Code, while divorce is the object of special law, with inevitable duplication of procedures and some unresolved asymmetries.

Just as in the U.S., in Italy legal separation grants a change in some of the legal obligations flowing from marriage but does not alter the ultimate essence of the status. Hence, during legal separation, the marriage remains in effect, albeit in suspended animation. Just like in the U.S., neither party is free to remarry, property acquired during legal separation is still marital property, unless it is divided by the court during the separation proceeding, and if one of the spouses dies during separation, the other is the surviving spouse with respect to succession.

It is only through the institution of divorce that the civil marriage is dissolved, or, to use the politically palatable subtle distinction adopted by the Law of Divorce, the civil effects of a religious marriage cease. The practical effect of this system, if not to discourage a formal divorce proceeding in favor of staying bound in a failed marriage, is to slow down the process of attaining a divorce, to stimulate out-of-court negotiation and mediation between the parties, *de facto* taking the edge off the adversary posturing of the spouses by legal disincentives. Those couples who find a way to remain reasonable and work out their differences through the trial period of separation, and reach a workable joint divorce petition are rewarded with a more expeditious and more economical outcome. The legal order has accepted a hands off posture vis-à-vis the spouses or ex spouses, while maintaining its vigilance as *pater patriae* on the interests of the children to education, maintenance, shared parental role during their upbringing, and even continued involvement with the respective extended families, notwithstanding the fact that the spouses may have chosen to become ex spouses.

Divorce in Italy can be characterized as no fault. In fact, the reform operated by L. 87/74 (Law 6 marzo 1987 n. 74, Gazz. Uff. 11 marzo 1987, n. 058) eliminated all traces of a fault basis by abrogating the possibility for the spouse not at fault to object, reducing the required separation period to three years, and introducing the procedural expedient of a joint petition. The law of divorce affirms the principle of dissolubility of the legal matrimonial bond in line with a tendency to privatize family relationships. Sesta, at 3205. The model apparently adopted by the legal system is divorce as a remedy (as opposed to divorce-sanction, consensual divorce, or divorce-repudiation), which seems to better reconcile the countervailing needs: to protect the stability of matrimony and to safeguard the freedoms of the individual. *Id.* at 3207. However, at least in theory, dissolubility is still configured as the exception because divorce remains limited to the specifically enumerated causes identified by law.

Based on Arts. 1 and 3, L. 868/70 dissolution or cessation of the civil effects of marriage is available on the basis of an ascertainment by the judge that the material and spiritual communion of the spouses can no longer be re-established based on one of the causes (cases, or premises as they are interchangeably referred to) enumerated in Art. 3. In Art. 3, the law provides a non-homogeneous list hard to categorize and reconcile, which has generated and continues to generate endless doctrinal debate and jurisprudential variations. The focus of the law seems to be on the inclusion of all those instances where a criminal violation by one spouse is antithetical to the possibility of a matrimonial communion. The emphasis however, is not on the time of the crime, or even on whether the other spouse was aware of the commission of the crime at the time of marriage, but on the juridical event of the adjudication of guilt, or the imposition of a sentence of a specific duration. Therefore, we find in the list sentences of fifteen years to life imprisonment (there is no capital punishment in Italy, and life imprisonment generally does not exclude the possibility of parole), the enumeration of voluntary homicide or its attempt against a child or the spouse (no matter if no sentence was in fact applied), and a specific list of crimes. In case of indictment of any crime, including against a child or the spouse not ending in adjudication of guilt, it would seem that the spouse who survived would be left with the catch-all remedy of the three years separation like everyone else as the only avenue to end the marriage.

Other causes for divorce are the annulment, divorce or a new marriage abroad obtained or celebrated by the foreign spouse. This norm is intended to avoid a situation of moral and judicial disparity, and to offer a remedy to the one-spouse-marriage situation where Italian law would have obligated the Italian spouse to remain bonded to a promise unilaterally while the foreign spouse would free himself by recourse to the law of his country of origin. SESTA, at 3227. In these cases, the cessation of the material and spiritual communion and the impossibility of re-establishing it, which is at the basis of the petition for divorce, is self evident.

Another divorce ground is the non-consummation of the marriage, which represents another attempt to equalize the legal field for catholic and non-catholic citizens. Catholics who had contracted matrimony under the Concordat (before a catholic priest and then transcribed) had and continue to have access to the remedial arsenal of ecclesiastic annulment before the Ecclesiastic Courts, featuring opportunities to disengage from the bonds centered on the sexual "rights and duties" inherent to it. SESTA, at 3229. The Constitutional Court declared Art. 1 of the Concordat unconstitutional in the portion that prescribed the executory nature of the dispensation relative to the civil effect of the dual rite matrimony creating an alternative jurisdiction to the civil jurisdiction for dual rite matrimony. *Id.*; CCost 2 feb. 1982/18, FI, 1982 I, 934. This is one of the key points where the Law of Divorce implements the separation of Church and State and sanctions their respective independence. Conversely and perversely, this stance ends up influencing the civil configuration of matrimony possibly attributing to the aspect of sexuality, which in the secular sphere is seen as a mere component of marriage, still a predominant importance.

Another cause for divorce is identified in the case where one of the spouses undergoes a sex change procedure. This norm correlates to L. 82/164 (Law 14 aprile 1982 N. 164, Gazz. Uff. 19 aprile 1982, n. 106) which succinctly regulates the procedure and the effect of obtaining a sex reassignment.

However, as we have seen, the one cause for divorce that is used most often is legal separation for a minimum of three years and the ensuing failed attempt at reconciliation, at the time of filing for divorce, accounting for over 99% of the cases. There are two mandatory components: a final decree of judicial separation or a homologation (official recognition) of the consensual separation, and the passage of the prescribed period of time. In practice, separation has become an almost universal cause of divorce, morphing from the temporary remedy of legal separation that ends in reconciliation, to a stepping stone toward divorce three years later. SESTA, at 3237. In addition, as mentioned in the previous chapter, the President of the Tribunal will personally meet with the spouses, both at the time of separation and again at the time of the divorce, to attempt reconciliation.

As seen previously, judicial legal separation is premised on the existence of facts that render intolerable to the spouses the prosecution of their life in com-

mon, or such as to be gravely prejudicial vis-à-vis the education of their children. C.c. Art. 151. The consensual is based on the spouses' agreement: the
law only requires judicial oversight of that agreement. There are very limited
grounds on which the judge would have grounds to refuse homologation (official recognition) of a consensual.

On the other hand, marital fault has been eliminated as a foundation for
divorce, even though it may be relevant for the determination of the financial
and personal consequences. Indeed, the reform of the institution of separation has configured it as a remedy of wide breadth, for the protection of the
individual right to self determination, thereby providing a wide receptacle for
multiple individual circumstances. SESTA, at 498. The very spouse who, with
his behaviors, causes the intolerability of life in common is in no way precluded from taking advantage of the institution of separation. Likewise, a decision of judicial separation is not precluded because one of the spouses re-
sists, hoping that the other will reconsider at a later date. One interpretive
trend takes the individualistic approach to mean that the evaluation of intolerability is subjective to the petitioning spouse and not objective for the judge
to ascertain. *Id.* at 499. Another trend maintains that the intolerability and
the prejudice have to be grounded in behaviors contrary to the duties arising
from marriage. *Id.* Because of this interpretation ambiguity, it is customary
for an attorney in a petition for separation to list specific facts constituting an
alleged breach of the matrimonial contract. Therefore, the point of reference
for the petition in a judicial separation is the rights and duties arising by law
in favor of and for each spouse, including loyalty, moral and material support,
cooperation in the interest of the family, and cohabitation. C.c. Art. 143. A
judicial petition will state how specific behaviors of the other spouse failed to
meet his obligations with a view to identify "fattispecie" (grounds) that may
be more likely to constitute the basis for a possible charge (*addebito*) against
the other spouse. For example, Mario's temporary abandonment of the marital home in view of the difficulties he and his wife were experiencing may
constitute a *de facto* separation, but it does not start the clock ticking for the
three year period required for the subsequent divorce petition, nor does it per
se constitute a violation of the duty of cohabitation. C.c. Art. 146. The factual basis for *addebito (charging one spouse with responsibility for the separation)* cannot be just violations of the duties imposed by marriage, the consequence of an already active and progressive disintegration of the moral and
material communion of the spousal relationship. Instead, instances justifying
addebito must be at the root of the marriage disintegration, and must have a
direct causal connection to it. The judge in the evaluation will look at the conduct of both spouses and undertake a comparative evaluation. The judge will

also examine the conduct of the spouses in its entirety, rather than focus on just one episode. Either or both spouses can present a request for *addebito*. *Addebito* is relevant to the determination of the maintenance check. C.c. Arts. 548 and 585. Otherwise, the obligation of support of the legally separated spouse is based on the financial abilities and the need of each spouse, just like before separation. After the order of the tribunal or homologation (official recognition) in the consensual, the spouse who owes a maintenance check and fails to pay it, is criminally liable.

As a matter of course then, the parties will start separation proceedings with an eye towards the final objective of obtaining a divorce. The issues that normally confront spouses at the time of their divorce petition in the U.S. will be broached and mediated (or litigated), at least in great part, at the time of separation. Separate attorneys, or even the same attorney, if Lily and Mario choose the consensual, will work to mediate differences out of court and reach a structured agreement that includes custody, visitation, and child support. Routinely, the attorneys will advise their clients about the economic, emotional, and time-saving advantages of a consensual petition followed by a joint divorce petition. Indeed, only a very small percentage of judicial separations end with "*addebito*" to one spouse, resulting in financial consequences different from what a consensual would have produced while also requiring a much higher cost in representation, emotional aggravation for spouses and children, and extended time frames for resolution. Mario and Lily, through a consensual in Italy, have relatively ample latitude to set the conditions of their separation. Later, a joint divorce petition is the logical progression after a consensual and provides the advantage of saving time and money.

Summary Chart—Grounds for Divorce

	U.S. (Tennessee)	China	Italy
Legal separation as remedy.	Yes	No	Yes
No fault divorce by consent.	Irreconcilable differences divorce only by consent in TN. Parties have to wait sixty or ninety days.	Yes, it is called breakdown of mutual affection, dissolving the marriage in just a few minutes.	Yes to no fault divorce, but not by consent. Requires judicial verification that the material and spiritual communion of the spouses can no longer be reestablished based on enumerated "causes" the most common of which is three years of legal separation.
Divorce through registration by mutual consent.	No	Yes	No
Mediation.	Available as an alternative dispute resolution process and mandatory in most cases in Tennessee.	Mandatory.	Mandatory reconciliation attempt by the President of the Tribunal. Available out of court mediation.
Reconciliation attempt by the court.	Not routinely, although a judge could choose to do so in a given case.	Yes, through mandatory mediation.	Yes, by the President of the Tribunal, both at the time of legal separation and at the time of the divorce.
No fault grounds.	Yes, in TN, if there are no minor children and the parties live separately for two years. Also in some form in most other states.	Yes, called breakdown of mutual affection.	Yes
Mutual affection as ground.	No	Yes	No

continued	U.S. (Tennessee)	China	Italy
Party at fault has standing to sue.	No	Yes	Yes
Void and voidable marriage.	Yes	Yes	Yes
Hybrid ground.	Two years of legal separation as ground.	Two years of separation as grounds for divorce.	Three years of legal separation is the most common ground (cause).

CHAPTER 7

CHILD CUSTODY
AND VISITATION

United States

Historical Background

Historically, in the United States, mothers were generally awarded primary custody of the children under the tender years doctrine, which was based on the theory that it was in a young child's best interest to be placed in the mother's custody. The doctrine was expanded to the point that mothers enjoyed a presumption of custody, absent rebuttal of that presumption by proof of unfitness, exigent circumstances, harm to the child, etc. Beginning in the 1970s, courts began to strike down the tender years presumption on equal protection grounds. Various state legislatures also passed statutory prohibitions concerning the tender years presumption. TENN. CODE ANN. 36-6-101(d) ("It is the legislative intent that the gender of the party seeking custody shall not give rise to a presumption of parental fitness or cause a presumption or constitute a factor in favor of or against the award of custody to such party."). Some states substituted a presumption in favor of the child's primary caretaker, but most states now require the court to consider a number of factors and to award custody based on the best interests of the child, using a comparative fitness standard which compares the parties' fitness as parents. A few states impose a presumption in favor of joint custody, or equally shared custody.

Terminology

Historically, custody was divided into physical and legal custody. In most instances, physical custody was given to one parent, usually the mother, and visitation was given to the other parent, usually the father. In this scenario, the children would live primarily with the mother and would visit periodically with the father. Other possibilities included joint physical custody, where the child spent equal or nearly equal amounts of time with each parent, and, in cases involving multiple children, split physical custody, where one parent was the custodial parent of one or more children and the other parent was also the custodial parent of one or more children (*i.e.*, girls live with Mom, boys live with Dad).

Legal custody (decision making authority) could be allocated to the custodial parent or shared. Custody could also be allocated for specific issues, such as religious custody (where one parent would be responsible for the child's religious training), or medical custody (where one parent would be responsible for making medical decisions for the child).

Use of the custody/visitation designations led to a claimed perception that the custodial parent was the "real" parent, post divorce, and the other parent was just the "visitor." In addition, because custody was awarded based on the comparative fitness of the parents, there was the perception that the custodial parent was the "good" parent and the other parent was the "bad" parent. There was also the perception of a winner and a loser in the custody battle. More recently, a number of states have adopted more inclusive language designed to decease parental acrimony and to encourage post divorce cooperation regarding parental duties. Instead of granting custody to one parent and visitation to the other, courts "allocate parenting responsibilities," designating one parent as the primary residential parent and the other as the alternate residential parent, for instance. Legal custody is termed "decision making authority."

Tennessee has adopted inclusive terminology, replacing "custody" and "visitation" with "parenting responsibilities," which are allocated between the "primary residential parent" (PRP) and the "alternate residential parent" (ARP). A "residential schedule" designates where the child will reside on any given day of the year. TENN. CODE ANN. §36-6-402.

Agreement

Most parents are able to reach an agreement on custody and visitation. Settlements are encouraged, but must be approved by the court, based on the best interests of the child. Courts generally defer, however, to the parties' judgment about what is best for their child, if the terms appear reasonable. In Tennessee, the agreement would be set forth in a document called a parenting plan (see discussion below). Once the parenting plan is approved by the court and incorporated by reference into the court's decree, it becomes an order of the court and must be followed by the parties. If one parent wants to modify the plan, over the objection of the other parent, a petition must be filed with the court showing the need for the change.

Parenting Plans

Historically, custody orders and agreements were very general in nature, usually granting custody to one party and liberal or reasonable visitation to the other. This approach gave the parents a great deal of flexibility but burdened the court with multiple petitions where the parents were not able to cooperate post divorce. A number of jurisdictions now require the use of parenting plans. These plans may be temporary, during the pendency of the divorce proceedings, or permanent, governing post divorce parenting. The agreements are designed to assist the parents in allocating parental responsibilities during and after the divorce and to emphasize the continuing parental roles of both parties. The plans are very specific and require the parties to allocate parenting responsibilities for every day of the year, including holidays, birthdays, vacations, etc. The parenting plan must also allocate decision making authority and typically requires dispute resolution mechanisms that the parties must utilize, prior to returning to court, when disagreements arise concerning the interpretation of the parenting plan provisions, post divorce.

Tennessee has enacted legislation that requires the use of both temporary and permanent parenting plans. If the parties are not able to reach agreement on the terms of the temporary and permanent parenting plans, the court will devise one for the parties, taking into account a number of statutory factors. At a minimum, the permanent plan must include a residential schedule, which clarifies the residential time allocation between the parents, including vacations and holidays, and must also include a process for resolving future disputes prior to bringing a court action. TENN. CODE ANN. § 36-6-404(a).

If Lily and Mario can agree on the terms of a temporary parenting plan while the divorce is pending, no written plan is required to be entered with the court. If they cannot agree, as is likely to be the case here, either party may request the court to order dispute resolution. TENN. CODE ANN. § 36-6-403. In that event, the court will most likely order the parties to attend mediation in an effort to help the parties reach an agreement on a temporary parenting plan. If dispute resolution is not available, the statute allows either party to request an expedited hearing to establish a temporary parenting plan.

At the time of the final divorce hearing, the court must approve or order a permanent parenting plan. If the parties are not able to submit an agreed plan, the court can order the parties to attend mediation again. If mediation is unsuccessful, each party will be permitted to submit a proposed permanent parenting plan and the court will craft a permanent parenting plan, considering the statutory factors that the court believes are in the child's best interests. If only one party submits a proposed permanent parenting plan, the court may simply adopt that plan, if the court finds that it is in the child's best interests to do so. If abuse or abandonment is found, special rules apply to prohibit or limit the use of court ordered dispute resolution.

Parenting Coordinators, Domestic Relations Decision-Makers ("decision-makers"), and Arbitrators

Social science research has indicated that exposure to parental conflict is correlated to poor developmental outcomes in children. In high conflict cases, courts are using a number of intervention techniques to assist the parties in co-parenting and to provide the parties with additional assistance designed to help them resolve disputes, particularly those related to the children. The goal is to identify the high conflict cases early in the divorce process, to implement various techniques designed to lessen the conflict before it escalates, to prevent or at least minimize the potential harm to the child. *See, i.e.*, Colo. Rev. Stat. §§ 14-10-128.1 to 14-10-128.5.

Tennessee does not have statutory authority for parenting coordinators, but some judges have appointed parenting coordinators in complex and acrimonious custody cases. The facts of our case are not likely to warrant the appointment of a parenting coordinator, although the court will probably order the parties to mediation.

Mediation

Mediation is growing in popularity as a vehicle for settling divorce cases. Mediation involves the use of a trained neutral party (lawyer, financial analyst, psychologist, etc.) who guides the parties through the negotiation process to assist them in reaching an agreement on some or all of their divorce related issues. Some courts mandate mediation (referred to as court annexed mediation) for virtually all divorce cases, in an effort to move the parties toward settlement and to prevent escalation of conflict between the parties. Exceptions generally exist for cases involving domestic abuse. The cost of mediation is usually assessed against the parties by the court as costs, dividing the amount equitably, with provisions for reduced fees or *pro bono* mediation for indigent litigants.

In Tennessee, either party may request the court to order mediation, or the court may do so on its own motion. Some Tennessee courts mandate mediation in their local rules, absent a waiver by the court. *See*, Tenn. 25th District Chancery Court Rule 17.02. The court may not order mediation in cases involving abuse, except under limited circumstances which are designed to protect the victims of abuse. Tenn. Code Ann. §36-6-107. There is no order of protection or finding of abuse in our facts, so the court would probably order the parties to mediation if they are not able to agree on a parenting plan on their own. The parties can choose their mediator or select from a list provided by the court. The court will award the mediator's fee as costs in the divorce case.

Parent Education Classes

As noted previously, parental conflict can be very detrimental for children, especially for children of divorce. In an effort to reduce the exposure of children to post divorce parental conflict, many courts require parents to attend parental education classes. The assumption is that most parents love their children and want to do what is best for them, but that many parents are not aware of the special needs of their children after the divorce or perhaps the parents are so focused on their own issues that they fail to recognize the children's needs. The classes usually last several hours and address such topics as the perception among many children that they are somehow to blame for the divorce, the detrimental effect on the child when one parent disparages the other parent in front of the child, and child's need to have a loving relationship with both parents.

Tennessee requires parents to attend a four-hour parent educational seminar. It is statutorily required to educate parents concerning how to protect and enhance the child's emotional development and to inform the parents regarding the legal process. The seminar must include a discussion of alternative dispute resolution, marriage counseling, the judicial process, and common perpetrator attitudes and conduct involving domestic violence. Tenn. Code Ann. §36-6-408. The seminar is educational in nature and is not designed for individual therapy. Children may not attend. The court may waive the seminar requirement upon a showing of good cause. Fees for the seminar may be assessed by the court as it deems equitable and may be waived for indigent persons. *Id.* The court may hold a party in contempt for refusal to attend the educational seminar and may consider the refusal as evidence of lack of good faith in determining custody, but the court cannot refuse to grant a divorce based on the failure of either or both parties to attend the educational seminar. TENN. CODE ANN. § 36-6-101 (e). The parties are required to attend the seminar as soon as possible after filing the complaint for divorce and prior to attending any mediation sessions.

In our case, Lily and Mario could attend the seminar together or separately. Hopefully, the information conveyed in the seminar will better equip them to work toward a plan for coparenting during and after the divorce proceeding that will foster cooperation and support the healthy emotional development of both Jade and Dino.

Factors

When the parties are not able to reach agreement on custody and visitation issues, the court must decide based on the best interests of the child. Courts are typically given a great deal of discretion in making custody awards and are generally guided by statutory factors.

In Tennessee, the court must make a custody determination based on the best interests of the child and, in doing so, must consider all relevant factors, including the following, where applicable:

(1) The love, affection and emotional ties existing between the parents or caregivers and the child;

(2) The disposition of the parents or caregivers to provide the child with food, clothing, medical care, education and other necessary care and the degree to which a parent or caregiver has been the primary caregiver;

(3) The importance of continuity in the child's life and the length of time the child has lived in a stable, satisfactory environment; provided, that, where there is a finding ... of child abuse ... or child sexual abuse ... by one (1) parent, and that a nonperpetrating parent or caregiver has relocated in order to flee the perpetrating parent, that the relocation shall not weigh against an award of custody;

(4) The stability of the family unit of the parents or caregivers;

(5) The mental and physical health of the parents or caregivers;

(6) The home, school and community record of the child;

(7) (A) The reasonable preference of the child, if twelve (12) years of age or older; (B) The court may hear the preference of a younger child on request. The preferences of older children should normally be given greater weight than those of younger children;

(8) Evidence of physical or emotional abuse to the child, to the other parent or to any other person; provided, that, where there are alle-

gations that one (1) parent has committed child abuse ... or child sexual abuse ... against a family member, the court shall consider all evidence relevant to the physical and emotional safety of the child, and determine, by a clear preponderance of the evidence, whether such abuse has occurred. The court shall include in its decision a written finding of all evidence, and all findings of facts connected to the evidence. In addition, the court shall, where appropriate, refer any issues of abuse to the juvenile court for further proceedings;

(9) The character and behavior of any other person who resides in or frequents the home of a parent or caregiver and the person's interactions with the child; and

(10) Each parent or caregiver's past and potential for future performance of parenting responsibilities, including the willingness and ability of each of the parents and caregivers to facilitate and encourage a close and continuing parent-child relationship between the child and both of the child's parents, consistent with the best interest of the child. TENN. CODE ANN. § 36-6-106.

Lily will probably focus her evidence on the fact that she has been the primary caregiver, that only she made the effort to learn sign language, that Mario is ashamed of Dino's deafness, and that Mario bullies Jade into playing sports, indifferent to the distress it causes her.

Mario will argue that he is a very involved father, especially in light of his job responsibilities; that he is not ashamed of Dino but only wants to pursue all viable medical alternatives; that he is not bullying Jade but is just encouraging her to face challenges that will help her build character; that Lily wants to keep Dino dependent on her by limiting him to sign language and not pursuing medical alternatives; and that Lily is overly protective of Jade and doesn't make her do anything she doesn't want to do, especially when it serves to undermine his relationship with Jade. If the parties are not able to work out their differences and agree to a parenting plan, the court will have to sort out a residential schedule that it deems to be in the children's best interests, taking into account the relevant statutory factors listed above.

Representation for the Child

Representation for children in divorce cases is generally not required, but is left to the judge's discretion. Most courts will appoint representation in difficult cases and in cases involving allegations of abuse. The representation may take the form of a guardian *ad litem* or an attorney *ad litem*. Although there are multiple variations of each role, strictly speaking, the guardian *ad litem* represents the child's best interests and need not be an attorney. The attorney *ad litem*, however, must be an attorney and is appointed to represent the child client. In some cases, where the child's wishes and the child's best interests differ, the court may appoint both a guardian *ad litem* and an attorney *ad litem*.

In Tennessee, the only formalized rules concerning the duties of the child representative are limited to juvenile court cases involving allegations of neglect or abuse. Those rules were extended to divorce cases by the legislature for a short period and were then repealed. Currently, the role of the child's representative in Tennessee divorce cases is determined by the court when making the appointment. TENN. CODE ANN. §36-4-132 authorizes the court to appoint a guardian *ad litem* for the child in a divorce proceeding, upon the court's own motion or upon the motion of either party. The court may assess the costs and fees of the guardian *ad litem* against the parties as the court deems equitable, but the costs and fees may also be waived, upon motion by an indigent party. The guardian *ad litem* is presumed to be acting in good faith and while so doing is immune from liability that might otherwise attach while acting within the scope of the appointment. TENN. CODE ANN. §36-4-132. Any report filed by the guardian *ad litem*, as a result of his or her investigation may be reviewed by the court and the parties, but the report is not admissible against a hearsay objection. *Toms v. Toms*, 98 S.W.3d 140, 144 (Tenn. 2003). Case law has sanctioned the appointment of an attorney *ad litem* in a divorce case, at least for purposes of representing the guardian *ad litem* on appeal, as being within the trial court's discretion. *See Toms v. Toms*, 209 S.W.3d 76, 81 (Tenn. Ct. App. 2005).

The Child's Voice

Children are rarely called upon or permitted to testify in contested custody matters. There are two primary reasons for this approach. The first is that children are generally not sufficiently mature to make a considered judgment regarding custody preferences. The second is that courts do not want to put the burden on the child of having to choose between parents. The decision concerning the child's ability to testify is usually left to the court's discretion, but older children may have a statutory right to testify. The child's testimony, if allowed, is generally given *in camera*, with only the parties' attorneys present, along with the judge.

In Tennessee, the reasonable preference of a child of twelve years of age or older is a factor that must be considered by the court. TENN. CODE ANN. §36-

6-106. The court also has the discretion to hear the preference of a younger child, if requested. Even though the court may be required to consider the reasonable preference of a twelve-year-old, that preference is not outcome determinative. It is only one factor among many that the court must consider in making a custody determination.

Jade, who is nine, and Dino, who is five, are too young to have a right to be heard on the custody issue in Tennessee. The court has discretion to receive testimony from the children regarding their preferences, but it is unlikely that the court would ask such young children to testify, or that the court would grant the request of either parent to allow the children to testify. If critical facts were contested that the court felt could be clarified by the children's testimony, the court might consider an *in camera* examination. If, for instance, Lily insists on a provision precluding Mario from forcing Jade to play sports and Mario objects, the court may want to examine Jade to determine the validity of Lily's claim that Mario's demands are endangering Jade's health. The court will probably attempt to make that determination without involving the child, though, if possible.

Jurisdiction

The United States has both federal and state laws that govern subject matter jurisdiction to determine custody issues. The statutes were passed to address the serious problem of parental kidnapping in which one parent would be granted custody of the children in state A and the other parent would kidnap the children and take them to state B and obtain a court order granting custody to the kidnapping parent. The federal law, the Parental Kidnapping Prevention Act (PKPA), 28 U.S.C. § 1738A *et seq.*; and the state laws, the (UCCJA) Uniform Child Custody Jurisdiction Act and the more recent Uniform Child Custody Jurisdiction and Enforcement Act (UCCJEA) TENN. CODE ANN. § 36-6-201 *et seq.*; are designed to identify the one state court with jurisdiction to enter an initial custody order, to determine whether that initial court has continuing exclusive jurisdiction over the initial decree or whether that continuing exclusive jurisdiction has been lost and another state court has jurisdiction to modify the initial decree. The acts also address matters concerning emergency jurisdiction and various enforcement procedures.

The United States is also a signatory to the Hague Convention on the Civil Aspect of International Child Abduction which governs international abductions of children under sixteen years of age. The Hague Convention applies when one parent wrongfully removes a child from the country that is the child's "habitual residence," in breach of the other parent's custody rights, and takes the child to another country that is a signatory country. The convention only applies between countries that have ratified it. This convention has been ratified by more than seventy-five nations, including the United States.

In our case, both of the parents and the children live in Tennessee, so there are no other states or nations that have a claim of jurisdiction to determine custody. If the Tennessee court grants custody to Lily and Mario wrongfully takes the children to Italy, Lily could use the Hague Convention to get the Italian court to return the children. If custody is granted to Mario and Lily wrongfully takes the children to China, Mario could use the Hague Convention to get the Chinese courts to return the children only in Hong Kong and Macao. The rest of China is not a signatory to the Hague Convention on the Civil Aspect of International Child Abduction.

China

Historical Background

In China, the concept of "parents' right to child custody" did not appear in Marriage Law 1950, Marriage Law 1980, and the amended Marriage Law 2001 (Current Divorce Law). However, all the laws mentioned above clearly provide that, after divorce, both parents have the right and duty to bring up and educate their children. Furthermore, GENERAL PRINCIPLES OF THE CIVIL LAW OF PEOPLE'S REPUBLIC OF CHINA, (1986) (hereinafter referred to as General Principles of the Civil Law 1986) and relevant judicial interpretations all describe the parents' rights to child custody.

More specifically, Article 21 of the current Marriage Law states that parents shall have the duty to bring up and educate their underage children; parents shall also have the right and duty to protect and educate their children who are minors. Article 23 provides that if underage children cause damage to the state, the collective, or individuals, their parents will be civilly liable. Nonetheless, to safeguard the best interest of the child and reduce child custody disputes, law commentators in China suggested that provisions regarding determination of parents' rights to child custody should be added to the Marriage Law.

As for the parent's rights to visitation, neither the Marriage Law 1950 nor the Marriage Law 1980 mandate this right. The current Marriage Law, for the first time, specifically provides for this right. Article 38 of the law states that: "after divorce, the parent that does not directly raise the child has the right to visit the child, and the other party has the obligation to give assistance." In addition, this provision provides that parties must first attempt to reach an agreement on visitation. If no agreement is achieved, the people's court will then make a judgment. If visitation is not conducive to the physical and mental health of the child, the people's court has the discretion to terminate the right to visit. However, courts will reinstate of the right of visitation after the party seeking invitation proves that the reasons for suspending the visitation have been eliminated.

Terminology

In China, custody and visitation are two separate issues regulated in different provisions in the Marriage Law and its related statutes. The parents' rights to child custody refer to the parents' legitimate rights to supervise and protect the person, property, and other lawful rights and interests of a minor after divorce. The parents' rights to visitation are also called the rights to visit or the parents' rights to communicate with their children, which means that, after divorce, the father or the mother who does not directly raise and live with the child will have the right to visit and communicate with the child. Post divorce, the children usually live with one parent in any given period. The parent who does not live with the child has the right of visitation.

When exercising parents' rights to child custody after divorce, the Chinese law follows the principles of both sole and joint parental custody. Under Article 36(2) of the current Marriage Law, both father and mother shall, after divorce, have the right and obligation to raise their children. The provision indicates that both parents are entitled to child custody after divorce. In practice, courts first consider joint custody if it is for the best interests of the child. If, in courts' discretion, joint custody is harmful for the child, courts will award custody to one party, based on the court's initiative or upon the request of the child, other interested persons, child protective institutions, or guardian institutions. Thus, the parents' rights to child custody or parental authority are awarded to either or both parties according to the court's decision or the agreement reached by the parents, as the case may be.

Custody and Guardianship

As mentioned previously, the concept of "child custody" first appeared in the GENERAL PRINCIPLES OF CIVIL LAW 1986. The Chinese equivalent of the U.S. "child custody" is the guardianship mandated in GENERAL PRINCIPLES OF CIVIL LAW 1986, which provides that a guardian shall fulfill his duty to protect the person, property, and other lawful rights and interest of his wards. In

addition, Article 10 of OPINIONS ON SEVERAL ISSUES CONCERNING THE IM-
PLEMENTATION OF GENERAL PRINCIPLES OF THE CIVIL LAW 1988 states that
the duty of the guardian shall include three aspects: the first is personal custody, which includes protecting the personal health of his ward, taking care
of the life of the ward, and teaching the ward to behave; the second is property custody, which includes managing and protecting the property of the
ward; and the third is the right to act as an agent of the ward, which includes
conducting civil activities, and filing litigation.

When a guardian fails to fulfill his or her duty or infringes upon the lawful rights and interests of the ward, Article 18(3) of GENERAL PRINCIPLES OF
CIVIL LAW 1986 provides that the guardian shall be held responsible. In addition, if a guardian causes any property loss for the ward, the guardian must
compensate for such loss. The people's court may disqualify a guardian on the
application of a concerned party or unit.

Article 16 of the GENERAL PRINCIPLES OF CIVIL LAW 1986 identifies the
persons who may serve as guardian for minors. First, the parents of a minor
shall be his guardians. Second, if the parents of a minor are dead or lack the
competence to be his guardian, a person from the following categories may
act as a guardian: 1) paternal or maternal grandparent; 2) elder brother or sister; or 3) any other closely connected relative or friend willing to bear the responsibility of guardianship and having approval from the working units of
the minor's parents or from the neighborhood or village committee in the
place of the minor's residence. In the event of a dispute over guardianship,
such as where several legal guardians are reluctant or eager to serve as
guardians, the working units of the minor's parents or the neighborhood committee or village committee in the place of his residence must appoint a
guardian from among the minor's near relatives. If disagreement over the appointment leads to a lawsuit, the people's court has jurisdiction to rule on the
appointment of a guardian.

In addition, the GENERAL PRINCIPLE OF CIVIL LAW 1986 expressly requires
the guardian to be competent. Competence refers to mental and physical
health, as well as the economic conditions of the person serving as guardian.
Article 11 of OPINIONS ON THE IMPLEMENTATION OF GENERAL PRINCIPLES OF
THE CIVIL LAW 1988 lists the categories of person that can not serve as a
guardian: a) a person with limited capacity for civil conduct; b) a person who
lacks the competence of guardianship for physical or economic reasons; c) a
person who was sentenced and is in prison; d) a person with bad behavior or
under other circumstances that are not conducive to the healthy growth of the
ward. (*See* CHEN WEI: RESEARCH ON LEGISLATION OF CHINA'S MARRIAGE AND
FAMILY LAW (Beijing: the Masses Press) (2000) (373).

Factors for Custody

As mentioned above, the current Marriage Law and its related statutes and regulations did not explicitly provide factors for courts to apply in determining parents' rights to child custody. However, the current Marriage Law offers guidance for courts to decide the child-rearing responsibilities, which are the functional equivalent of child custody in practice. Similar to the tender years doctrine, in China, Article 36 of the current Marriage Law indicates that the mother shall have custody of breast-fed infants after divorce, and a breast-fed infant means a child under the age of 2. In the following cases, the father may be awarded custody of the child: 1) the mother is suffering from a communicable disease or other serious disease for a long time, such that it is not suitable for the child to live with her; 2) the mother is able, but unwilling to provide child support, and the father requests custody; 3) for other reasons, it is not suitable for the child to live with the mother. In addition, courts must grant an agreement reached by the parents giving custody of a child under the age of two to the father if the agreement is in the best interests of the child.

For children over two years of age, the parents must first attempt to reach an agreement to determine which party will raise the children. If they fail to reach an agreement, the people's court will decide in accordance with the rights and interests of the child and the actual conditions of both parents. In addition, if the father and the mother both desire to live with the child above the age of two, courts give priority to the party who satisfies one of the following conditions: 1) where the party has lost reproductive capacity due to a sterilization surgery or for other reasons; 2) where the child lives together with one party for such a long time that the change of living environment will be significantly harmful to the health and growth of the child; 3) where one party has no other children, while the other party has other children; 4) where the child lives with one party, who is conducive to the growth of the child, and the other party is suffering from a communicable disease or other serious disease for a long time, or there are other circumstances not conducive to the physical and mental health of the child, so that it is not suitable for the other party to live with the child. Furthermore, unlike in the U.S. where courts focus exclusively on the parents' conditions in determining child custody, in China, the grandparents' relationship with the child is an important factor for courts to consider in awarding custody. When the economic conditions of both parties are similar and both of them desire custody, but the child has lived with one set of grandparents for a long time, and the grandparents are willing and able to help take care of the child, that factor may be a deciding factor in determining custody between the father and mother.

Visitation Rights

The visitation right in China resembles the Parenting Plan in the U.S. in regulating parental responsibility after divorce. Under the provision of Article 38 of the current Marriage Law, after divorce, the parent that does not directly bring up the children has the right to visit the children, and the other parent has the obligation to give assistance. Parents should first attempt to reach an agreement on how to exercise the right of visitation. If they fail to reach an agreement, the court will decide based on the best interests of the child. When the parent who does not live with the child visits the child, the other parent has the duty to cooperate with that visitation.

Under some circumstances, if the visitation by the parent is harmful to the physical and mental health of the child, the court will suspend the right to visit. However, there is no provision in the existing law to define the harmful situation that would justify terminating visitation altogether. In general, in any of the following situations, visitation will be considered to be detrimental to the physical and mental health of the child:

(1) Where the parent who has right of visitation is suffering from a communicable disease, such that it is inappropriate to visit the child;

(2) Where the parent who has right of visitation violates the visitation agreement or order in such a way that it seriously influences the life and study of the child;

(3) Where the parent who has right of visitation takes the child to a pornographic place or lets the child watch harmful films, television programs, books, or periodicals;

(4) Where the parent who has right of visitation morally degenerates, commits adultery, has a concubine, prostitutes, takes drugs, or gambles, where such conduct is not conducive to the physical and mental health of the child;

(5) Where the parent who has right of visitation commits domestic violence, abuses, or abandons the child;

(6) Where the parent who has right of visitation instigates, coerces, or tempts the child to carry out a misdeed or criminal act; or

(7) Where the parent who has right of visitation discovered but did not prevent, the misdeed or criminal act of the child, or educate the child regarding such actions.

When the above situations are found to occur, the court will suspend the parent's right of visitation. Under Article 26 of Supreme Court's Interpretation I of the current Marriage Law, the parent who directly rears the children, or any other legal custodian who bears the obligation of upbringing and ed-ucating the underage children has the right to request the court to suspend the visitation right. After accepting the request to suspend visitation, the court has a great deal of discretion in ruling whether it is necessary to suspend the parent's right to visitation. A suspension, if granted, only temporarily pro-hibits the right of visitation. When the reasons for the suspension are removed, the court will order a resumption of the right of visitation.

The parent's right to visit the child is a legal personal right that parents enjoy. To protect the parents' legitimate rights and the interests of the child, when any person refuses to perform the judgment or decision on the visita-tion right of the child, the court may take mandatory measures such as de-taining and fining the relevant individuals and enforcing the right.

Agreement

Similar to the U.S., during the divorce process, parents first attempt to reach an agreement on custody and visitation. Once the agreement is approved by the court, the divorced couples have to follow the terms in the agreement and file a petition to modify the agreement.

The Child's Voice

Similar to the U.S., in China, children are not permitted to express their opinions in court to contest custody or visitation matters. However, if the child is aged ten or older, the court should consider the preference of the child in determining which party shall take custody of the child. The primary rea-son for this approach is that the court should award custody based on the best interests of the child, and a ten-year-old has gained a certain ability of recog-nition. Similar to the U.S., this preference is only one factor that the court will consider in determining which parent should take custody.

In our case, under the spirit of Article 36 of the current Marriage Law, at the time of divorce, either Lily or Mario could take sole custody of one child or both, or both parents could obtain joint custody of both children. First, Lily and Mario must attempt to reach an agreement regarding custody issues at the time of di-vorce. Because both Jade and Dino are younger than ten years old, the prefer-ence of the children will not be considered by the court. Second, if Lily and Mario fail to reach an agreement, the court will award custody in accordance with the rights and interests of the child and the actual conditions of both parents.

If the court awards both children's custody to Lily after the divorce, Mario will be awarded the right to visit the children. However, Mario and Lily must seek an agreement on how to exercise the right to visit, including the manner, time, place and other issues on the exercise of the right to visit. If they fail to reach an agreement, the people's court will make a judgment on visitation. In addition, when exercising the right to visit, Mario must act properly in accordance with the agreement or judgment of the court. At the same time, Lily, who lives with the children, has the duty to assist Mario in exercising his right of visitation. If Lily fails to perform the obligation of assistance, without justifiable cause, Mario has right to request the court to enforce the visitation rights. If the children refuse to be visited by their father, Mario, the court will not enforce the physical visiting act of the children.

In addition, if Mario's visitation is harmful to the physical and mental health of the children, Lily has a right to file a petition to suspend Mario's right to visit. The court will suspend Mario's visitation right if deemed necessary. After the cause of such suspension is removed, the court must, upon Mario's request, resume his right to visit.

Italy

Overview

There are many similarities between Italy and the U.S. regarding custody of minor children after a legal separation or divorce, including the guiding principles that govern the courts' decision making process in custody determinations ("the moral and material interest of the children" which is akin to the U.S. term of art "best interest of the child." and the age of twelve, beyond which the child, in Italy and Tennessee must be audited (heard) by the judge in making the custodial determination). Italian child custody law is influenced by solutions implemented in other countries that have a more established experience in designing and working with custody orders for minor children, resulting in legislative reforms in Italy.

As such, for example, out-of-court settlement of the terms for the continued exercise of each parent's proper role in the educational and emotional upbringing of the children is favored, with the court's involvement preferably limited to a minimum. Historically, just like in the U.S., custody of minor children following a separation or divorce was predominantly given to the mother, especially when the children were young. However, both changes in societal attitudes and recent reforms are combining to reshape the meaning of the role, or in Italian legal parlance, the duty of parenting after separation and divorce. In resolving difficulties, Italian courts exercise a great deal of discretion, mostly guided by principles enunciated by the Civil Code and the Constitution, humanity, and common sense.

One overarching difference between Italian and U.S. custody processes is dictated by the Italian two step system where separation, as the precursor of divorce, is the time when the initial custody decisions are made. Other peculiarities follow from this structure. At the time of separation, animosity between the parents regarding their failed marriage runs high, and yet the fact that, in many cases, the separating spouses live in the same *Comune* [municipality] makes it logistically plausible to legislate a preference for joint custody and feasible to implement it. The separation period serves as a trial and error arena for the parents to work out a system whereby they can each stay involved in their children's lives, while they each make a separate life for themselves. A forced cooperation may be brought about by the sheer necessities of keeping up with educational and vocational routines of the minor children when both separating spouses work. By the time a consensual, the most common separation process, satisfies the three year legal requirement for a joint divorce, most custody decisions, formal and informal adjustments, and mutual concessions have taken hold, while the parents have accumulated some experience at being parents without being a couple. At the time of the actual divorce, one or both parents may have moved, or may be interested in forming another family, making the somewhat aspirational shared parenting principle less feasible, and exclusive custody may become the only option, as a practical matter.

Historical Background

Until recently in Italy, because the law contemplated primary custody, or the Italian equivalent, exclusive custody to one of the parents, as the most common solution to the issue of custody after separation and divorce, in the vast majority—over 90% of cases—custody of minor children in both separation and divorces was awarded to the mother, with a slight increase of custody awards to the father when the children were older, close to the age of majority. *See* ISTAT, Matrimoni Separazioni e Divorzi [Marriages Separations and Divorces] (2003), *available at* http://www.istat.it/societa/struttfam. Over the last ten years, the number of custody determinations in favor of the mother have decreased somewhat, even though they still represent over 80% in both separations and divorces, with a proportional increase of joint custody decisions, and only a slight increase in exclusive custody orders in favor of the father. ISTAT, Separazioni e Divorzi in Italia [Separations and Divorces in Italy], 6 (2005), *available at* http://www.istat.it/societa/struttfam. Therefore, although there was never a legally formulated presumption in favor of one of the parents, like the tender-years doctrine in the U.S., the practical result was the same.

A drastic change was recently implemented by law, in essence making shared custody the norm and exclusive custody the exception. In fact, Law 54/2006, which rewrote C.c. Art. 155 marked a complete turnabout in favor of shared custody and joint parenting or, better stated, the legal recognition of the right of children to continue to have a meaningful relationship with each of the parents even after the spouses' life in common has ceased. Once more, the Italian legislature has expressed its interest in protecting the rights of the child notwithstanding the choices made by parents relative to their marriage or life together.

Terminology

Before Law 54/2006 was passed, exclusive custody by one parent was the norm, joint custody was the exception, and joint custody required complete cooperation between the parents. With the passage of Law 54/2006, joint custody has replaced exclusive custody as the norm, and joint custody has been relabeled "shared custody," to emphasize that parents do not have to be together physically at any point in the process. Now, the exercise of legal and physical custody can take place in a segregated manner, which may be the only way possible when there is conflict between the parents, assigning specific responsibilities at different times and in different places between the parents. Naturally, the ability of the separated parents to communicate consistently and to spend a few minutes together during the exchanges, makes the process of shared custody smoother, more natural, and less cumbersome.

In addition, the reform has introduced the principle of *bigenitorialità* (joint parenting), mandating that both parents exercise their parental power. The functional equivalent of U.S. legal custody in Italy is by law a "function"—a term of art which includes a right and a countervailing duty—which parents, whether separated or divorced, have to exercise in common. Pedagogical consultants are available and recommended, similar to parenting coordinators in the U.S., to prevent problems of contradictory educational directions.

Shared Custody and Joint Parenting

The law now provides that with respect to the custody of minor children, the judge is required first to consider the possibility of the children remaining in the custody of both parents during separation. C.c. Art. 155(2) Alternatively, the judge may decide to which parent the children are assigned. *Id.* In cases where shared custody is appropriate, unless the parents have already reached a shared custody agreement, the judge also decides the times and modalities with respect to the permanence of each child with each of the parents. *Id.* Shared custody orders are geared to establish equilibrium between the times that the children spend with each of the parents. However, the law does not prevent shared custody determinations that give a preponderance of the permanence of the children to one of the parents, when specific conditions make that allocation a more desirable solution, whether temporarily or permanently.

With respect to parenting power (legal custody in the U.S.), the new code provision simply states that it is exercised by both parents. C.c. Art. 155 (3). The major decisions with respect to instruction, education, and health care are made in common, considering the aptitude, the natural inclinations, and the aspirations of the children, and of course, in case of disagreement, the judge will decide. *Id;* C.c. Art 147. The rules of law in the Civil Code seem to gloss over the change in status of the parents with respect to each other, advocating a seamless continuum for the parents in carrying out their role as parents where, notwithstanding their disagreements at the core of their failed relationship, they would presumably be in blissful agreement with each other with respect to the myriad of issues involved in raising their children. Indeed, the reform intends to impose on the parents a duty to strive to reach a consensus, notwithstanding their separation or divorce, to further the interests of their children. SESTA, at 558. The doctrine (respected legal scholarship) has noted that aspirational content of Art. 155 is somewhat betrayed by the fact that the "legislator" (legislature) finds it necessary in the same article to provide that the decisions of greatest importance are to be taken by the parents jointly (Art. 155 (3)), a specification that should have been superfluous in light of the general principle of joint parenting introduced by the reform. *Id.* The same latent contradiction is evidenced by the further explanation that the judge, relative to the matters of ordinary administration, may order that the parents exercise their parental powers separately. Art. 155 (3) C.c.; SESTA, at 558.

In light of these mandates, it is unlikely that either Lily or Mario could prevent the other from exercising their respective parental powers, or that Lily would be able to make all parenting decisions independently, no matter how grave the discrepancies at the outset. With the preference for shared custody and joint parenting, unless there is a clear scientific basis for the extreme preferences of Mario and Lily with respect to the upbringing of Dino and Jade, for example with respect to working with the hearing impairment of Dino, the court may even allow each parent to interact with the children in their preferred manner, if it does not interfere with a balanced development of the children and is not otherwise unmanageable logistically.

The reform has not been in effect long enough to see how it percolates through the decisions and how it translates into practice. Some critics have pointed out that it stands in sharp contradiction with the institutions of separation and divorce. Critics say that if these two institutions sanction the right of the parents to make choices relative to their life in common, then the judge cannot, in his decision relative to the children, ignore the changes that have taken place in the life of the separated or divorced parents and sanction the right of each parent to interfere in the child's every-day activities even when the child is physically with the other parent. SESTA, at 541.

Obviously, exclusive custody is still alive and well in the reform: only it is the option less favored by the legislator (legislature). The judge can still grant exclusive custody when the specific situation calls for it. Exclusive custody may still be preferred where the parents reside in different cities or regions so that the consistent transfer of the children from one to the other parent cannot be easily arranged or when the parents belong to different ethnic groups or different cultures.

Exclusive custody can also be granted when the conflict between parents is so high that shared custody may be detrimental to the development and well being of the children. The judge can opt for exclusive custody *sua sponte* or based on a parent's petition when joint custody is contrary to the interests of the children. The court's order must set forth the bases and reasoning supporting the same. C.c. Art. 155-*bis*. Either parent can petition the court for exclusive custody at any time. Both Mario and Lily could go this route at any time based on allegations similar to what their U.S. counterparts would present in a U.S. court. With respect to both Dino and Jade, Lily would emphasize the fact that granting exclusive custody to her will maintain continuity in care giving with their mother, considering that both children have developed strong love and affection ties with her. Lily will emphasize that Dino needs her. Because she knows sign language, she can best communicate with Dino, and has embraced and learned to work with his condition, she is the better choice as caregiver and custodial parent for the continued development and well being of young Dino during his formative years. Additionally, she may argue that Mario has never cared for the children, resents Dino's condition, and refuses to learn sign language, all of which will be detrimental to the educational and physiological development of the child if Mario remains involved day to day. Mario, Lily will point out, does not have the aptitude to be the custodial parent because he pressures Jade into activities she is not predisposed to for his own purposes, not for Jade's best interests. While these arguments may convince the court that Mario should not get exclusive custody, under the new provisions, it is not certain that Lily or Mario would be able to put forth a sufficiently compelling argument to exclude the other from shared custody.

Further, assuming that Lily could obtain exclusive custody, it is not likely that a judge would exclude Mario from visitation. Indeed, when the judge orders exclusive custody he has to safeguard the interest of the child in maintaining a balanced relationship with both parents. C.c. Art. 155(1). Here is where custody decisions become even more challenging, as the visitation provisions must be adopted not only with an eye towards the satisfaction of the selfish interests of the non custodial parent, but mainly with an eye to the interests of the minor, because depriving minors of one of their parents may have grave psychological consequences on their development. Sesta, at 559. Therefore, the non custodial parent must be afforded an opportunity to spend significant time with his children to maintain and reinforce their relationship, and substantially partake in their life. *Id.* Hence, Lily would likely not be able to exclude Mario from visitation based on the facts of this case, in light of the rights of her children to continue a relationship with both parents. As pointed out by multiple decisions of the Court of Cassation, the reform of the custody provisions has codified what the jurisprudence had previously emphasized: that the responsibility of the parents towards their children in times of separation or divorce is, as always, not a mere right, but a right with an annexed duty (a right-duty), in line with the constitutional provision of Art. 30 (it is the duty and the right of parents to maintain, instruct, and educate their children) and of Art. 147 of the Civil Code (*Duties towards children.* Marriage imposes on both spouses the obligation to maintain, instruct, and educate their children, taking into account their abilities, natural inclinations, and aspirations). *See, e.g.* Cass. 19 apr. 2002/5714.

Doctrinally, it has been pointed out that the right of visitation is a right-duty as well, because of the public interest it fosters, and because it can only be infringed by the court upon finding grave and proven conditions of conflict with the fundamental interests of the minor. However, while the non custodial parent can petition the judge if his visitation rights are infringed, the duty portion of visitation is not enforceable, as there is no corresponding remedy afforded the custodial parent to obtain by judicial order that the non custodial parent be "forced" to stick to his visiting responsibilities. One extreme remedy for failure to exercise the right-duty of visitation may be termination of parental rights under Art. 330 of the Civil Code which is available when one parent neglects his parental duties with grave prejudice to his children.

Also non-visitation could constitute the extremes of the crime of "violation of the obligation to assist the family" of Art. 570 of the Penal Code.

The right of visitation is likely to receive more detailed treatment in custody decisions involving high conflict divorces while more generic terms may be sufficient when the parents demonstrate the ability to manage the continuing family relationships. *See* Cass. 3 maggio 1986 n. 3013. The case of Mario and Lily may require specific modalities as the starting point is specific disagreement, each parent vying for exclusive custody, to the point of intending to exclude the other from interacting with the children. Lily would like to at least preclude overnight stays of her children with the father after separation. Italian courts tend to view as pretext many of the reasons that the custodial parent attempts to use to prevent the children from spending the night with the noncustodial parent. Doctrinally, an arrangement with overnight stays is favored because it recasts visitation not as a marginal event but as an integral part of the everyday life of the child. Sesta, at 563–564. The reform follows the doctrinal inclination, even though tribunals in the first years after introduction may still tend to follow pre-reform patterns. Even if Lily is granted exclusive custody, Lily's desire to preclude Mario from obtaining overnight visitations is not likely to be viewed favorably.

Art. 155 of the Civil Code is also applicable when parents, after the requisite separation, obtain a divorce. Shared custody had been first introduced among the custody options by L. 1987/74, Art. 6 and heralded as a way of making the effect of divorce imperceptible for children, lessening, if not eliminating, the conflict of loyalties that prevails in situations of exclusive custody. Conversely, some commentators pointed out that the judge should not order shared custody in those cases where conflict among the parents runs too high for them to be able to manage daily contact without it becoming an occasion for daily skirmishes. One of the logistical prerequisites of shared custody, that the homes of the parents not be too far from one another, tends to be less likely to exist at the time of divorce, than at the time of separation.

Parental Educational Project

The equivalent of the U.S. Parenting Plan is the Parental Educational Project which must be presented as an addendum to the separation petition and has to divide the physical presence of the minor child with each parent maintaining equilibrium, and also has to assign duties and items of expense to each parent. The minor child can therefore continue to live with each of the parents independently from the relationship the parents maintain with each other. If one of the parents prevents visitation by the other or discredits the other parent, these actions can be used as a valid reason for exclusive custody. Lily, therefore, should exercise restraint and be very cognizant of the rights of Mario, absent evidence that Mario's approach is indeed detrimental to children's moral and material interests.

Typically, the minor children will rotate from one parent to the other every other day during the week and every other weekend to allow enough time to maintain a routine in each home and avoid feelings of longing for the absent parent. If the parents have an acrimonious relationship, pick ups can be coordinated around the school routine so that the parents actually avoid, as much as possible, occasions and triggers for open conflict displays in front of the children, which are notoriously detrimental to the children's emotional well being. Based on the availability and willingness of the parents, encounters with one parent can be organized during the time that the child lives with the other parent. The purpose of the parental educational project is to allow each parent to stay involved in the everyday activities of the child. These very frequent interchanges are possible in many cases because separated or divorced parents continue to live in the same municipality. Mario and Lily, going through a separation in Bologna, would most likely follow the same patterns, making shared custody and joint parenting a possibility, at least logistically.

Even in exclusive custody, though, both parents have to decide on the issues of critical importance to their children's education and upbringing, such as education and religion. When the conflict between the parents is high, the visitation agreements should strive to create a situation where the child still has the opportunity to spend quality time with the noncustodial parent as well. The goal is for the child to maintain a direct relationship with the noncustodial parent as opposed to the image projected willingly or involuntarily by the other parent. The conflict situation is normally expected to resolve within the first two or three years of separation, during which time pedagogical counseling of each parent by trained professionals on the children's education (parental counselors in the U.S.) is highly recommended to prevent uncomfortable situations for the children. The consultation with the pedagogical counselors is advisable before filing the separation petition, but can also be ordered by the judge when she finds a situation of heightened conflict. In the case of Lily and Mario, counseling may be ordered by the court due to the multiple issues raised by the parents regarding the upbringing of the children where there exists a strong divergence of opinions. These issues include the best way to work with Dino's hearing impairment, the religious foundation to provide for both children, and the role of sports in Jade's psycho-physical development. The issues of custody and parental planning are addressed at the stage of separation, when theoretically at least, the spouses could reconsider and decide not to proceed with divorce. As Italian law and decisions make abundantly clear, the fact is that even though there may be a separation and eventually a divorce between the parents, there remains a parental relationship and the requirement on both parents to find a manageable coordinated solution relative to the exercise of parental responsibilities.

Agreement

Like in the U.S., most parents, upon separation, do reach an agreement on custody and visitation, which is then approved by the court, and, once approved, together with the parenting plan, is incorporated into the court's decree and has to be followed by both parties.

Mediation

Art. 155-*sexies* of the Civil Code provides that the judge may, in his discretion, postpone consideration of the decision about custody to allow the parents to reach an agreement in the furtherance of the moral and material interests of the children, with the help of a panel of experts in family mediation. The new norm adds to the judge's arsenal in facilitating a custody solution, the choice, after consulting with the parties, to rely on the help of experts, and on the support of the centers of family mediation. Mediation is not mandatory but is an available alternative which is gaining more and more momentum. Mediation can be attempted in the mediation centers as well as before private consultants. The judge can order a continuance of the hearing to allow the independent process to produce a solution relative to the post separation coordination of duties, activities and decision making opportunities for both parents with respect to their children. The judge maintains communication with the experts during the process, but has no other involvement in it. The process of mediation is otherwise independent of the judicial process and confidential. Once the mediation has produced an outcome, the parties will again appear before the judge reporting an agreement reached, agreement not reached, or an agreement in process, whereupon the judge will order one last continuance to endeavor to conclude the process.

Mediation is favored as a less institutional solution that is more likely to achieve the objectives of lessening conflict and facilitating communication among the parents. Indeed, separating or divorcing couples are normally in situations of open, ongoing personal conflict fueled by family and friends who, siding with one or the other, tend to increase polarization and prevent resolution. Mediation, a non juridical time-out taking place under the guidance of family professionals, can help the parents disengage from the issues that caused the failure of the relationship, and become fully engaged in their continuing common responsibilities as parents.

Evidence Obtained by the Judge *ex Officio*

The judge can obtain evidence *ex officio* to support his decision relative to custody by relying on the investigations of the social services with territorial competence (jurisdiction). C.c. Art. 155-*sexies*. Even before the reform, court decisions were affording the examining judge inquisitorial powers analogous to those of the juvenile judge, because of the belief that the examining judge is acting in the furtherance of the public interest to the protection of children. *See* SESTA, at 557. As such, an instrument that has become common in practice and is credited with good results is the adoption of the technical consultation, in which an expert in child psychology examines the child, identifies the child's preferences, fears and hopes, and general outlook to assess development and psychological make-up. The technical consultation affords the court the benefit of the child expert's opinion and provides a voice to the minor at the same time. *Id.*

Factors

The polestar for the judge in custody decisions is "exclusively the moral and material interest of the child," (C.c. Art. 155) the Civil Code equivalent of the ubiquitous best interest of the child standard in U.S state statutes on the same subject. As observed above, Italian judges get little guidance, and therefore ample discretion, in this process, as the Code does not get into the factors the judge should consider in making custody determinations. The judge will rely on his experience, humanity, and sensibility, but will also follow the general principles of the Constitution and the Civil Code with respect to children's maintenance, instruction, and education. Not surprisingly, the love and affection between parent and child are key factors used unanimously and consistently by judges in making custody determinations. Court decisions also echo very closely some of the other factors used in U.S. state statutes such as how a parent exercised his role in the past, especially relative to his emotional and affective ties; the attention paid to the child; his ability to understand and educate; his disposition to continue to provide a consistent relationship; the personality of the parent; the parents' style of living and ability to provide the child a conducive environment for her development. *See e.g.* Cass. Civ. 22 giugno 1999, No. 6312. Not relevant to a custody determination is whether the separation was charged to one of the parents, as custody is definitively not a prize for having been found legally the innocent spouse. Indeed, the less successful spouse can be the preferred candidate for custody purposes when she is more apt to take care of the children and when there is already a strong rapport of love and affection with that parent.

Grandparents

Unlike in the U.S. where grandparents' visitation is subject to the parents' right to the care and custody of their minor children, the Italian "legislator" (legislature) has made a clear choice with respect to the importance of a sustained and meaningful relationship with grandparents to a child's development. Parents cannot arbitrarily deprive their children of the benefit of the love, affection, knowledge, and experience that grandparents can contribute to their grandchildren. Minor children have a right to maintain meaningful relationships with their grandparents. C.c. Art. 155 (1). The judge can intervene *ex officio* or by initiative of the *Pubblico Ministero* (the representative of the state), upon information by the interested parties. Grandparents can also petition the judge where the parents' behavior is prejudicial to the maintenance of their relationship with the grandchildren, so that their visitation right-duty, the counterpart to the absolute right of minors to maintain their bond with their grandparents, can be guaranteed even after custody determination has altered the original structure of the nuclear family.

Representation of the Child and the Child's Voice

In its previous text Art. 155 of the Civil Code did not make it mandatory for the child to be heard, but court decisions and the doctrine (respected legal scholarship) stressed that taking into account the child's moral and material interests imposed by law could hardly be accomplished without reference to the other key provisions of the Code, such as, for example, Art. 147 which emphasizes the inclinations and aspirations of the children, elevating children from mere objects of the rights of their parents to subjects having their own interests. Sesta, at 551. Thus, even though the law before or after 2006 does not expressly mandate a guardian for the child or that he be heard, in light of the requirements of the international conventions that Italy is a signatory to (namely the International Convention on the Rights of the Child of 1989), the courts frequently have taken into account the desires expressed by children in custody determinations, especially if the children showed awareness, if they were able to formulate and articulate their aspirations even cautiously, and when they were adolescents. *Id.* The courts have developed a legal framework to name a special representative for the child, to avoid involving the child in situations of direct conflict between the parents, and to perpetuate an attitude of protection. *Id.* 552–553. Decisions of the Court of Cassation on the topic have run the gamut between holding that the preference expressed by the child is irrelevant, to holding that the custody decision cannot be made without reference to the opinion of the child relative to which parent they prefer. *Id.* 554.

The reformed Arts. 155 *et seq.* make it mandatory for the judge to interview the minor child twelve and older, and in case the child is younger, if he has reached sufficient maturity. *See* C.c. Art 155-*sexies*. The interview must be done before making custody determination: however, the code provisions do not set forth the consequences for failure to interview the minor. *Id.* It likewise is not clear whether the parents can jointly waive the requirement for the court to interview the child. SESTA, at 555. Like in Tennessee, in Italy, Jade and Dino at nine and five respectively are too young to be heard, and it is unlikely the court would ask their opinion relative to the activities or the education and treatment options their parents disagree on.

Gender Violence and False Accusations of Pedophilia

A research project commissioned by the Ministry of Equal Opportunities on violence against women uncovered that a large number of women are subjected to gender violence in Italy: 6,743,000 were the victims of physical and/or psychological violence in 2007. ISTAT, *La Violenza e i Maltrattamenti Contro le Donne Dentro e Fuori la Famiglia [Violence and Mistreatments against Women Inside and Outside the Family]* (2007) *available at* http://www.pariopportunita.gov.it/DefaultDesktop.aspx?doc=1058. Conversely, there are also instances in which women seek to exclude men from custody through false accusations of pedophilia, and the propagation of defamatory statements tending to justify allegations of violence. Children suffer from both direct violence on them and from the exposure to these forms of indirect violence.

Summary Chart—Child Custody and Visitation

	U.S. (Tennessee)	China	Italy
Preference for parental agreement on custody and visitation, subject to court approval.	Yes	Yes	Yes
Grandparent's relationship with child recognized as a factor in deciding custody.	No	Yes	Yes
Parenting Plans.	Yes	Yes	Yes
Mediation.	Yes	Yes	Yes
Representation of child.	Yes, if the court so orders.	Yes	Guardian not exclusively mandated.
Preference of child for custody.	Twelve years or older.	Ten years or older.	Twelve years or older.
Tender years doctrine once recognized.	Yes, historically, but no longer recognized.	Yes	Yes, although not formally stated in the law.
Tender years doctrine currently recognized.	No	Yes	No
Primary custody in one parent in most cases.	Yes	Yes	Yes, although there is a recent legislative change that preferences joint custody.
Joint custody.	Yes, if the parents agree.	Yes, courts first consider joint custody if it is in the child's best interests.	Yes, by legislative preference.
Guiding principle for determining custody.	Best interest of the child.	In accordance with the rights and intents of the child and the actual conditions of both parents.	The moral and material interests of the children.

CHAPTER 8

CHILD SUPPORT

United States

Parents have a co-equal duty to support their children, according to each parent's ability. Unfortunately, a number of children still live in poverty. Recent census figures show that approximately 18% of the children in Tennessee between the ages of five and seventeen live in poverty. U.S. CENSUS BUREAU, CURRENT POPULATION SURVEY, *Poverty Status by State: 2006.* Many of those children live in single parent homes. When parents divorce, the court orders the parents to continue to support their minor children, usually designating a specific sum that must be paid each month.

Child support obligations typically continue until the child reaches the age of majority, but can continue indefinitely when the child is severely disabled. In Tennessee, the court can order the parents to pay child support until the child reaches the age of eighteen. If the child is still in high school at the age of eighteen, the support obligation continues until the child is graduated, or until the class of which the child is a member when the child attains the age of eighteen is graduated, whichever occurs first. TENN. CODE ANN. § 34-1-102.

Post-Majority Support Obligations

If the child is disabled, as defined by the Americans with Disabilities Act (ADA), the court can order child support to continue until the child reaches the age of twenty-one. If the child is severely disabled, however, the court may, in some instances, continue support obligations indefinitely. TENN. CODE ANN. § 36-5-101(k)(1, 2).

Dino, because of his deafness, would qualify for child support until the age of twenty-one, but probably would not meet the requirements for unlimited child support because he is not severely disabled. Jade's child support would end when she is graduated from high school or attains the age of eighteen, whichever occurs later. If she falls behind the class that she is in when she turns eighteen, her child support will end when that class is graduated.

A few states allow divorce courts to order post majority support, particularly costs associated with college. In Tennessee, however, there is no post majority support obligation, unless the parties agreed to it in the marital dissolution agreement (MDA). The only exception to this rule arises in the case of high income obligors, where the court may order the obligor to contribute to an educational trust fund during the child's minority. This money reverts to the obligor, to the extent of any funds not used for the child's education.

Because Mario is not a high income obligor, Lily's only chance of getting Mario to be responsible for post majority expenses for Jade, such as college tuition, is to get Mario to agree to include such an obligation in the parties' MDA. Mario may not be willing to agree, or may do so only in exchange for other concessions. Barring an agreement in the MDA, any contribution by Mario or Lily to Jade's post majority education expenses will be voluntary. Because Dino's support obligation continues until age twenty-one, due to his deafness, both parents can be ordered by the court to contribute to his post majority education expenses, until Dino attains twenty-one years of age.

Pre-Majority Termination of Child Support Obligations

Parental support obligations may terminate before the child reaches the age of majority in a few circumstances where the child is presumed not to be financially dependent on the parents. The most common of these are marriage, military enlistment, judicial emancipation, adoption, and death. Neither bad conduct on the part of the child nor non-judicial agreement between the parents is sufficient to eliminate the support obligation. Death of the parent also terminates the support obligation in most instances, unless the court order or the parties' MDA provides otherwise. For that reason, it is important for the parents to obtain life insurance policies with the children named as beneficiaries. Courts typically have the authority to order the parents to obtain life insurance as well as health insurance for the benefit of the child. TENN. CODE ANN. §34-1-101(i) (life insurance) and TENN. CODE ANN. §34-1-101 (h) (health insurance).

Child Support Guidelines

In order to promote uniformity in child support awards, each state has passed Child Support Guidelines that direct the courts in calculating the appropriate amount of child support to award, based upon the income of one or both parents. Tennessee's Child Support Guidelines originally considered the income of the alternate residential parent (ARP) only, but in 2005, Tennessee switched to an income shares model, which considers the income of each parent and assigns pro rata responsibility for child support. TENN. COMP. R. & REGS. Ch. 1240-2-4.

In determining the proper amount of child support, the court must apply the Child Support Guidelines as a rebuttable presumption. The court may not deviate from the Child Support Guidelines unless the court makes a written finding that the application of the Child Support Guidelines would be "unjust or inappropriate in that particular case, in order to provide the best interest of the child(ren) or the equity between the parties." TENN. CODE ANN. §34-1-101 (e)(1)(A). The court must also state the amount of support that would have been ordered under the guidelines and a justification for the variance from the guidelines. *Id.*

The Child Support Guidelines do provide for deviations in limited instances, such as 1) where the alternate residential parent spends significantly more or significantly less visitation time than is considered the norm; 2) where the child has extraordinary medical or educational needs; and 3) where one parent has relocated with the child, causing the other parent to incur substantial travel expenses in order to spend time with the child. TENN. COMP. R. & REGS. Ch. 1240-2-4-.07. The guidelines also contain special provisions for very high and very low income parents. TENN. COMP. R. & REGS. Ch. 1240-2-4-.07 (low income) and TENN. COMP. R. & REGS. Ch. 1240-2-4-.04(3)(d) (high income). If either of the parents is supporting other children who are not before the court, those children will be considered in the calculations, as well. TENN. COMP. R. & REGS. Ch. 1240-2-4-.04(5)(a).

The Tennessee Department of Human Services website contains a calculator for determining child support which attorneys can download. www.state.tn.us/humanserv/is/incomeshares.htm. The income and certain expenses of each parent are uploaded and a corresponding child support amount is calculated, based upon the number of children eligible for support. That support figure is allocated to the parents, pro rata, based on their income. The alternate residential parent pays his or her share to the primary residential parent (PRP). If the child spends exactly equal time with each parent, the lower income parent is usually designated the primary residential parent for purposes of the child support order. If the parties have split custody, each parent will owe child support to the other parent for the child that does not live primarily with that parent, and the court will net out the payments, so that only one parent will be paying.

The child support amount will be subject to income assignment, meaning that the ordered amount of child support will automatically be taken from the parent's paycheck by the employer and sent to the state's central collection agency for distribution to the other parent. Income assignment is required, except in cases where there is a written agreement by both parties that provides for alternative arrangements, which must be reviewed by the court and entered in the record. Tenn. Code Ann. §36-5-501(a)(2)(B).

Although parties generally have a great deal of autonomy in divorce proceedings and are encouraged to reach out-of-court settlements, the general rule does not apply in child support matters. Any agreement by the parties must be approved by the court and will be subject to the child support guidelines presumptions. Thus, the court is not likely to approve any agreement reached by the parties that provides for less child support than would be ordered pursuant to the child support guidelines.

In our case, if the children live primarily with Lily, Mario will be ordered to pay his share of the child support obligation to Lily for the benefit of the children, and vice versa. If the children spend substantially equal amounts of time with Lily and Mario, Lily, as the lower income parent will be designated the primary residential parent, for purposes of child support, and Mario will pay her the difference between their pro rata shares of child support. If one child lives primarily with each parent, Jade with Lily and Dino with Mario, for instance, Lily will owe Mario child support for Dino and Mario will owe child support to Lily for Jade. The amounts would be netted out and Mario would be ordered to pay the difference to Lily. After Jade reaches the age of majority, Mario would no longer be liable for her support, and Lily would begin paying her pro rata share of child support to Mario for the benefit of Dino.

Insurance

The parents will be required to provide health insurance coverage for the children. Tenn. Code Ann. §36-5-101(h)(1). If health insurance coverage is provided though the alternate residential parent's place of employment, the attorney for the primary residential parent may want to get the court to approve a Qualified Medical Child Support Order (QMCSO) which will allow the non-employee parent to obtain forms and reimbursements directly from the plan, without requiring the assistance or cooperation of the employee parent.

The court can also order the parents to obtain and maintain life insurance policies with the children as named beneficiaries. Tenn. Code Ann. §36-5-101(h)(i). Life insurance is important because the parent's estate is not generally responsible for the child support obligation, absent agreement by the parties.

Modifications

Once the income amount is determined, it may be modified only when either party can show a significant variance between the current amount of support and the amount that would currently be due pursuant to the Child Support Guidelines. That amount is currently 15%, with a lesser standard for low income obligors. A modification increase may be sought by the recipient, based on a significant increase in the obligor's income, or a modification decrease may be sought by the obligor, based on a significant decrease in the obligor's income. TENN. COMP. R. & REGS. Ch. 1240-2-4-.05. Retroactive modifications of child support arrearages are not allowed. The court can modify prospectively only, from the time of the filing of the petition to modify and the mailing of notice to the other party. TENN. CODE ANN. § 36-5-101(f)(1). For this reason, it is important for the attorney representing the obligor parent to emphasis the need to file a modification petition immediately if the obligor parent has a significant drop in income.

Jurisdiction

The court must have personal jurisdiction over the obligor parent before ordering that parent to pay child support. Personal jurisdiction can be obtained by personal service within the state, or by substituted service under the long-arm statute. After setting the initial support order, the court retains jurisdiction over the matter until the child reaches the age of majority, all the parties leave the state, or the parties agree in writing to have the matter heard in another state. A child support matter can also be transferred to another county within the state if all the parties leave the original county. TENN. CODE ANN. § 36-5-3001 et seq.

Jurisdiction to modify the child support of another state is governed by federal law, the Full Faith and Credit for Child Support Act (FFCCSOA). 28 U.S.C. § 1738B. The court that renders the original child support order retains continuing exclusive jurisdiction over the matter, to the exclusion of other states, unless all of the parties and the child move out of the state or the parties agree in writing to transfer jurisdiction to another state.

Because this divorce is taking place in Memphis, Tennessee, any future petitions to modify the child support obligation must be brought in Memphis, as long as either Lily or Mario remains a resident, unless they agree in writing to transfer jurisdiction to another court.

Enforcement

Unpaid child support obligations may be enforced like any other judgment, except that child support arrearages are not subject to a statute of limitations.

TENN. CODE ANN. §36-5-103(g). In addition, because the court has ordered the obligor parent to pay, the obligation can be enforced through the contempt powers of the court. If the recipient parent can show that the obligor parent has the ability to pay the child support arrearages and is simply refusing to do so, the court can hold the parent in civil contempt and order the parent to jail until the parent pays the child support arrearage. The jailed parent is said to "hold the keys to the jail" in that the parent can be released at will, upon payment of the existing debt.

Child support and parenting time are deemed to be independent obligations. Thus, it is not a defense to nonpayment of child support to show that the other parent interfered with the delinquent parent's time with the child. If Mario is ordered to pay child support to Lily, as the primary residential parent, it will not be a defense to his failure to pay that Lily denied him access to the children. His remedy is to file a petition with the court seeking to hold Lily in contempt, not to deprive the children of support.

There are numerous other tools available to assist in enforcing child support arrearages, including 1) revocation of the obligor's license, including drivers' licenses, hunting licenses, and professional licenses; 2) interception of federal income tax returns; 3) attachment of the person; 4) requirement of security by bond; 5) imposition of liens against real or personal property; 6) sequestration of rents and profits; and 7) entry of Qualified Domestic Relations Orders (QDRO's) to access retirement funds. Nonpayment of support can also result in state and federal criminal charges in extreme cases. TENN. CODE ANN. §36-5-104; TENN. CODE ANN. §39-15-101; 18 U.S.C. §228.

China[*]

In China, after divorce, the parent who does not have child custody has the obligation to support the child. Under the current Marriage Law and relevant judicial interpretations of the Supreme People's Court, child support should be conducive to the physical and mental health of the child, protect the legitimate rights and interests of the child, and consider specific conditions such as the rearing ability and actual conditions of both parents, etc.

Child support includes two major aspects. The first is the determination of child support payments. Parents should attempt to determine the amount and manner of child support payments. If they fail to reach an agreement, the people's court will make a judgment. The second aspect is the modification of

---

[*] This part is written by Chen Wei, Pi Xijun, and Ran Qiyu.

child support payments. If the actual situations of the parents or the child change after divorce and the execution of the original agreement or judgment with relation to the child support is difficult or obviously unfair, the parties concerned may request a modification of the amount and manner of child support payments.

Post-Majority Support Obligations

Unlike the U.S. where most states do not require post majority support of able bodied children who have completed high school, Chinese family law specifically provides for child support in some situations, even after an able bodied child reaches majority and completes high school. Article 12 of the SEVERAL OPINIONS ON HANDLING CHILD REARING ISSUES (1993) lists three circumstances in which parents still have the obligation to support their adult children "without the ability to live an independent life." The first circumstance is when a disability causes the adult child to completely or partially lose his ability to make a living; the second circumstance is when the adult child is still attending high school or inferior education; and the third circumstance is a catch-all situation that means the adult child is unable to maintain a normal life for whatever non-subjective reasons.

Pre-Majority Termination of Child Support Obligations

Similar to the U.S., in China, there are also a few situations in which support could be terminated before the child reaches majority. Generally, child support should be paid until the child reaches the age of eighteen. However, Article 11 of the SEVERAL OPINIONS ON HANDLING CHILD REARING ISSUES (1993) provides that, if the child has reached the age of sixteen, but is under the age of eighteen, and his main source of income is his own labor, then if he is able to keep the average standard of living of the local place, the parents may terminate the payments of child support. The provision applies to both male and female children.

Child Support Guidelines

The primary statutory authority for child support is Article 37of the current Marriage Law. Section 1 of Article 37 provides that, after divorce, if the child is to be brought up by either party, the other party should undertake part or all of the child's necessary living and educational expenses. Both parties should agree upon the amount and term of payment. If they fail to reach an agreement, the people's court should decide the amount and term of the child support. Additionally, the agreement or judgment concerning the living and education expenses of the children does not prohibit the children from making reasonable requests for an increased amount beyond the amount determined in the agreement or judgment.

Moreover, Article 21 of the current Marriage Law provides that parents are obligated to rear and educate their children, and the children also have the obligation to support their parents. Where the parents fail to perform their obligations, the underage children and the children without the ability to live an independent life are entitled to ask their parents to pay. With regard to the scope of child support payments, Article 21 of Interpretation I of the current Marriage Law also provides that the scope includes the expenses for living sustenance, education, medical care, etc.

Under Article 37 of the current Marriage Law, the amount and manner of child support payments can be decided as follows:

(1) *According to agreement.* Unlike in the U.S. where courts usually will not approve any child support agreement that deviates from the child support guidelines, in China, the parents should first seek an agreement on the amount and manner of child support payments. If they fail to reach an agreement, the people's court shall make a judgment. Here, it should be noted that under Article 10 of Several Opinions on Handling Child Rearing Issues (1993), parents can make an agreement allowing the custodial parent to pay all the costs of the child support. However, if the people's court discovers that the rearing capacity of the custodial parent can not guarantee the costs of the child, the agreement should not be permitted because the agreement would badly harm the healthy growth of the child.

(2) *According to judgment.* At the time of decision, the people's court shall determine the amount of child support payments based on the actual needs of the child, the paying ability of the parents, and the actual living standard of the places where the parents live, in accordance with Articles 7 to 12 of Several Opinions on Handling Child Rearing Issues (1993). Different from the U.S. pro rata responsibility, in China, if the payee has a fixed income, the amount of child support payment generally accounts for 20% of his or her total revenue. The amount paid for two or more children may be properly increased, but in general, may not exceed 50% of his/her total income. Where the parent has no fixed income, the amount may be decided in the light of the above provisions according to the total income in

that year or the average income of the same industry. Under special circumstances, when necessary, the above ratio may be appropriately increased or decreased. If the parent has no income or the parent's whereabouts are unknown, some property owned by the parent will be used to offset the support payments.

Typically, child support payments are paid periodically (monthly, quarterly or annually). Under special circumstances, such as when the payee needs to go abroad for a long time, the support may be paid in a lump sum.

Insurance

In China, for children under six years old, the state offers prophylaxis medical services for some serious diseases. For example, according to the government's requirement, children under six years of age must have free injections or free medicine offered by the health and medical department to prevent some serious diseases, including DPT vaccine for diphtheria and tetanus and some vaccines or medicine to prevent measles, hepatitis B, epidemic meningitis, and other diseases. Beyond the free vaccines, there is no national free health insurance for children provided by the Chinese government. Based on their economic ability, to safeguard the healthy growth of their children, parents can buy life insurance or health insurance at different levels for their children from life insurance companies, such as accidental injury insurance, serious disease insurance, accidental death insurance, etc.

In relation to the divorce case *Lily v. Mario*, as their son Dino is under six years old, he is entitled to enjoy the prophylaxis medical services offered by the government for the prevention of some serious diseases. In addition, if Mario buys health insurance for Dino, and both parents agree at divorce that Mario shall bear the obligation to pay the annual premium for the health insurance, then he shall continue the obligation after divorce. Of course, if the circumstances of Mario change and it is difficult for him to shoulder this obligation, and Lily has become employed and is capable, the obligation to pay the premium can be changed, based on their mutual agreement. Lily shall then bear the financial responsibility for Dino's health insurance.

Modification of Child Support Payments

Paragraph 2 of Article 37 of the current Marriage Law provides that the agreement or court judgment on the payment of a child's living and educational expenses shall not prevent the child from making a reasonable request, when necessary, to either parent for an amount exceeding what is decided upon in said agreement or judgment. This is a general provision of the Marriage Law on the modification of child support payments. Article 18 of SEVERAL OPINIONS ON HANDLING CHILD REARING ISSUES (1993) states that, in one of the following circumstances, if the child requests for more child support payments and the parent has the ability to pay, the request should be granted: 1) the original payments of child support are not sufficient to maintain the actual living standard of the local place; 2) the actual needs have exceeded the original amount because of medical expenses or educational expenses; (3) for other legitimate reasons. However, the current Marriage Law and relevant judicial interpretations only provide for the increase of child support payments, but the provisions regarding decrease or remission of child support payments are ignored. In judicial practice, if the payments of child support should be reduced or dismissed under objective circumstances, the people's court should support the claim.

It should be noted that, in accordance with some social surveys, some commentators in China pointed out that the vast majority of children, particularly minor children, lived with their mothers after the parents divorce, but the amount of child support payments decided by the court were too low and some judgments were difficult to enforce, which were the main reasons for the falling of some divorced women's living standards. Taking Beijing as an example, many payments of child support paid monthly by divorced fathers were only 200–300 Yuan, while the minimum living standards of Beijing, at the time of the social survey, was 290 Yuan. If these mothers had low incomes, their family lives were kept at the level of basic food and clothing. And because some divorced fathers refused to pay or delayed paying their children support payments, the lives of divorced single mother families got even worse. *See* Xia Yinlan, *On the Protection of the Interests of Divorced Women*, 217 *in* INVESTIGATION ON THE IMPLEMENTATION OF THE MARRIAGE LAW, (Wu Changzhen ed., Beijing: Central Literatures Press) (2004). Therefore, the Chinese authors believe that, in determining the amount of child support payments, the people's court should pay more attention to the actual needs of children healthy growth, instead of merely considering the actual living standards of the local places (that is, the common living standard) when the payees have the ability to support.

Jurisdiction

In China, although there is no legal provision addressing jurisdiction to change a parent's custody in the current Marriage Law, according to the spirit of the provision that both parents share equal rights to the child's support and education, the issue of changing custody after divorce may be addressed by parents through agreement at first. Where agreement is not possible, one party may institute an action to the people's court for varying the child custody, then the people's court shall make a judgment according to law.

In accordance with Article 16 of SEVERAL OPINIONS OF THE SUPREME PEOPLE'S COURT REGARDING THE TREATMENT OF CHILDREN REARING ISSUE IN TRIAL OF DIVORCE CASES BY THE PEOPLE'S COURTS (1993), in any of the following cases, the modification of the child rearing relationship (including the modification of a parent's direct custody to the child), requested by either party, shall be supported: 1) the party living with the child is unable to continue rearing the child due to suffering from serious diseases or disability; 2) the party living with the child fails to perform his or her duty of rearing the child (including custody to the child) without reasonable reasons, or abuses the child, or such party living together with the child has an adverse influence on the normal growth of the child; 3) the minor child over ten years old is willing to live with the other party and the said party has the capacity of rearing the child (including custody to the child); or 4) for other reasonable reasons, it is necessary to modify the child rearing and custody. In addition, Article 17 of this judicial interpretation describes that where the parents reach an agreement to vary custody to the child, it shall be supported. If parents neither meet the above conditions to change the child custody nor reach an agreement on the modification of their child custody, the custody to the child shall not be varied.

In relation to the divorce case *Lily v. Mario*, according the above provisions, where both Mario and Lily reach an agreement about their child custody, the custody can be changed. However, if Mario wants to change the custody relationship, but Lily objects, Mario may lodge a complaint to the people's court. If one of the justified reasons in the above judicial interpretation exists, then the people's court shall make a judgment to change the custody to the children. But if Mario petitions the court to change custody solely because Lily moves to live in a different part of China, the people's court shall not support his claim where it is satisfied that Mario meets none of the just reasons in Article 16 of the above judicial interpretation.

As to the jurisdiction over the cases dealing with child custody at divorce, in the Chinese mainland, there are two methods to divorce as mentioned in Chapter 5, one is divorce at a registry, and the other is divorce through litigation. That is, if both parties divorce at a registry, the custody to child shall be dealt with in the marriage registration office. Where the parties divorce through litigation, the people's court shall have jurisdiction over and make a decision on the issue of child custody. According to Article 22 of the CIVIL PROCEDURE LAW OF PRC (2008), a divorce lawsuit shall be under the jurisdiction of the people's court of the place where the defendant has his domicile; if the place of the defendant's domicile is different from that of his habitual residence, the lawsuit shall be under the jurisdiction of the people's court of the place of his habitual residence. In addition, Article 35 of the Civil Procedure Law provides that when two or more people's courts have jurisdiction over a lawsuit, the plaintiff may bring his/her lawsuit in one of these people's courts; if the plaintiff brings the lawsuit in two or more people's courts that have jurisdiction over the lawsuit, the people's court in which the case was first entertained shall have jurisdiction.

Further, according to Article 306 of Opinions of the Supreme People's Court on Several Issues on the Execution of the Civil Procedure Law of PRC, when the Chinese People's Courts and a foreign court have jurisdiction over a lawsuit, if one party institutes the action in a foreign court, and the other one lodges a complaint to a court of PRC, the people's court may accept the case. After the judgment, an application or request of the foreign court or the party for recognition and enforcement of a judgment or written order of a foreign court shall not be permitted by the people's court , unless otherwise provided by the international treaties concluded or acceded to by both China and the country concerned.

Under Article 266 of the Civil Procedure Law, in the case of an application or request for recognition and enforcement of a legally effective judgment or written order of a foreign court, the people's court shall, after examining it in accordance with the international treaties concluded or acceded to by the People's Republic of China or with the principle of reciprocity, and arriving at the conclusion that it does not contradict the basic principles of the laws of the People's Republic of China nor violate the state sovereignty, security, social, and public interests of the country, shall recognize the validity of the judgment or written order, and, if required, issue a writ of execution to enforce it in accordance with the relevant provisions of this Law. If the application or request contradicts the basic principles of the law of the People's Republic of China or violates the state sovereignty, security, social, and public interests of the country, the people's court shall not recognize and enforce it.

Enforcement

On the issue of enforcement of child support payments, both in situations where the amount of child support payments was reached by an agreement and those where it was decided by the court, if the payor refuses to pay or does not pay on time, the other party may request the people's court to enforce the agreement or the judgment of the people's court.

If the people's court decides that the two minor children of Mario and Lily are under the custody of their mother Lily, under the current Marriage Law and relevant judicial interpretations, the father Mario should pay for the two children's support. The parents shall seek an agreement on the amount and the duration of child support payments. If they fail to reach an agreement, the people's court will make a judgment. According to the facts in the case, if Mario and Lily fail to reach an agreement, the people's court should decide that Mario should pay all the costs of upbringing, while Lily has no such obligation. The reason is that Lily does not work, so she has no salary or other sources of income. As to the specific amount of child support payments, it should be determined on the actual needs of the cost of living, educational expenses, medical expenses, and other expenses as well as Mario's actual paying ability and the actual local living standards.

Further, under Article 7 of SEVERAL OPINIONS ON HANDLING CHILD REARING ISSUES (1993), because Mario has a fixed income and pays for two children's support payments, a reasonable amount of child support payments should be determined within the scope of 30–50% of his total monthly income. Of course, the above ratio may be increased or decreased under special circumstances. As the son Dino was born deaf, special costs such as the costs for recovery treatment and language training are needed, and the monthly wages of Mario are high enough to pay the support payments, so the above ratio can be increased. With regard to the duration of child support payments, the payments to the daughter Jade shall end when Jade reaches the age of eighteen, unless she is unable to live independently at that time. However, the payments to the son Dino should not be limited to his reaching majority at age eighteen. After the son Dino reaches the age of eighteen, his child support payments should continue until he can maintain an independent life. Of course, the support payments of Mario to the two children should be paid monthly.

Even after Mario pays the child support payments in accordance with the agreement reached by the parents or the judgment of the court, when necessary, the children still have the right to request their parent Mario to pay beyond the original amount stipulated in the agreement or the judgment, and can also file a petition to the people's court to increase the child support payments. Certainly, Mario can also file in the people's court for decreasing or remission of child support payments under special circumstances. If Mario fails to pay the child support payments in accordance with the agreement or the judgment, in the future, the child under the age of eighteen or the child who can not live independently, or their custodial parent, Lily, has the right to request the people's court to enforce the judgment or agreement.

In China, Article 48 of the current Marriage Law prescribes, "in case any person refuses to execute the judgment or decision on the payment of expenses for upbringing, supporting or maintenance, the partitioning or inheritance of property or visiting the children, the execution may be enforced by the people's court in accordance with the law. Relevant persons and entities shall be responsible for giving assistance to the enforcement." Judging from this provision, the people's court may decide to enforce the child support obligation from the wages or pension of the obligor parent, on the application of the parent entitled to receive the child support. The units concerned may deduct the child support from the wages or pension of the obligor parent directly and deliver it to the other parent who shall receive the financial support according to law.

As for the divorce case *Lily v. Mario*, where Mario has ability but fails to perform the support obligation, Lily may claim to the people's court to enforce Mario's obligation. The employer of Mario shall cooperate to deduct the child support monthly from the wages of Mario based on the enforcement ruling of the people's court and deliver it to Lily, the mother of the two minors, to meet the two children's needs for living and study and to safeguard their healthy growth.

Criminal Liability for Willful Nonsupport of Child

In China, as in the U.S., if one parent doesn't perform the support duty to the child, the child or the child's legal representative may claim to the people's court to enforce the support order from the property of the obligor. Where the parent refuses to fulfill his duty to support his/her child and neglects his/her child, if the circumstances are flagrant (threatening the life and health of the victim, and the criminal motives are evil, the crime is cruel, and the consequences are serious), a crime is constituted, then the parent shall be sentenced to fixed-term imprisonment of not more than five years, criminal detention, or public surveillance according to the provision on abandonment crime in Article 261 of CRIMINAL LAW OF PRC.

In the divorce case, *Lily v. Mario*, if Mario is capable but fails to perform the support obligation to his child, neglects his child so that the son Dino suffers from some life threatening disease, lives in poverty, or suffers malnutrition, a crime is constituted. Lily may claim to the people's court to investigate Mario's criminal responsibility in accordance with the provisions of the Criminal Law.

Italy

In the Italian legal system each parent's duty to provide for the maintenance of their minor children is prescribed by Art. 147 of the CIVIL CODE as one of the consequences of marriage. Parents have a right-duty of maintenance towards all their children alike, whether born within or outside of marriage. COST. Art. 30. Much like in the U.S., both parents must comply with this obligation proportionally to their respective financial position and their ability to work professionally or at home. C.c. Art. 148. Each parent has a coequal duty commensurate to his or her financial ability. Cass. Civ. Sez. I, 8 marzo 1983 n. 1687.

After separation or divorce, the couple's children have a right to be afforded, as much as possible, the style of life they were enjoying before. Cass. Sez. I, 22 marzo 2005 n. 6197. Therefore, no matter whether there is exclusive or shared custody, the role of the judge with respect to the children, if there is no satisfactory agreement between the parents, is to establish a maintenance check in favor of the custodial parent that is sufficient to continue to provide for the education, medical expenses, clothing, food, general living expenses, extra-curricular activities, ordinary, and extraordinary expenses related to the children's upbringing so they continue to enjoy, to the extent possible, the conditions they were accustomed to prior to their parents' separation or divorce. This obligation results in a maintenance check for the children (as opposed to the maintenance check for the spouse).

There are several major differences between the U.S. and Italy with respect to the reach of child support obligations, due to the state's interest in the protection of children, the family solidarity obligations imposed by law on close relatives based on need, and the less clearly established end point for child support obligations.

First, the obligation to maintain one's children is clearly defined as an obligation not within the control of the parties, and subject to a ruling by the judge *ex officio*. Cass. Civ. Sez. I, 23 agosto 1990, n. 8582. The maintenance contribution cannot be disposed of, and it is not based on the "principle of petition" (meaning that it would arise only when someone files a petition for it), as in ordinary civil proceedings, but it arises by law: if the parents do not take action regarding child support, the judge has the power and duty to defend the interest of minor children. Cass. Civ. Sez I, 26 febbraio 1988, n. 2043. The judge can force the non-performing parent to pay his share of the children's maintenance to the other parent or to anyone who is taking care of the children. Art. 148. C.c. Hence, the judge, during separation proceedings, will consider the agreement of the parties with respect to child maintenance, but if none exists, the judge will make a determination relative to the payments owed for that purpose at the very first hearing, an interim ruling which is immediately enforceable.

Second, unlike Tennessee and most other states, the law clearly attributes a positive role to grandparents in providing for the children: it falls on the grandparents to help the parents fulfill their financial obligations towards the children when the parents do not have sufficient means. C.c. Art. 148. Any interested party can petition the court to obtain an order garnishing a portion of a parent's wages for the payment of child support. *Id.* The same procedure can be used to force the grandparents to support the parents who lack sufficient financial means, so they in turn can fulfill their obligations towards the children. Cass Civ. Sez. I, 23 marzo 1995, n. 3402.

Third, although the maintenance obligation is finalized to support children to the age of majority, it does not end automatically at majority. *See* Cass. Sez. Civ. I, 19 ottobre 2006, n. 22491. Instead, the parents' obligation has a variable duration, predicated upon the circumstances of the case and lasting until the child reaches financial independence. For example, unlike in Tennessee and most other states, it is well established that the obligation of the parents continues when the child, although over eighteen, is engaged in university studies. Cass., Sez. Civ. I, 17 gennaio 1977, n. 210.

The payment of a maintenance check for children is primarily ordered during a legal separation or divorce. However, it can also be ordered against the unmarried parent who is not otherwise fulfilling his obligations towards his natural children. Instead, during marriage, each parent's share of their maintenance obligation towards their children is simply referred to as a contribution.

Alimenti (Basic Maintenance)

Maintenance should be distinguished from the related though more limited concept of *alimenti*, a term that is sometimes used interchangeably with maintenance, but technically refers to a more limited obligation of basic support, to provide for food and shelter when the person who is legally entitled to it is in a state of need and files a petition seeking *alimenti* (basic support). The two concepts overlap because the obligation of maintenance, and consequently the maintenance check, is inclusive of the obligation of *alimenti*. Conversely, maintenance extends beyond mere basic needs with the goal of perpetuating the lifestyle the children were enjoying during their parents' marriage so they are not suffering, at least in terms of comfort, because of the decision of their parents to lead separate lives.

The obligation of *alimenti*, derives from family solidarity principles, and obtains to (and falls on) family members in order of proximity provided by law. The obligation to provide *alimenti* falls to 1) the spouse; 2) the children; 3) the parents; 4) the sons-in-law and the daughters-in-law; 5) the father-in-law and the mother-in-law; and 6) the brothers and sisters, in this order. C.c. Art. 433. The list is exclusive. If one obligor satisfies the obligation, the others below him are exonerated. The obligation for parents to provide *alimenti* for their children, and for each spouse to provide *alimenti* for the other spouse, is residual, as they each normally owe the much more onerous obligation of maintenance.

The maintenance obligation arises by law from the relationships of spouse and child: the maintenance check is a mere pragmatic solution, in separation or divorce, to ensure that this obligation is fulfilled until the children reach financial independence. The right to maintenance obtains to the child; thus, during separation or divorce, the custodial parent has a right to receive a maintenance check to help provide for the child.

Conversely, *alimenti* may be requested only by a child who in a "state of need and is incapable of providing for his or her maintenance." C.c. Art. 438. *Alimenti* differs from the obligation of maintenance in that while maintenance does not require a petition, *alimenti* only arises if a petition is filed, and the petition can only be proposed by the obligee child, only to the extent of his basic needs. A child's right to *alimenti* may come into play after he has become financially independent and later finds himself in a state of need. Cass. Civ. Sez. I, 21 febbraio 2007, n. 4102 (post majority child who abandons his job loses his right to maintenance and may have a right to *alimenti* for which he has to petition personally, not through the custodial parent).

Post-Majority Support Obligations

While in Tennessee the obligation to pay child support stops automatically upon reaching the age of eighteen, or at graduation from high school, in Italy it has long been established that the parents' obligation to support their children does not automatically end when they reach the age of majority. Hence, a reduction of the maintenance check with respect to the children cannot simply rest on the mere fact that the child has reached majority but has to be based on the fact that, having reached majority, the child has become economically independent, or that even though he is in a position to be economically independent, he has failed to take advantage of that opportunity. Cass. Civ. Sez. I, 20 maggio 2006, n. 11891. The post majority child who is still financially dependent has to be without fault to be entitled to maintenance from his parents. In this context, the unjustified refusal to work constitutes fault. However, it is well established that the child does not have to take any available job. Indeed, the post majority child who has obtained a university degree, still has the right to a maintenance check until he finds an occupation consistent with his social condition and professional preparation, as long as he is actively searching for work and not negligent. Cass. Civ. Sez. I, 28 maggio 2007, n. 12457; Cass. Civ. Sez. I, 6 dicembre 2007, n. 25436. In the current economic climate with persisting high unemployment, this search could take a while. Then, if the child starts to work and reaches financial independence, he no longer qualifies to receive maintenance from the parents: the fact that he may later quit work or interrupt his career does not automatically revive the parents' maintenance obligation, but only the more limited obligation of *alimenti*. Cass. Sez. Civ. I, 28 gennaio 2008, n. 1761.

Law 84/2006 codifies post majority children's right to maintenance vis-à-vis each of their parents as previously identified by the Supreme Court. C.c. Art. 155-*quinquies* (1). The new Code provision goes a step further, identifying post majority children as the direct recipients of the maintenance check. When the parents separate, the judge, evaluating all the circumstances, can order, in favor of the children who have reached majority but are not economically independent, the payment of a periodic check to be paid directly to the children. C.c. Art. 155-*quinquies* (1). Notwithstanding the indication of the Code, courts tend to favor payment of the maintenance check for children to the custodial parent. For example, if the financially dependent post majority child is still living with the custodial parent, the maintenance check is owed to the custodial parent *iure proprio* (by his own right). The post majority child who lives with the custodial parent but is absent periodically because of study or work, is still deemed as living with the custodial parent if the custodial parent's home remains his permanent residence, for purposes of the right of the custodial parent to receive the maintenance check from the noncustodial parent *iure proprio*. Cass. Civ. Sez. I, 27 maggio 2005, n. 11320.

Law 84/2006 also codifies the continuing parental obligation of maintenance towards post majority children who are severely handicapped as defined by Art. 3 (3) Law 5 febbraio 1992, n. 104, Gazz.Uff., 17 febbraio 1992, n. 39. C.c. Art. 155-*quinquies* (2).

In sum, the approach of the Italian system to the issue of post majority child support is opposite to that prevalent in the U.S. As a rule, the parents' duty of maintenance—in the form of a separation or divorce maintenance check for children—continues post majority. It may, therefore, be relatively easy for Lily, if she is the custodial parent for purposes of the children maintenance check to continue to receive the check after their majority. The fact that Mario may not be a high income obligor would not prevent his continued obligation. Mario's check may not be for a large amount, but some child support is likely to continue. Other factors would be relevant, such as whether Dino and Jade engage in post majority university level studies and continue to live in Lily's home. In fact, if the child has not reached financial independence, the parents' post majority contribution is not voluntary—as it would be in most cases in the U.S.—but a mere extension of the same duty of maintenance parents have towards minor children. Unless an agreement is reached between the parties, Mario would have to petition the court as per Art. 710 of the CIVIL PROCEDURE CODE to obtain a change with respect to his maintenance check obligation, and would have the burden of proving that the children have indeed reached financial independence, or that although in a position to reach it, they have been negligent about it.

It is uncertain whether Dino would be classified as severely handicapped based on the definition of Law 104/1992. The determination of the level of severity is made by the local units of the National Healthcare Systems through a process involving the participation of multiple physicians and experts. Art. 4 Law104/1992. If Dino is found to be severely handicapped, Mario will continue to be responsible for his maintenance, and thereby owe a maintenance check, for the rest of his life. However, even if Dino's disability is not severe, if Dino thus remains unable to achieve financial independence, Mario's, as well as Lily's, responsibilities with respect to Dino's maintenance could still continue indefinitely.

Pre-Majority Termination of Child Support Obligations

As in the U.S., in Italy child support obligations can terminate before the child reaches majority in a few cases such as marriage, emancipation, adoption, or death of the minor child. On the other hand, courts do not customarily order parents to obtain life insurance in favor of the children to provide for them financially in case of one or both parents' untimely demise. Solidarity principles, such as the obligation of *alimenti* imposed on close family members in favor of one another in case of need, as highlighted above, social insurance, and social services continue to provide the fall-back mechanisms for children's sustenance in the event of their parents' death.

Child Support Guidelines

Unlike in many states in the U.S., in determining the amount of the maintenance check with respect to minor children and post majority children who are still unable, without their fault, to achieve financial independence, Italian judges do not have as detailed statutory guidelines as U.S. judges. Law 84/2006 added further guidance in the CIVIL CODE, modifying Art. 155 listing several factors the judge must weigh in determining the maintenance check. They are: 1) the needs of the child; 2) the lifestyle the child was accustomed to when living with both parents; 2) the times the child spends with each parent after separation or divorce; 4) the financial resources of both parents; and 5) the economic value of domestic contribution and care undertaken by each parent. C.c. Art. 155.

The agreement between the spouses or former spouses has to be considered by the judge in reaching his determination but it does not limit his discretion. Imputability (finding one spouse responsible for the separation) of the separation or divorce to one parent is not a factor to be weighed. If only one of the spouses is employed, and the income earning parent is noncustodial, the calculation of the maintenance check will be based on his income. The calculation is more complex when both parents have income. The court has to calculate the income of each of the working spouses or ex spouses and then determine the amount of the respective contribution. Under the principle of proportionality to the financial condition of each parent, the Supreme Court has held that courts, in determining the financial position of each parent, have to take into account every type of income accruing to the spouse: ordinary income from work activities, real estate lived in or otherwise utilized, every other income stream, stock, and other form of business ownership. *See* Cass. Civ. Sez I, 3 luglio 1999, n. 6872; Cass. Civ. Sez. I, 5 ottobre 1992, no. 10926.

The Court has thus been interpreting and extending Art. 148 of the CIVIL CODE which takes into account every kind of activity (professional, employee, homemaker, etc.) and attributes value to the functional as well as the financial contribution of each parent. Clearly, the duty of maintenance is not limited to food, housing, and education but extends to assistance in all aspects of child rearing. Even in situations of shared custody, attempts to satisfy the children's maintenance obligation by allocating payment of individual expenses to each parent have been found to create continuous friction. The practical solution remains to quantify the parents' contributions and establish proportionality via the payment of a periodic check, generally to be paid monthly in favor of the custodial parent. The right to a maintenance check for the children belongs to the parent/spouse independently, *iure proprio*, and not on behalf of the children. The entitlement does not change when the children reach majority, if they continue to live with the custodial parent, and are still incapable of financial independence. *See* Cass. Civ. Sez. I, 16 giugno 2000, no. 8235. The maintenance check owed for the children to the custodial parent does not get reduced if the custodial parent starts to live "more uxorio" (common law marriage) in a situation of relative stability. Cass. Civ. Sez. I, 24 febbraio 2006, n. 4203. It can be adjusted due to changes in the financial conditions of the obligor, or changes in the needs of the child taking place during the pendency of the petition, without the need to submit a new petition

Even with the more precise guidelines of the reform, the determination of the appropriate maintenance check to be contributed by separated or divorced parents remains fraught with difficulties, especially in the current regime of joint parenting with liberal visitation and permanence of the children with both parents. The maintenance check is automatically adjusted based on the ISTAT indexes, unless the parents or the judge have otherwise agreed or disposed. Art. 155 C.c.

Family Checks

Family checks were originally introduced in 1934 to guarantee workers and their families sufficient income to live with dignity and freedom, a principle later (1946) constitutionally guaranteed. *See* Cost. Art. 36. The system of family checks has been modified multiple times since then, but it maintains the characteristics of a fund, a type of insurance funded by the contribution of all workers, and paid out by the Instituto Nazionale Previdenza Sociale (INPS) to the beneficiaries, identified through ever changing and increasingly more complex criteria, through their employers. The family check is calculated based on the total income received by the worker; the size and composition of his family; whether any of the family members, who because of partial or total mental or physical disability, cannot temporarily or permanently engage in work; and whether there are in the recipient's family minor children who cannot engage in activities typical of their age. In cases of legal separation involving children, the custodial parent has the right to receive the family checks for the children, even though they may be based upon the other spouse's employment relationship. L. 151/1975, Art. 211. Oddly, when there are no children, the family checks for the separated spouse belong to the worker spouse so that he can use them to fulfill his obligations under Arts. 143 and 156 of the Civil Code, and the Supreme Court has held that if nothing is said with regard to the checks in the separation agreement, they presumptively have been taken into account in calculating the maintenance check due from the worker spouse to the other. *See* Cass. Civ. Sez. I, 2 aprile 2003, n. 5060.

Medical Insurance

Medical insurance is generally not an issue in determining the child support check because Italy has the *Sistema Sanitario Nazionale* (National Healthcare System) funded with government moneys which purports to afford to anyone present on the territory at a minimum, emergency medical care, and to all citizens, preventive and medically necessary acute and long term catastrophic care. However, medical expenses have to be considered in determining the maintenance check for the children. Even with the National Healthcare System, elective procedures and treatment can be obtained in private hospitals and clinics by paying out of pocket. Also, because of the overburdened National Healthcare System, the only way to receive care for most diagnostic tests, and most specialist outpatient consults, without significant delays, is to pay out of pocket to private service providers. In addition, even when using the National Healthcare System many services require a co-payment. Lastly, certain procedures such as elective care or certain ongoing treatment for non-life threatening conditions can only be obtained from private service providers, and by out-of-pocket payments.

In attempting to guarantee to the children of separated or divorced parents the same lifestyle they were accustomed to during the intact marriage, the opportunity to seek privately offered medical care is one discriminating factor between different financial strata in the population. The issue of medical care available only through the private sector could be relevant in Dino's case if the parents decide to seek specialty and ongoing treatment which is only available by recourse to the private sector, to alleviate the consequences of Dino's hearing impairment. Another expense item to be considered in deciding on child support obligations in the same general category is orthodontic care, as quality orthodontic care is often available only through the private sector, as well. In the case of Jade and Dino, both children are likely to need those services at some point given their ages.

Modifications and Jurisdiction

As previously mentioned, the concept of jurisdiction translates imprecisely in the Italian legal order in *competenza per materia*. Jurisdiction to rule on maintenance checks normally belongs to the ordinary tribunal with jurisdiction for separation or divorce, and only exceptionally to the juvenile courts. The applicable rules are those for proceedings in camera. The petition is by *ricorso*, (a style of pleading) as opposed to complaint and summons [*citazione a guidizio*] and the resulting judgment is by decree (*decreto*)with written reasoned opinion (*decisione motivata*). Arts. 710 and 737 *et seq.* C.p.c.; Cass. Civ. Sez. I, 12 novembre 1994, n. 9527. The judge has ample inquisitorial powers, and is not limited by the requests and submissions of the parties, but can make inquiries at his discretion. C.p.c. Art. 738. The decree of the judge in this proceeding is subject only to the remedy of a limited appeal to the Court of Appeal, called *reclamo* (limited appeal), within the peremptory deadline of ten days from the notice of the decree, and the Court of Appeal in turn will decide on it *in camera* as well. C.p.c. Art. 739. No further judicial review is permitted.

As already pointed out, the right to a maintenance check for the children belongs to the parent/spouse by his own right, *iure proprio*, and not on behalf of the children. The entitlement does not change when the children reach majority, if they continue to live with the custodial parent, and are still incapable of financial independence. *See* Cass. Civ. Sez. I, 16 giugno 2000, no. 8235. The fact that the custodial parent starts to live *more uxorio* (common law marriage) in a situation of relative stability is not a basis to seek a reduction of the maintenance check owed for the children. Cass. Civ. Sez. I, 24 febbraio 2006, n. 4203. On the other hand, the maintenance check can be adjusted due to changes in the financial conditions of the obligor, or changes in the needs of the child. If changes of this type occur during the pendency of the petition, they can be presented without submitting a new petition (after a divorce petition is filed, quite some time may pass from before a decision is reached: interim changes are taken into account within the same proceeding). The maintenance check is automatically adjusted based on the ISTAT [previously defined] indexes, unless the parents or the judge have otherwise agreed or ordered. C.c. Art. 155.

Consequences of Nonpayment to the Obligor

The separation or divorce decree or decision is enforceable without more. The wages or pension of the obligor can be garnished based on it. The spouse entitled to the maintenance check for the children based on the separation or divorce decree can summon the obligor spouse's employer or Pension Fund so that they are ordered to contribute a portion the obligor's wages or pension directly to obligee spouse every month according to the terms set by the recipient. Thereafter, the obligor will be unable to block deductions and payments. The same enforcement procedures apply to the maintenance check which may be temporarily set by the President of the Tribunal during the first hearing in a separation or divorce. Even these interim rulings are enforceable, and the obligee can immediately proceed to execution without waiting for the separation decree or decision. Civil as well as criminal liabilities can accrue to the non-performing parent. The parent who fails to pay the maintenance check in favor of the children can lose parental power (C.c. Art. 330); he can be indicted for the crime of intentional failure to obey a judicial order (criminal contempt) (C.P., Art. 388), and for the crime of violation of his obligation of assistance to his family (C.P., Art. 570).

Summary Chart—Child Support

	U. S. (Tennessee)	China	Italy
Co equal duty of parents to support child according to one's ability.	Yes	Yes	Yes
Normal expiration of support obligation.	Age of majority, eighteen in TN, graduation from high school, or when the high school class, of which the child is a member upon attaining the age of majority, graduates —whichever is later.	Generally upon reaching eighteen years of age, but parents still have obligation when adult children "without the ability to live an independent life."	Upon reaching financial independence.
Grandparents can be liable to help pay child support if they are able.	No	No	Yes
Parents liable for post majority support for university students.	No, except by agreement at divorce. Courts can also order the divorced parent to contribute to an education account during the child's minority.	Yes	Yes
Pre-majority termination of child support obligation.	Military enlistment, marriage, judicial emancipation, adoption, death.	Age sixteen, if the child can maintain a average standard of living by his own labor.	Marriage, emancipation, adoption, death.
Application of child support guidelines which limit the judge's discretion in setting child support amounts.	Yes	Yes	No, the judge has discretion, guided by consideration of statutory factors.
Requirement of Health Insurance for the child provided by the parents.	Yes	No, except by agreement. Government provided vaccines	No, because there is a National Healthcare System.

continued	U. S. (Tennessee)	China	Italy
		for children under six years of age.	
Basis for Modification of child support obligation.	Significant variance between the support paid and the amount that would currently be due under the child support guidelines.	The current needs have exceeded the original amount.	Subject to the judge's discretion. (Judge also has inquisitorial power).
Recognition of the obligation to pay basic support to a post majority child in need, when petitioned by the adult child.	No	Yes	Yes, (Alimenti).
Parental liability for post majority support of a handicapped child.	Yes	Yes	Yes
Government assistance checks paid for the benefit of children of workers with low wages.	No	No	Yes, family checks paid to the custodial parent.
Child support enforceable by garnishment of parent's wages or pension.	Yes	Yes	Yes
Criminal liability for willful nonsupport of child.	Yes	Yes	Yes

CHAPTER 9

PROPERTY DIVISION

United States

Background

Historically, states followed two very different approaches in dividing marital property. Most states followed the common law, which divided property based on title ownership. Eight states, however, known as community property states, viewed all property acquired through marital labor as belonging to the marital community, to be shared by the spouses at the time of divorce without regard to title. Later, a ninth state adopted the community property regime by statute. In the common law states, the monied spouse usually held the title to most of the marital assets and was awarded those assets at the time of divorce. In the community property states, the property was typically divided equally between the spouses, or in some cases, "equitably."

The title doctrine followed by the common law states resulted in great inequities, eventually leading all of the common law states to adopt the doctrine of "equitable distribution." Equitable distribution allows the court to divide the marital property equitably, without regard to title ownership, taking into account several statutory factors. The adoption of equitable distribution by the common law states resulted in greater similarity between the common law states and the community property states regarding division of marital property. Currently, only three community property states require equal division of marital property (California, Louisiana, and New Mexico). The other six community property states (Arizona, Idaho, Nevada, Texas, Wisconsin, and Washington) allow the court some discretion to make an equitable distribution of the community property. Among the common law states, the doctrine of equitable distribution is sometimes interpreted to require an equal division of marital property, absent a reason for deviation. In Tennessee, the court is required to apply several statutory factors to divide

171

the marital property equitably, though not necessarily equally. Tennessee requires the courts to divide marital property before considering the issue of spousal support. One of the statutory factors in determining spousal support is the "provisions made with regard to the marital property." (TENN. CODE ANN. § 36-5-121(i)(8)).

Three-Step Approach

Most courts follow a three-step approach in dividing marital property. The first step is to classify the property. The second step is to value the property and the third step is to divide or distribute the property.

Classification

Most common law states classify the parties' property as either separate or marital, although there are a few "hotchpot" states that divide all of the property owned by the parties at the time of divorce. The community property states will determine whether the property is communal or separate. Tennessee is a common law state that recognizes both marital and separate property.

Marital Property. Most of the property acquired during the marriage is considered marital property, subject to certain exceptions. In Tennessee, marital property is broadly defined to include all real and personal property, tangible and intangible, acquired during the course of the marriage up to the date of the final divorce hearing, and owned by the parties at the time the complaint for divorce is filed. Other states use different cut off dates such as the date the divorce complaint is filed, the date that the parties separate, or a date within the court's discretion.

In Tennessee, if either of the parties has fraudulently conveyed any property in anticipation of the divorce, the transaction may be set aside by the court and the property will be included in the marital estate. Marital property also includes property as to which either spouse acquires a right, up to the date of the final divorce hearing. Unfortunately, for Lily, this means that her casino winnings will be considered marital property, even though she won them after the parties separated and filed for divorce. (TENN. CODE ANN. § 36-4-121(b)(1)(A)).

Separate Property. A spouse's separate property is not subject to distribution by the court. Separate property includes all real and personal property owned by the spouse prior to the marriage, as well as property acquired by gift, bequest, devise, or dissent, at any time. Separate property also includes pain and suffering awards, victim of crime compensation awards, future medical expenses, and future lost wages. (TENN. CODE ANN. § 36-4-121(b)(2)).

Mario's antique coin collection, which he inherited from his father, will be classified as separate property and will not be subject to equitable distribution by the divorce court.

Pensions. Pensions are considered marital property, in most states, to the extent that they were earned with marital labor. In Tennessee, both vested and unvested pensions are considered marital property, along with all other fringe benefit rights relating to employment that accrue during the marriage. (TENN. CODE ANN. §36-4-121(b)(1)(B)). Tennessee, like most states, uses the coverture fraction to determine the portion of the pension that will be considered marital property. The coverture fraction is obtained by dividing the number of years of employment during the marriage by the total years of employment. In our case, Mario's years of employment during the marriage are the same as his total years of employment at the time of the divorce, so the entire pension would be considered marital property. In a case where the employed spouse worked for a company for ten years before marrying, and then continued to work for that company for ten more years before divorcing, the coverture fraction would be one half, so half of the value of the pension would be considered marital property, to be divided between the two spouses. It is possible, in most cases, for the court to order that pension payments be paid directly to the nonemployee spouse through the use of Qualified Domestic Relations Orders (QDRO's).

Statutory Transmutation. Income from and appreciation in value of separate property during the marriage is also classified as separate property, unless the doctrine of statutory transmutation applies, in which case the income and appreciation are classified as marital property, but the separate property, itself, remains classified as separate property and not subject to equitable distribution by the court. Statutory transmutation occurs when each spouse substantially contributes to the preservation and appreciation of the separate property. The substantial contribution may include the direct or indirect contribution of a spouse as homemaker, wage earner, parent, or family financial manager. (TENN. CODE ANN. §36-4-121(b)(1)).

Intentional Transmutation. Property can also be transmuted from marital to separate, from separate to marital, or from the separate property of one spouse to the separate property of the other spouse, based on the intention of the parties. The intention of the parties may be presumed based on their actions. For instance, if one spouse owns a home prior to the marriage and subsequently retitles that home in both parties' names, the home will be presumed to be marital property. The presumption is rebuttable, however. Mario's great-grandmother's diamond ring would have been classified as his separate property if he had kept the ring, because he inherited it and because he owned it prior to the marriage. Most states consider engagement rings to be conditional gifts that are contingent upon the marriage taking place. After the marriage, the gift is complete, and the ring becomes the separate property of the wife. Some states consider the ring to be marital property, but Tennessee classifies the engagement ring as the wife's separate property.

Tracing. Most states apply the doctrine of tracing when classifying marital property. Tracing allows the court to "trace" a piece of property back to its source, for purposes of classification. For example, Mario's gold watch can be traced back to the parties' joint savings account, which would be considered marital property. Normally, the watch would also be classified as marital property, due to tracing, but here we also have to consider the doctrine of intentional transmutation. It appears that Lily intended to make a gift to Mario of the watch which she purchased with marital funds, thus transmuting the marital funds which were used to purchase the watch to Mario's separate property in the form of the watch.

Commingling. If marital property and separate property become inextricably commingled, such that the court cannot separate out the marital property, all of the commingled property will be classified as marital property and subject to equitable distribution by the court. For example, if the parties have one joint bank account into which they deposit both marital and separate funds and from which they pay both separate and marital debts, the court will classify the entire account as marital property if the parties cannot identify which funds in the account are marital and which are separate.

Debts. Debts must also be classified and, to the extent that they are classified as marital, will be subject to equitable distribution by the court. Some states consider marital debt as those debts that are traceable to the acquisition of marital property. In Tennessee, all debt incurred during the marriage is classified as marital debt. In making an equitable distribution of the marital debts, the court will consider four factors: 1) the debt's purpose; 2) which party incurred the debt; 3) which party benefited from the debt; and 4) which party is better able to pay the debt.

All of Mario's and Lily's debts: Mario's educational loans, the mortgage on the home, and the credit card debts for general living expenses will be considered marital debts. The court will allocate those debts between the parties, taking into account the four factors outlined above.

Deferred Compensation. When one of the parties has expended marital labor but has not been compensated for that labor at the time of the divorce, the court may confront both allocation and valuation issues. The allocation issue arises when the party will also have to expend post divorce labor in order to earn the compensation at issue. For instance, if one of the divorcing parties is a plaintiff's personal injury lawyer who has won a contingent fee case at trial, which is on appeal at the time of the divorce, the attorney's contingent fee, when collected, will represent both marital and post divorce labor. Because the fee is contingent, it also presents valuation issues. The Court does not know at the time of the divorce what the value of the contingent fee will be. It may be zero, if the case is lost on appeal. In such cases, the court will hear expert testimony concerning the number of marital labor hours already expended on the case at the time of the divorce, as well as evidence concerning the expected number of post divorce hours anticipated for the appeal. The court can then assign percentages of the recovery, if any, to each spouse, or the court can reserve jurisdiction to decide the matter once the amount of the actual fee is determined.

Personal Injury and Worker Compensation Awards. Personal injury, worker compensation, and other similar awards generally include compensation for past and future medical expenses, past and future pain and suffering, and past and future lost wages. Oftentimes, the awards are lump-sum amounts and do not designate specific amounts for the various elements of damage. To the extent that the award is specific, however, those amounts that represent compensation for loss of marital assets will be classified as marital property. In Tennessee, the statute defines marital property to include "recovery for personal injury, workers compensation, social security disability actions, and other similar actions for the following: wages lost during the marriage, reimbursement for medical bills incurred and paid with marital property, and property damage to marital property." TENN. CODE ANN. §36-4-121(b)(1)(C)). Separate property, on the other hand, includes "pain and suffering awards, victim of crime compensation awards, future medical expenses, and future lost wages." TENN. CODE ANN. §36-4-121(b)(2)(E)).

Professional Credentials and Goodwill. Most states do not consider professional credentials, such as a medical license or license to practice law, to be marital property, even if the credential is earned during the marriage, and even if the other spouse contributes to the ability of the other spouse to earn the professional credential. Those factors may be considered, however, in the distribution of the property that is classified as marital. In our case, Mario's Ph.D. will not be classified as marital property, but Lily's support of the family while Mario completed his degree is a factor that the court will consider in making an equitable distribution of the property that is classified as marital property. TENN. CODE ANN. §36-4-121(c)(3)).

The net assets of any business associated with the professional credential will be considered marital property, such as the accounts receivable, furniture, etc. in the medical or law office of the spouse. The goodwill of the professional practice will not be considered marital property, as a general rule, because the professional practice is usually deemed personal to the professional and does not have an independent market value. To the extent that the goodwill of the profession does have a market value, such as in the case of dental practices, courts will classify the goodwill as marital property.

Valuation

States also differ as to when marital property should be valued but generally seek to have the property valued close to the time that the court will make its decision regarding distribution of the marital property. In Tennessee, the statute provides that the property must be valued as of the date as near as reasonably possible to the final divorce hearing date. TENN. CODE ANN. §36-4-121(b)(1)(A)).

Distribution

Trial courts are usually required to consider certain statutory factors in making an equitable distribution of the marital property. The exception, of course, are the three community property states that mandate an equal division of the community property. In Tennessee, the court must make an equitable, though not necessarily equal, distribution of the marital property, taking into account all relevant factors, including the following statutory factors:

(1) The duration of the marriage;
(2) The age, physical and mental health, vocational skills, employability, earning capacity, estate, financial liabilities, and financial needs of each of the parties;
(3) The tangible or intangible contribution by one party to the education, training or increased earning power of the other party;
(4) The relative ability of each party for future acquisitions of capital assets and income;
(5) The contribution of each party to the acquisition, preservation, appreciation, depreciation, or dissipation of the marital or separate property, including the contribution of a party to the marriage as homemaker, wage earner, or parent, with the contribution of a party as homemaker or wage earner to be given the same weight if each party has fulfilled its role;
(6) The value of the separate property of each party;
(7) The estate of each party at the time of the marriage;
(8) The economic circumstances of each party at the time the division of property is to become effective;

(9) The tax consequences to each party, costs associated with the rea-
     sonably foreseeable sale of the asset, and other reasonably foresee-
     able expenses associated with the asset;
(10) The amount of social security benefits available to each spouse; and
(11) Such other factors as are necessary to consider the equities between
     the parties. TENN. CODE ANN. §36-4-121(c).

The Tennessee court cannot consider marital fault in making an equitable distribution of the marital property, except to the extent that factor five (listed
above) applies and the marital fault results in depreciation or dissipation of marital or separate property (i.e., where one spouse uses marital funds to take a paramour on a vacation). TENN. CODE ANN. §36-4-121(a)(1). The Tennessee statute
also contains a specific provision concerning the family home and providing that
the court may award the family home to either party, but must give special consideration to the primary residential parent. TENN. CODE ANN. §36-4-121(d).

In our case, Lily will ask for the family home, and will rely on the statutory
preference given to the primary residential parent for the children, assuming
that she is named the primary residential parent. Lily will also argue factors
two and four, pointing out that Mario will have a greater income earning capacity than she, after the divorce. Under factor three, Lily will offer proof that
she supported Mario while he finished his advanced degree. Under factor five,
Lily will offer proof of her contributions to the marriage as homemaker and
wage earner while Mario was a student. Under factor six, Lily will introduce
evidence of Mario's antique coin collection.

Mario, on the other hand, will focus on factor one, the duration of the
marriage, in that this was not a marriage of long duration. He will also offer
evidence under factor five, of his contributions to the marriage as wage earner.

Legal Separation. If the parties are not ready to end the marriage permanently, but do not wish to continue living together, they may ask for a legal
separation. Under an order of legal separation, the parties are still married,
but live separately. The parties may later decide to reconcile, to get divorced,
or to remain legally separated indefinitely. (See further discussion of legal separation in chapter 6.)

When the parties obtain a legal separation, the court can either divide the
marital property at the time of the decree of legal separation or at the time of
the divorce. If the marital property is divided at the time of the legal separation, any after acquired property by either spouse is classified as separate property of that spouse, even though the parties are still legally married. The property must be valued as closely as possible, to the date of the entry of the order
finally dividing the marital property. TENN. CODE ANN. §36-4-121(b)(1)(A)).

China*

The division of marital property at the time of divorce is intimately related with the marriage property system. In the Chinese mainland, because of the limitation of historical factors, the provisions on the marital property system in Marriage Law 1950 were not detailed. The provisions on the marital property system in Marriage Law 1980 were amended and supplemented according to the needs of new situations. But the Marriage Law 1980 lacked the explicit provisions on the scope of separate property, as well as the contents, the time, forms, and the effects etc. of contractual property of spouses, which resulted in practical difficulty. The Supreme People's Court of China issued a series of judicial interpretations to guide the judicial practice successively. After entry into the twenty-first century, the current Marriage Law clearly provides for the scope of marital community property (hereinafter referred to as marital property) and separate property of the husband and the wife (hereinafter referred to as separate property), as well the contents, forms, and effects, etc. of the contractual property system.

With regard to the division of marital property, Article 39 (1) of the current Marriage Law states that, "At the time of divorce, the husband and the wife shall seek agreement regarding the disposition of their joint owned property. If they fail to reach an agreement, the people's court shall, on the basis of the actual circumstances of the property and on the principle of taking into consideration the rights and interests of the child and the wife, make a judgment." Furthermore, SEVERAL OPINIONS OF THE SUPREME PEOPLE'S COURT ON HOW TO DEAL WITH THE PROPERTY DIVISION ON THE DIVORCE CASE UNDER THE TRIAL OF THE PEOPLE'S COURT (1993) (hereinafter referred to as Opinion on the Property Division 1993) provide that:

> For the division of the property jointly owned by the spouses in divorce case, pursuant to the Marriage Law of PRC, the Law on Protection of the Rights and Interests of Women of PRC and other laws concerned, the people's court shall clarify the property that is respectively owned by individuals, jointly owned by the husband and wife as well as jointly owned by the family. Then the people's court shall fairly and reasonably hear the case based on the principles of the equality of the men and women, of protecting the legal rights and interests of women and children, giving consideration to the party without fault, respecting the willingness of the litigants, helping the production and offering convenience to living.

---

* This part is written by Chen Wei, Pi Xijun, and Lai Wenbin.

The first step is to define the scope of jointly owned property, then divide the property on the principles of equality between men and women, of protecting the lawful rights and interests of the women and children.

Five concepts regarding marital property will be considered below: the classification of marital property, the division of marital property, the discharge of debts incurred jointly by spouses, the case when one party invades the other party's property rights at the time of divorce, and economic compensation for housework at the time of divorce.

Classification of Marital Property

Like the U.S., only marital property is subject to division upon divorce, so the first step in the process is the classification of property as marital (community property) or separate. Parties are encouraged to seek an agreement on their property relationship that shall be granted priority over the statutory property system. That is, the statutory property system will apply only in the case of no agreement between the parties.

Marital Property

Marital property falls into two categories, statutory marital property and contractual marital property.

Statutory Marital Property. Under Article 17(1) of the current Marriage Law, the following property acquired by both husband and wife during the marriage shall be jointly possessed property:

(1) wages and bonuses;
(2) proceeds of production and business operation;
(3) income gained from intellectual property;
(4) property inherited or bestowed, with the exception of such property that is designated to only one of the parties. (If the parents of the husband or the wife spent money on purchasing a house for the spouses, the money shall be determined as a gift to both of parties, except when the parents clearly expressed that the money was only gifted to one party); and
(5) other property which should be in their joint possession.

Moreover, with regard to a house rented by one party before marriage and purchased with jointly owned property after marriage, even though the house ownership certificate is registered under one party, the house shall be classified as property jointly owned by the husband and the wife.

The property earned after the marriage that is separately managed and used by the husband or the wife living in two separate places shall be deemed as the property jointly owned by the spouses, too. Any increase in value of property owned by one party before marriage shall be treated as marital property. Like in the U.S., where both parties repair, decorate, and rebuild the house owned by one party before marriage the enhanced part or the expanded part should be determined to be the property jointly owned by the husband and the wife for distribution. In case it is hard to make a distinction between the individual-owned property and the property jointly owned by the husband and the wife, the claiming party has the obligation to shoulder the burden of proof. Where the litigant is unable to give convincing evidence and the people's court is unable to verify, the property shall be dealt with as the property jointly owned by the spouses. (See: Article 4, 7 and 12 of OPINIONS ON PROPERTY DIVISION (1993) This approach is similar to the commingling doctrine in the U.S.

Contractual Marital Property. Under Article 19 of the current Marriage Law, husband and wife may come to an agreement on the ownership of property incurred in the duration of marriage or prior to marriage. It also states: "The agreement shall be made in written form. Where there is no such an agreement or it is not explicitly agreed upon, the provisions of Article 17 (being marital community property) and 18 (as separate property) shall be applied. The agreement concerning the property obtained in the matrimonial duration and the pre-marital property shall be binding upon both parties." Thus, if the spouses reach an agreement that the separate property acquired by one party during the marriage or prior to the marriage will be jointly owned, the property concerned belongs to marital community property.

It is noteworthy that the husband and the wife have equal rights and obligations to their marital property, similar to community property states in the U.S. They have equal ownership of their community property and enjoy equal rights and assume equal obligations regardless of shares in the jointly owned property. Both spouses have the equal rights to possess, use, seek profits from, and dispose of marital property according to law.

Separate Property

Separate property of one spouse, also called unique property owned by the spouse, refers to certain property owned respectively by husband or wife after marriage in accordance with the law or an agreement reached by the spouses. In the Chinese mainland, under the current Marriage Law and the judicial interpretations, although there is no concept of "special property of one spouse," either of the spouses is permitted to retain certain separate property in accordance with a spouses' agreement or the law.

Statutory Separate Property. As to the scope of statutory separate property, Article 18 of the current Marriage Law provides that, "The following property shall be owned by either the husband or the wife:

(1) the pre-marital property that is owned by one party;
(2) payment for medical treatment or living subsidies for the disabled arising from a body injury on either party;
(3) the property to be in the possession of one party as determined by a will or an agreement on gift;
(4) articles of living specially used by either party;
(5) other property that shall be used by either party."

Contractual Separate Property. Under Article 19 of the current Marriage Law, husband and wife may seek an agreement on the ownership of property obtained during the marriage and premarital property. Any such agreement is binding on third parties only after notice to them, however.

With regard to the rights and obligations of the spouses to separate property, either spouse has the right to possess, use, seek profits from, and dispose of his/her own separate property at will, without the consent of the other party. Meanwhile, the separate debts of either party or debts incurred by his or her separate property during the term of marriage or prior to marriage, shall be paid off by the party concerned with his or her separate property.

As to the divorce case of *Lily v. Mario*, if the parties have no agreement on the property acquired by the spouses during marriage, the community property system shall be applied. Under the current Marriage Law and the judicial interpretations, the ownership of the property acquired during marriage by Lily and Mario, including the ownership of the house and car, is not controlled by the title to the property. Thus, the ownership of the property acquired by the spouses during marriage shall be determined as follows:

The Ownership of Housing and Its Ancillary Decoration Facilities and Other Attachments and Furniture etc. Purchased after Marriage. As to the housing purchased by the spouses after the marriage, if it was purchased with marital property, it shall belong to jointly owned property; and if purchased with the separate property prior to marriage of Lily or Mario, shall belong to the separate property of the purchaser. As for the ancillary decoration facilities and other attachments of the housing, household electronic appliances, and furniture purchased during the marriage, and so on, in principle, belongs to the statutory community property of the husband and the wife. If these were purchased with separate property of either party, they belong to the party's separate property.

The Ownership of Other Assets Acquired during the Marriage. All other assets acquired by either or both spouses during the marriage, including cars and pensions belong to the statutory community property. If Mario worked for a company for ten years before marriage, and then continued to work for the company for ten years before divorcing, the coverture fraction would be one half, and half of the value of the pension would be considered marital property. However, if the car was purchased by Lily or Mario alone before their marriage, it shall belong to the separate property of the party concerned.

In short, as to the housing and car registered in the name of Mario, if they were purchased with the couple's jointly owned property, they should be marital community property. Conversely, if they were purchased by Lily or Mario alone prior to their marriage or purchased with separate property during the marriage, they should be separate property of the purchaser. It should be noted that, although the housing and car were registered in the name of Mario, Mario shall bear the burden of proof to prove whose property it is. If Mario cannot prove that the two kinds of assets were purchased by him alone prior to their marriage or with separate property during the marriage, they shall be presumed to be purchased with jointly owned property, so that they shall belong to marital community property.

Property Interests Gained from Health Insurance and Personal Insurance. As to the health insurance and personal insurance of Mario offered by his employer, the ownership of the insurable interests shall belong to the person designated as beneficiary, or by Mario himself, in accordance with the insurance agreements if there is no specific beneficiary. Therefore, the property interests arising from health insurance and personal insurance do not belong to marital community property.

The Property Inherited by Mario during the Marriage. The ownership of the ancient coins inherited by Mario from his father during the marriage should be determined based on whether there was a succession will appointing a successor. If there was a will which said the ancient coins should be inherited only by Mario, they shall belong to Mario's separate property. Conversely, if no a will designated that only Mario could inherit the ancient coins, they shall belong to the community property of Lily and Mario.

In addition, note that Lily and Mario may conclude a written agreement that some property acquired by the spouses during the marriage is owned by one party according to the law. For instance, both parties may reach an agreement that the 20,000 Yuan of bank deposits accumulated by both parties during the marriage and the car purchased with community property belong to Lily's separate property. These assets will be Lily's separate property under the agreement.

Distribution of Marital Property

Article 39 of the current Marriage Law provides that, "At the time of divorce, both husband and wife shall agree upon the disposal of the jointly owned property; if they fail to come to an agreement, the people's court shall decide the disposal thereof, taking into consideration the actual circumstances of the property and following the principle of favoring the child and the wife." As stated in the previous chapter, in the Chinese mainland, there are two approaches to divorce, one is divorce at a registry, and the other is divorce through action. Thus, there are two approaches to divide marital property at the time of divorce.

Distribution of Marital Property When the Parties Divorce at a Registry

The distribution of marital property when the parties divorce at a registry is a method of distribution by agreement. If either party goes back on the agreement concerning partitioning of property, Article 9 of JUDICIAL INTERPRETATION II OF MARRIAGE LAW (2004) states that, "within one year after the husband and wife were divorced on the basis of agreement, if they change ideas on the issue concerning the partitioning of property and file a suit for modifying or canceling the agreement on the partitioning of property, the people's court shall accept their application. After the people's court has accepted the suit, if it finds that no circumstance of fraud or coercion exists when the agreement on the partitioning of property was reached upon, it shall dismiss the pleading of the party concerned." Conversely, if circumstance of fraud or coercion exists, the people's court may modify or cancel the agreement according to law, even mediate or make a decision on the re-division of marital property.

Distribution of Marital Property When the Parties Divorce through Action

With regard to the distribution of marital property in the case of divorce through action, under Article 39 of the current Marriage Law and OPINIONS

ON PROPERTY DIVISION (1993), the people's court shall fairly and reasonably hear the case based on the principles of the equality between men and women, of protecting the legal rights and interests of women and children, favoring the party without fault, respecting the willingness of the litigants, helping the production, and giving convenience to living. Each of these concepts will be explained below. Accordingly, at the time of divorce through action, there are two methods to divide marital property: distribution pursuant to an agreement by the parties or, if the parties are not able to agree, a judgment by the court.

Principles of Distribution Pursuant to a Judgment

When dividing marital property, the people's court shall comply with the following principles:

Principle of equality between men and women. That is, at the time of divorce, husband and wife shall enjoy equal rights in the distribution of their jointly owned property. As to the property acquired during marriage, if neither party is found to be at fault, the property shall be typically divided equally between the spouses, regardless of whether it is acquired by either or both parties or how much property either or both parties have earned.

Principle of protecting the legal rights and interests of children and women. The court shall take into consideration the reasonable requirements of the child and the wife, thus, the wife who has no income or has lower income shall get more property in order to maintain her living after divorce. Either party who lives together with the child shall get more reasonable property to enable the healthy development of the child materially.

Principle of giving consideration to the party without fault. That is, when dividing marital property at the time of divorce, the no fault party shall be awarded more property than the party found to be at fault.

Principle of helping the production and giving convenience to living. That is, at the time of divorce, the distribution of jointly owned property of the husband and the wife should be based on the needs of production and living of both parties. Housing, furniture, household electronic appliances, cars, and high-valued daily necessities such as professional equipments for personal use, computers, and library materials, shall be typically distributed to the party who needs them. In short, at the time of divorce, the property of production or business operation or daily necessities, such as housing

and furniture, should be valued as marital property to be distributed reasonably. If the value of the housing, furniture, and other
materials is more than the due share of the party should get, he/she
shall compensate the other party with cash, securities, or other
property.

In the divorce case *Lily v. Mario*, at the time of divorce, the spouses should
seek agreement regarding the distribution of their marital property. If they
fail to reach an agreement, the people's court shall, on the basis of the actual
property and on the principle of equality between the men and women and
of taking into consideration the rights and interests of the child and the wife,
make a judgment. From the specific facts of the case we can know that Mario
has a high income job. On the other hand, Lily has no income because of time
spent engaging in housework. According to the analysis of support for children in the chapter 8, for the rearing and healthy development of the children,
the people's court shall decide that Lily will directly bring up the two children,
and thus shall give more marital property to her and for the convenience to
living, she shall be granted the ownership of the housing, furniture, and the
car needed to transport the child to school and hospital. The other property,
Mario's expected pension as well as the ancient coins inherited from Mario's
father, belong to the defendant Mario.

Remember that after Lily gets the housing and car in accordance with the
court's judgment, she enjoys the ownership of them. If Lily remarries in the
future, her second spouse is entitled to live in the house without housing ownership, because the housing is Lily's premarital separate property. In addition,
if the housing, furniture, and other household property are allocated to Lily
by the people's court, but Mario has no other housing, at the same time, the
people's court may order Mario to live temporarily in the housing for no more
than two years.

The Repayment of the Marital Debts

Article 41 of the current Marriage Law states that, "at the time of divorce,
the debts jointly incurred by both husband and wife for the common life shall
be paid out of the jointly owned property. If the jointly owned property is not
enough to pay the debts or if the property is individually owned by the husband and the wife, both parties shall agree upon the repayment of the debts.
If both parties fail to reach an agreement, the people's cCourt shall decide on
the repayment of the debts." At the time of divorce, the first step is to classify
marital debts and personal debts, then pay off the debts accordingly.

On the aforementioned *Lily v. Mario* divorce case, if during the marriage, in order to maintain family living or repay the expenses of medical treatment for his son Dino or the education cost of daughter Jade, either Lily or Mario or both spouses owed a debt of 20,000 Yuan to a third person, the debt shall be community debts which will be paid off with marital property at the time of divorce. If marital property is insufficient to pay off the debt, both parties shall seek an agreement on the repayment, or the people's court will make a judgment. On the basis of the specific circumstances of the case, taking into account the specific conditions of Lily who has less separate property and is without other income at the time of divorce, the people's court may decide that Mario should be responsible for the marital debt. However, it is worth noting that the handling of marital debt at the time of divorce, either by the agreement of both parties or by the judgment of the court, has no external legal effect to the creditor, just as in the U.S. Even though the marital debt is determined to be paid off by Mario, the creditors still have the right to require Lily to bear responsibility jointly and severally. If Lily does do that, she has the right to request for recovery from Mario under the terms of the agreement or the judgment of the people's court. In addition, if Lily or Mario owed a personal debt to a third party prior to their marriage or at the time of marriage, the debt should be paid off by the party in debt, with his or her separate property.

Infringement upon the Property Rights of the Other Party at the Time of Divorce

Article 47 of the current Marriage Law stipulates that, "If, at the time of divorce, any party conceals, transfers, sells or destroys the property jointly owned by both the husband and the wife, or fabricates any debt in an effort to seize the property of the other party, the party who did one or several illegal acts mentioned above may, in the partition of jointly owned property, have a smaller or even no share." Under Article 31 of JUDICIAL INTERPRETATION OF MARRIAGE LAW (2001), when either party discovers that the other party has engaged in the above acts after divorce, he or she may initiate a lawsuit in the people's court within two years from the next day when the party discovers the acts.

Economic Compensation at Divorce

Article 40 was newly supplemented in the current Marriage Law, providing that, "where the husband and the wife agree in writing that the property acquired by them during marriage is in their separate possession, if one party has performed more duties in respect of bringing up the child, taking care of the old and assisting the other party in work, he or she shall, at the time of divorce, have the right to request the other party to make compensation, and the other party shall do so accordingly."

Requirement of Claim for Economic Compensation at Divorce

Under the current Marriage Law, at the time of divorce, either spouse shall enjoy the right to claim for economic compensation if he or she meets the following requirements:

Written Agreement Adopting the Separate Property Regime. There must be written agreement that the separate property system is applied after marriage, that is, both spouses agreed in writing that property acquired respectively by them during their marriage was in their separate possession, which is the premise to claim for economic compensation. If statutory community property applies, there is no right to request economic compensation, even though one party performed more household duties during their marriage.

Performance of More Household Duties By One Party. One party must have performed more household duties, that is, one spouse has performed more duties in undertaking housework, bringing up the child, taking care of the old, and assisting the other party in work, study, and so on.

Claim Made at the Time of the Divorce. Economic compensation must be claimed at the time of divorce.

Determination of Economic Compensation at Divorce

Both parties shall seek agreement on the specific amount and method of the economic compensation at first. If they fail to reach an agreement, the people's court shall make a judgment properly and reasonably, on a basis of taking into account such facts as the duration that one party performed more household duties, how much he/she contributed to the family, to what extent it influences the professional development, income, and ability to earn money, as well as the age, health, and property situation of the party, taking into consideration the economic interests (including expected economic interests) earned by the other party during the marriage, his/her professional improvement in occupation, income, and ability to earn money, as well as his/her current property situation and coming financial burden.

As to the divorce case of *Lily v. Mario*, Lily may require Mario to pay economic compensation for her housework, if she meets the following three

statutory requirements: first, both Lily and Mario must have agreed in writing to adopt separate property system after marriage. Second, one spouse must
have performed more household duties. Third, the party who performed
more household duties shall claim for economic compensation at the time of
divorce. Where Lily meets the requirements, she is entitled to claim the compensation at divorce from Mario. Both parties shall seek an agreement on the
specific amounts and payment methods of the compensation, if they fail to
reach an agreement, the people's court shall enter a judgment. The people's
court shall consider the following two reasons for Lily's claim for economic
compensation at divorce; in particular, the second reason shall be paid more
attention to:

(1) the separate property respectively acquired by the husband and the
     wife during the marriage: the property acquired by Mario is six times
     as that by Lily.
(2) the separate contributions of the husband and the wife to the family:
     as to the family and the children, Lily performed more household du-
     ties while Mario earned more wealth. However, as Lily was mainly
     engaged in housework during the marriage, this had an adverse in-
     fluence on her job, income, occupation in the future, pension, ex-
     pected economic interests, and so on. On the contrary, Mario's job,
     income, occupation in the future, pension, expected economic in-
     terests, and so on benefited from the assistance of Lily in housework.

From the above two aspects we can see that during the marriage, as Lily
performed more household duties, she lost her job and wages. She acquired
less separate property during the marriage and no housing, no pension, no
health insurance, and no life insurance. Even her ability to earn money has
been reduced and she requires an education and training costs for re-em-
ployment. Mario gained his doctoral degree with the assistance of Lily, and
improved his ability to earn money. He has a very good job and his separate
property acquired during the marriage is six times that of Lily. He also has a
bright professional development prospect and considerable expected economic
interests of health insurance, life insurance, and pensions. Therefore, we believe that, based on the fairness principle of civil law and the opinion of recognizing the value of housework and protecting the legitimate rights and interests of women, under Article 42 of the current Marriage Law in relation to
the economic compensation at divorce, the judge may award the compensation offered by Mario to Lily, valuing 320,000 to 390,000 Yuan when granting
a divorce. In other words, as to the property with a total value of 700,000 Yuan
acquired by Lily and Mario during the marriage, Lily may actually get

420,000–490,000 Yuan, accounting for 60%–70% of the total; Mario may actually get the property of value 280,000–210,000 Yuan, accounting for 30%–40%. In addition, as Lily needs housing to reside, consideration should be given to her by the judge in the property division. The judge may decide that Lily shall be granted priority to such daily necessities as housing and furniture which shall be converted into money in the property distribution for maintaining the normal life of her and the children.

In the real life of the Chinese mainland we know that, due to the impact of traditional values and habits, a few spouses adopt the system of contractual separate property, but the majority of husbands and wives agree to apply the system of statutory community property. Therefore, in the current judicial practice, only a few divorced parties meet the requirements to request for economic compensation at divorce. For instance, in the 398 cases investigated in Xiamen city during the years 2000 to 2002, there was only one case in which the wife claimed that she performed more duties in the custody of the child and requested for economic compensation. However, the request was not granted because the spouses did not agree to apply contractual separate property system during the marriage, failing to meet the statutory requirements.

Italy

Property distribution after separation or divorce is directly linked to the system of marital property adopted by the spouses during marriage. The Family Law Reform of Law 151/1975 introduced community property during marriage as the default system unless, at marriage or at any time thereafter, the spouses specifically contract for their property to be held separately. *See* C.c. Arts. 159 and 162. The separation decree, or the homologation (official recognition) in the consensual, coupled with the divorce decree operate the dissolution of the legal community with respect to property. C.c. Art. 191.

Like in the U.S., at the time of separation (and divorce when not preceded by separation) property owned by the spouses is classified as falling within or without community property, to then determine which spouse will retain it during separation and after divorce. It has been noted that the regime of community property, which is regulated as part of the consequences of marriage, is indeed a dynamic regime which oddly perfects itself only at the time of dissolution. Sesta, at 759. In this view, the property subject to community rules would be a mere expectation during marriage.

Community Property

Community property identifies both the system of property that flows from marriage by operation of law, unless derogated by the spouses, and more specifically the categories of items that under that regime are held in common during marriage, forming what is referred to in the U.S. as marital property. Community property is, in one sense, an inaccurate label because community does not affect property in general but is limited to those transactions affecting property that take place during marriage. In this system, most of the property, real or personal, acquired during marriage belongs to the community, and specifically: 1) property purchased by the spouses together or separately, with the exclusion of goods for strictly personal use of each spouse; 2) the interest earned and still not expended at the time of separation; 3) the business managed by both spouses and created after the marriage. C.c. Art 177. Marital property bears the burdens that were present on each item of property at the time it was acquired, bears the burdens of the property administration, bears the expenses for maintenance of the family for the instruction and education of the children, for every contractual obligation entered into by the spouses, even separately, if for the interest of the family, and for every contractual obligation entered into by the spouses jointly. C.c. Art. 186.

For all assets falling under it, the regime is akin to a tenancy by the entirety. It does not matter whose name is on the document incorporating the transaction and conferring title: if the asset is acquired during marriage, unless excluded by the Civil Code, or by a specific declaration of both spouses, the asset is included in the community by operation of law. There is the equivalent of a conclusive presumption that each spouse has equally contributed to the acquisition of property which occurs during marriage. Also, it does not matter that only one spouse actually took part in the transaction. Each spouse can manage the community property, and assert claims in court with respect to matters of day-to-day management, but the consent of the other spouse is required for those transactions that exceed "ordinary administration." C.c. Art. 180. However, transactions performed without the necessary consent, or ratification after the fact, are merely voidable, and they are voidable only if they involve real property or personal property subject to registration, such as vehicles, boats, and airplanes. C.c. Art. 184.

Community property loses this qualification at the time of separation, specifically when the separation becomes final. Cass. Civ. Sez. I, 25 marzo 2003, n. 4351. Notably, if the spouses reconcile, the community property system originally in place is re-established, but the purchases made during the period of separation are not part of the community property. Cass. Civ. Sez.

I, 12 novembre 1998, n. 11418. In order to give effect to the constitutional principle of protection of the good faith of the traders and to protect the freedom of private economic initiative (*See* Cost. Arts. 2 and 41) the reconstituted community, when there is no reliable system to publicize the reconciliation between the formerly separated spouses, is subject to the rights of the Italian equivalent of a third party purchaser in good faith for valuable consideration. Cass. Civ. Sez. I, 5 dicembre 2003, n. 11619.

The doctrine (respected legal scholarship) has expressed its opinion on the performance of this system after thirty years of experience with it, denouncing its substantial failure. Sesta, at 772. At the crucial moment of separation, the community property system can become a tangle of knots around the freedom of action of the spouses precisely when they are looking to the law to provide easy rules of disengagement, and it offers multiple opportunities for each spouse to exercise undue pressure on the other or even blackmail him. *Id.* The practical result has been that with the increased number of marriages experiencing crises, young couples are more often opting for the separate property regime, or even marital agreements in contemplation of divorce. *Id.* Indeed, while at the time of the Family Law Reform in 1975 about 1% of the couples chose the separate property regime, today the incidence of that forward looking choice is over 50% across the country with as much as 69% in Northern Italy. *Id.* at 773.

Separate Property

The categories of property which continue to remain the separate property of each of the spouses after marriage, and therefore are not subject to distribution by the court, are remarkably similar to those found in the corresponding statutory listings in the U.S. Thus in Italy, separate property includes: 1) the real and personal property of each spouse, i.e. the property the spouse owned, or with respect to which he had a right of enjoyment before marriage; 2) the property the spouse acquired after marriage by donation or devise, unless the document incorporating the donation or the will specifically bestows the property in common to the spouses; 3) each spouse's personal property, *i.e.* items strictly for the personal use of each spouse and their accessories; 4) the property needed for the exercise of the spouse's profession, unless they are used for the common business of the spouses; 5) property received as damage awards, and the pension received for loss of earning capacity, or the ability to work; and, 6) the property acquired by transfers of the property in the above categories. C.c. Art. 179.

Real property, or personal property such as cars, vessels, or airplanes, which are subject to registration (*See* C.c. Art. 2683) can be kept outside of the marital property if they are either devoted to strictly personal use, professional use of one spouse, or are purchased with the proceeds of property outside of community, and if at the time of purchase, with the participation of both spouses, such exclusion is noted on the transfer documents. C.c. Art. Art. 179.

The law does not provide much guidance for the judge to determine what items are "strictly" for personal use. Both doctrine (respected legal scholarship) and the courts consider the subjective intent of the spouse at the time of purchase as well as the actual use of the item as reasonable criteria to consider in deciding. For example, jewelry is an item of value commonly haggled over at separation as "strictly for personal use" of one spouse. Jewelry used by one spouse both every day and for special occasions has been deemed separate property, while jewelry purchased as an investment and held in a safety deposit box has been held to belong to the community. SESTA, at 830. Applying this reasoning, Mario's watch may be considered separate property and remain with Mario. By the same token, some decisions have considered the value of the good in question, especially if the value is high and disproportionate to the cumulative wealth of the couple, and the classification as "strictly personal" would have the effect of depriving the pool of community property of a substantial portion of its content to the detriment of one spouse. SESTA, at 830.

In Lily and Mario's case, the Civil Code identification of the above broad categories of property outside of community resolves the question relative to several items of personal property. For example, Lily's engagement ring, presumably given to her prior to marriage would be separate property of Lily's at dissolution. If donated to her after marriage, maybe to substitute or upgrade a ring of lesser value, both financial and sentimental, it would remain separate property of Lily's unless donated by Mario's great-grandmother specifically to both spouses. Conversely, just like his U.S. counterpart, Mario, in Italy, will be able to keep the antique coin collection he inherited from his father because all property received by a spouse *causa mortis*, be it by will or under the Civil Code, is outside of the community.

Damage awards and long term disability are separate property. However, a question arose with respect to the indemnity of companionship established by Law 11 febbraio 1980 n. 18, Gazz. Uff. 14 febbraio 1980 n. 44 in favor of certain categories of handicapped individuals: the Supreme Court held that such indemnity is not for the purpose of sustaining the severely handicapped on account of their diminished working ability but is intended to provide the family of the handicapped the means to support the family so that it will take charge of the handicapped member avoiding his institutionalization which would weigh on the public expense. Cass. Civ. Sez. I, 27 aprile 2005, n. 8758. As such, the indemnity of companionship is part of the community. These rules would not apply, however, in the case of Mario and Lily with respect to Dino because the indemnity for companionship is reserved to the severely handicapped, and it is very unlikely that Dino would qualify.

The judge cannot dispose of any property that belongs exclusively to one of the spouses (because it was acquired before marriage or because, although acquired after marriage, it falls into one of the excluded categories). The only exception, as will be further analyzed below, is that of the assignment of the family home to the spouse with exclusive custody of the children, even though he may not have title to it.

Marriage Fund

Each spouse or both together by means of a document with legal effect called "*atto pubblico*" as defined in Art 2699 of the Civil Code or someone other than the spouses by "*atto pubblico*" or by will can create a marriage fund by identifying real property, personal property subject to registration, and certain credit instruments to become part of the fund and be used exclusively to satisfy the family's needs. C.c. Art. 167. In order to be included in the marriage fund, credit instruments have to be incorporated in a document reflecting ownership. Therefore, stocks qualify while membership in partnerships would not. This institution is often compared to the more flexible trust. At the time of separation or divorce, the marriage fund is dissolved and the property divided.

Bank Accounts

The doctrine (respected legal scholarship) has amply debated the issue of whether rights that are characterized as personal in nature, as opposed to rights that pertain to a *res* should be included in or excluded from the community. The Supreme Court has addressed the debate, at least with respect to bank accounts, holding that Art. 177 of the Civil Code applies only to the acquisitions of property, real or personal, and does not apply to the creation of mere relationships of credit such as a checking account during the permanence of marriage. Cass. Civ. Sez. I, 27 aprile 2004, n. 8002. The practical relevance of the Supreme Court's position on this issue is that a petition to divide the balance of checking accounts can be presented immediately after the separation is started, without waiting for the separation to become final. Sesta, 788. Notably, the Supreme Court has also recognized that the owner

of the balance of the checking account cannot be determined by simply looking at the name appearing on the account. Instead an evaluation on a case-
by-case basis may result in assigning the funds to the other spouse, if she was
the only income producer in the family. Cass. Civ. Sez. I, 23 gennaio 2004, n.
1149. On the other hand, a portion of the doctrine (respected legal scholarship) continues to opine that money is property susceptible of being "acquired" so that it should fall under community property and not be divided
until the separation has become final. Sesta, 788.

Pensions

The Italian system provides social insurance for the events of disability, old
age, and death based on a complex system of contributions to a Fund administered by a state agency during employment whether as employee, independent contractor or member of a profession and whether the individual is
employed in the public or private sector. The worker matures a right to a pension for the events of disability or reaching retirement age. In addition, certain survivors have a right to receive a pension in the event of death of the
worker, namely the spouse, the children, the grandchildren, the parents, and
the brothers and sisters. If the worker was already receiving a pension due to
disability or retirement at the time of his death, the identified family members are entitled to a pension called "*di riversibilità*." If the worker was still
working at the time of his death, the pension to specified survivors is called
indirect pension. In order for the right to mature, certain minimum conditions of payments (contributions) must have taken place. The survivors have
a right to the pension *iure proprio*. The surviving spouse who is legally separated is entitled to the pension "*di reversibilità*" even if the separation was
charged (imputed) to him. In this case though, the surviving spouse's right is
subject to the spouse qualifying for "*alimenti*." As seen above, "*alimenti*" are
due when the separated spouse is in a condition of need and files the relevant
petition. The surviving divorced spouse also has a right to the pension "*di reversibilità*" if a) he was assigned a divorce check based on Law 1970/898, Art.
5; b) he did not get remarried; and c) the employment relationship which is
the source of the pension started prior to the divorce. Law 1970/898, Art. 9
as modified by Law 1987/74, Art. 13. When two or more surviving spouses of
the same decedent qualify for pension "*di reversibilità*," the tribunal will divide the pension and the other checks among all the individuals entitled to it
proportionally. *Id.* Thus, the pension "*di reversibilità*" accomplishes its solidarity purpose as to both the former and the current surviving spouses. Sesta,
3694. The determination of the amount owed in case of multiple beneficiar-

ies, according to the prevailing interpretation of the Supreme Court, is based exclusively on mathematical calculations, prorating the benefit based the number of years of marriage, but many decisions of the Supreme Court as well as of the lower Tribunals, while affirming the preeminence of the temporal criterion indicated by law, have negated its exclusivity considering other peculiarities of the case, such as the financial position of the parties. *Id.* at 3697.

Employment Severance

Unlike the U.S., in Italy, the spouse who is owed a divorce check acquires a right to the compensation the other spouse may receive at the end of his work relationship with his employer, whether in the private or public sector. Law 1970/898, Art. 12-bis. The right matures even if the ex spouse's own right with respect to his work relationship matures after the divorce decree, and it is 40% of the amount owed to the ex employee for the period of time that the labor relationship coincided with the duration of the marriage, unless the divorced spouse has remarried. *Id.*

Family Home

The specific rules applicable to the family home and its "assignment" at separation or divorce are inextricably interwoven with child custody determinations and the realization of the paramount interests of the children. Art. 155-*quarter* of the Civil Code introduced by Law 54/2006 specifically addresses the "assignment" of the family home and mandates that the judge consider first and foremost the interest of the children. C.c. Art. 155-*quarter.* The judge takes into account the assignment of the family home in regulating the financial relationship between the parents, considering when applicable, which one of the parents has title to the house. *Id.* The right to use and enjoyment of the family home ends if the beneficiary chooses not to live in it, or starts a cohabitation *more uxorio* (common law marriage), or gets remarried. *Id.*

The assignment of the family house favors the custodial parent specifically in order to maintain for the children the environment they are accustomed to, and to facilitate a seamless transition for them during a marriage crisis. Otherwise, the financial equalization post separation or divorce is regulated via the maintenance checks. However, since there are no other secondary criteria indicated by law in assigning the family home when there are no children or they are otherwise protected, commentators have suggested that, since inevitably the assignment of the marital house to one spouse provides a significant economic advantage to him, the judge should also be able to use the assignment of the family home as a way to equalize economic conditions between the spouses. Matteo Santini, *L'Assegnazione della Casa Conuigale in caso di Separazione, available at*: http://judicium.it/news/ins_04_07_07/Symp/Symposium%20Santini.html.

If there are no children, in the absence of guidance from the Civil Code, it seems that if one of the spouses has title on the house, he would get the use of it, unless exceptional circumstances apply such as a grave sickness of the other spouse requiring extensive treatment and when the spouse would not be able to leave the family home without grave health consequences. *Id.*

Distribution

If the separation is consensual, the distribution of marital and separate property is in fact accomplished by agreement of the parties which is then presented to the judge for homologation (official recognition). If the separation is judicial, the legal community is dissolved, but the property remains in common between the separated spouses for those items which, during marriage, were subject to community property, or remains separate property of each spouse if the asset was acquired before the marriage or falls under one of the categories excluded from community.

Judges find very limited specific guidance in a few terse dispositions of the Code when it comes to segregating the tangle of assets, liabilities, real property, and personal property commingled during marriage. The judge divides community property between the spouses by dividing equally the credits and the debits. C.c. Art. 194. There is no opportunity to prove that one spouse contributed more than the other because the law is a clear and inderogable application of the principle of equality between the spouses referenced also in Art. 162(3) and 210(3) of the Civil Code in conformity with Art. 29 of the Constitution. The only differentiation can be created with respect to the needs of the children, by establishing a right of use in favor of one spouse to a portion of the property belonging to the other spouse. C.c. Art. 194. This rule allows the judge to assign the family home to the custodial parent. The right of use and enjoyment thus established is sometimes called judicial because it is based on a judicial proceeding.

In general, to reassemble the assets so that their title reflects which spouse now has exclusive rights to them, there must be a process of division which can be consensual, through a contract, or judicial. However, when the title reflects the ownership rights of both spouses, the partition process is not mandatory in every case, as the spouses may very well decide to remain in a regime of property in common with respect to those assets which prior to the separation they owned under community, now dissolved.

With respect to personal property, the spouses have a right to take possession of the personal property that belonged to each prior to community or that they have each received as a gift or by inheritance during community. C.c. Art. 195.

Summary Chart — Property Division

	U. S. (Tennessee)	China	Italy
Property classification based on title/equitable division or community property principles.	Property held by title ownership but subject to equitable division, without regard to title, upon divorce in TN and most other states.	Community property unless the parties contract, at any time, for property to be held separately.	Community property unless the parties contract, at any time, for property to be held separately.
Recognition of separate property.	Property owned before marriage, gift, inheritance, pain and suffering awards, awards for future lost wages and medical expenses (occurring after the divorce), property acquired in exchange for other separate property (tracing).	Property owned before marriage, gift, inheritance during marriage (if specifically devised to only one spouse, in the will).	Property owned before marriage, gift, inheritance (unless specifically given or devised to both spouses in writing), items strictly for the personal use of each spouse, property needed for the exercise of the spouse's profession, certain damage awards, property acquired in exchange for other separate property.
Recognition of Marriage Fund to be used exclusively to satisfy the family's needs.	No	No	Yes
Pensions.	Treated as marital property based on the coverture fraction.	Treated as marital property based on the coverture fraction.	National government pension is available to a surviving ex spouse who qualifies for *alimenti* (basic maintenance based on need).
Allocation of the family home is influenced by the best interests of the child.	Yes	Yes	Yes

continued	U. S. (Tennessee)	China	Italy
Time when marital property is divided.	In a divorce, at the time of the divorce; in a legal separation, either at the time of the separation or at the time of the subsequent divorce, if one occurs.	At the time of the divorce.	At the time of separation, if consensual; at the time of the divorce if the separation is judicial, or if there is a divorce without a prior legal separation.
Principle governing division of marital property.	Equitably	Equally, with factors justifying deviation.	Equally

CHAPTER 10

Spousal Support

United States

Background

Historically, alimony was available only to the wife who was not found to be guilty of any of the fault grounds for divorce. Divorce itself was a remedy that was available only to the innocent spouse. Alimony was not available to the husband, even if he was the innocent spouse, because at common law only the husband had a duty of support. In 1979, the United States Supreme Court held that gender limitations on alimony were unconstitutional under the Equal Protection Clause. *Orr v. Orr*, 440 U.S. 268 (1979). In addition, with the introduction of no fault grounds for divorce, many states eliminated consideration of fault in the request for alimony. A number of states changed the terminology from alimony to spousal support or maintenance.

Eligibility for Alimony

There are a number of rationales that states have articulated as the basis for alimony, including the recipient's need, the recipient's contributions to the marriage, compensation for breach of the marital contract, restitution, and compensation for loss. Tennessee's legislature focuses on economic detriment as the basis for alimony, noting that "where one (1) spouse suffers economic detriment for the benefit of the marriage, the general assembly finds that the economically disadvantaged spouse's standard of living after the divorce should be reasonably comparable to the standard of living enjoyed during the marriage or to the post-divorce standard of living expected to be available to the other spouse, considering the relevant statutory factors and the equities between the parties." Tenn. Code Ann. § 36-5-121(c). In determining whether alimony is appropriate and in determining the type of alimony and the amount, the court must consider all relevant factors, including the following statutory factors:

(1) The relative earning capacity, obligations, needs, and financial resources of each party, including income from pension, profit sharing or retirement plans and all other sources;

(2) The relative education and training of each party, the ability and opportunity of each party to secure such education and training, and the necessity of a party to secure further education and training to improve such party's earnings capacity to a reasonable level;

(3) The duration of the marriage;

(4) The age and mental condition of each party;

(5) The physical condition of each party, including, but not limited to, physical disability or incapacity due to a chronic debilitating disease;

(6) The extent to which it would be undesirable for a party to seek employment outside the home, because such party will be custodian of a minor child of the marriage;

(7) The separate assets of each party, both real and personal, tangible and intangible;

(8) The provisions made with regard to the marital property, as defined in § 36-4-121;

(9) The standard of living of the parties established during the marriage;

(10) The extent to which each party has made such tangible and intangible contributions to the marriage as monetary and homemaker contributions, and tangible and intangible contributions by a party to the education, training or increased earning power of the other party;

(11) The relative fault of the parties, in cases where the court, in its discretion, deems it appropriate to do so; and

(12) Such other factors, including the tax consequences to each party, as are necessary to consider the equities between the parties. Tenn. Code Ann. § 36-5-121(i).

Courts traditionally focus primarily on the recipient's need and the obligor's ability to pay as the most important factors, coupled with the length of the marriage.

Types of Alimony

Once the court determines that alimony is appropriate, it must decide what type of alimony to award, the amount of the award, and the duration of the award. Tennessee recognizes four types of alimony: rehabilitative, *in futuro,* transitional, and *in solido.* Each of these types of alimony will be explained below.

In addition to these four types of alimony, the court may also award alimony *pendent lite* or nominal alimony. Alimony *pendente lite* means "alimony pending the litigation." The court may, in its discretion, at any time prior to the final divorce hearing, order the payment of alimony for the support of the other spouse and to enable the recipient to prosecute or defend the divorce. *Pendente lite* alimony may also be ordered to pay the expenses of job training and education of the recipient spouse. Nominal alimony is essentially a "placeholder," in that it allows the court to retain jurisdiction to increase the amount of alimony in the future, should circumstances justify doing so. Nominal alimony, of perhaps a dollar, might be ordered at the time of the divorce if the recipient spouse is facing some medical condition that may or may not result in permanent disability in the near future. The recipient spouse is not disabled at the time of the divorce, so alimony may not be warranted. On the other hand, if the court enters a final decree of divorce without awarding alimony, the court will lack jurisdiction to reopen the case to consider alimony if the spouse does become disabled shortly thereafter. *Vaccarella v. Vaccarella,* 49 S.W.3d 307, 316–17 (Tenn. Ct. App. 2001) *appeal denied.* By awarding nominal alimony of one dollar, the court retains jurisdiction to modify the alimony award if the recipient spouse later becomes disabled.

Rehabilitative Alimony

Tennessee has a statutory preference for rehabilitative alimony. Rehabilitative alimony is usually designed to maximize or at least increase one's earning capacity, usually by furthering one's education or training. To be rehabilitated means "to achieve, with reasonable effort, an earning capacity that will permit the economically disadvantaged spouse's standard of living after the divorce to be reasonably comparable to the standard of living enjoyed during the marriage, or to the post-divorce standard of living expected to be available to the other spouse, considering the relevant statutory factors and the equities between the parties." TENN. CODE ANN. §36-5-121(e).

Rehabilitative alimony is modifiable upon a showing of a substantial and material change in circumstances. In order to extend it beyond the term in the divorce decree, or to increase the amount, the recipient has the burden of proving that all reasonable efforts at rehabilitation have been made and have been unsuccessful. If a dependent spouse does not satisfactorily strive for self sufficiency, the Court may withdraw part or all of the support allocated to finance rehabilitation. *Loria v. Loria,* 952 S.W.2d 836, 838 (Tenn. Ct. App.

1997). On the other hand, if the spouse is not able to become rehabilitated, despite reasonable efforts to do so, the court may modify the rehabilitative award and order *in futuro* support.

Rehabilitative alimony terminates upon the death of the recipient. Because it terminates upon the death of the recipient, it is entitled to favorable tax treatment from the perspective of the obligor. It is deductible by the obligor and includible in the income of the recipient. Rehabilitative alimony also terminates upon the death of the obligor, unless otherwise specifically stated.

Alimony in futuro

Alimony *in futuro* is also known as permanent, periodic, or long-term alimony. This type of our money is paid on a long-term basis or until the death or remarriage of the recipient. In order to award alimony *in futuro*, the court must find that there is relative economic disadvantage and that rehabilitation is not feasible. An award of alimony *in futuro* may be made either in addition to an award of rehabilitative alimony, where a spouse may be only partially rehabilitated, or instead of an award of rehabilitative alimony, where rehabilitation is not feasible. TENN. CODE ANN. § 36-5-121(f).

Alimony *in futuro* is modifiable upon a showing of a substantial and material change in circumstances. It terminates automatically upon the death or remarriage of the recipient. It is deductible by the obligor and includible in the income of the recipient. The recipient is obligated to notify the obligor immediately upon remarrying. Failure to do so allows the obligor to recover all amounts paid to the recipient after the recipient's remarriage. Alimony *in futuro* also terminates upon the death of the obligor unless otherwise specifically stated.

Alimony *in futuro* is also subject to the "live-in lover" rule. If the alimony recipient lives with a third person, a rebuttable presumption arises that the third person is contributing to the support of the recipient, or that the recipient is contributing to the support of a third party, and that the recipient does not need the amount of alimony previously awarded. The presumption was originally designed to address the situation of a "live-in lover," but has been extended to other adults living with the recipient, including adult children. The presumption is rebuttable, however.

Transitional Alimony

Transitional alimony is an amount paid for a determinate period of time. Transitional alimony is appropriate when the court finds that rehabilitation is not necessary, but the economically disadvantaged spouse needs assistance to adjust to the economic circumstances of divorce.

Unlike rehabilitative alimony and alimony *in futuro*, transitional alimony is not modifiable, unless the parties agree, the court so orders, or the "live-in lover" rule applies.

Transitional alimony terminates upon the death of the recipient. It also terminates upon the death of the payor or unless otherwise specifically stated. The obligor quantifies for favorable tax treatment in that the payments are deductible from income. The court may provide additional conditions such as termination upon remarriage of the recipient.

Alimony in solido

Alimony *in solido*, also known as lump-sum alimony, is a type of support, the total amount of which is ascertainable when awarded, but which is not designated as transitional alimony. It may be paid in installments. The purpose of alimony *in solido* is to provide financial support to a spouse, but attorney fees may also be awarded as alimony *in solido*, where appropriate, generally when the recipient spouse does not have sufficient assets to pay for attorney fees but the obligor spouse does.

Alimony *in solido* is not modifiable, except by agreement of the parties. It does not terminate upon the death or remarriage of the recipient or obligor.

Mario and Lily

Mario will argue that their marriage is not of long duration; that the kids are now in school, so there is nothing to prevent Lily from working to support herself; and that Lily has a career to which she can return that will allow her to live in the marital standard of living. He will argue that he should not be ordered to pay any alimony, including Lily's attorney's fees, because Lily was awarded sufficient marital property from which to pay her attorney.

Lily will argue that she wants to be able to stay in the family home and to be home with the children when they are not in school. She will argue that she supported Mario while he worked on his degree and that it is only fair for him to pay rehabilitative alimony while she goes to law school, which will ultimately provide more support for the children and their college expenses. She will point out the legislative preference for rehabilitative alimony. Alternatively, she will argue that she will never be able to earn enough with her current degree to maintain the marital standard of living or the standard that Mario will be able to afford after the divorce, so she qualifies for alimony *in futuro* to bring her to that standard of living. As a last resort, Lily will argue for transitional alimony to help her transition back into the work force. Lily may also ask the court to award her Mario's separate property and his share of the marital property as alimony *in solido*, which she could then liquidate and invest, and use the income for support. Finally, Lily will ask the court to order Mario to pay Lily's attorney's fee, as alimony *in solido*, arguing that Lily lacks sufficient funds or property to do so.

Unless Mario and Lily can agree to support arrangements while the divorce is pending, Lily will have to file a motion for alimony *pendent lite*, to cover her living expenses and the cost of prosecuting the divorce.

Modifications

In construing the term "substantial and material change of circumstance," which is the threshold test for considering a petition to modify alimony, the courts have generally held that changed circumstances are "material" only when they arise after the divorce and were not within the contemplation of the parties at the time of the divorce. *Bogan v. Bogan*, 60 S.W.3d 721, 728 (Tenn. 2001). In order to be "substantial," the change must significantly affect either the obligor's ability to pay or the recipient's need for support. *Id.* Generally speaking, the following facts have not been found to constitute a substantial and material change of circumstance:

(1) The obligor increased expenses, absent proof of the obligor inability to pay the ordered support. *Elliot v. Elliot*, 825 S.W.2d 87, 92 (Tenn. Ct. App. 1991);

(2) An increase in either party income, standing alone. *Wright v. Quillen*, 83 S.W.3d 768, 774 (Tenn. Ct. App. 2002), *appeal denied*;

(3) Recipient reentry into the workforce. *Sannella v. Sannella*, 993 S.W.2d 73, 76 (Tenn. Ct. App. 1999);

(4) Income produced from the proceeds of the sale of property awarded to a spouse in the division of marital property. *Seal v. Seal*, 802 S.W.2d 617, 621 (Tenn. Ct. App. 1990);

(5) Obligor willful underemployment. *Watters v. Watters*, 22 S.W.3d 817, 823 (Tenn. Ct. App. 2000);

(6) Voluntary assumption of new financial obligations. *Sannella v. Sannella*, 993 S.W.2d 73, 76 (Tenn. Ct. App. 1999);

(7) Remarriage, alone, when the alimony is rehabilitative. *Isbell v. Isbell*, (816 S.W.2d 735, at 735 (Tenn. 1991);

(8) Cohabitation, alone, when the alimony is rehabilitative. *Stockman v. Stockman*, 1999 WL 617637, (Tenn. Ct. App., Aug 17, 1999) *perm. to appeal not sought*;

(9) Change in Income Tax laws. *Elliot v. Elliot*, 825 S.W.2d 87, 91 (Tenn. Ct. App. 1991);

(10) Recipient increased residential time with the parties children. *Wright v. Quillen*, 83 S.W.3d 768, 774 (Tenn. Ct. App. 2002), *appeal denied*; and

(11) Recipient receipt of Social Security Benefits. *Wright v. Quillen*, 83 S.W.3d 768, 774 (Tenn. Ct. App. 2002), *appeal denied.*

Retirement

States disagree as to whether the obligor retirement justifies an alimony modification. The Tennessee Supreme Court carved out a special test regarding modification of alimony obligations when the obligor retires. Instead of determining whether retirement was foreseeable at the time of the divorce, as other appellate courts had done, the Tennessee Supreme Court held that when the obligor's retirement is objectively reasonable, it does constitute a substantial and material change in circumstances respective of whether the retirement was foreseeable or voluntary o as to permit consideration of the alimony modification petition. The modification is not automatic, however. The trial court must examine the totality of the circumstances surrounding the retirement to ensure that it is objectively reasonable. The burden of establishing that the retirement is objectively reasonable is on the party seeking modification of the award, but a retirement cannot be deemed objectively reasonable if it was primarily motivated by a desire to defeat the support award or to reduce the alimony paid to the former spouse. *Bogan v. Bogan*, 60 S.W.3d 721, 729 (Tenn. 2001).

Once the threshold test of showing a substantial and material change of circumstance has been met, the petitioning party must then demonstrate that a modification of the award is justified. The court will apply the statutory factors on which an initial award is based, to determine whether a modification is warranted. *Wright v. Quillen*, 83 S.W.3d 768, 773 (Tenn. Ct. App. 2002), *appeal denied.* It is within the trial court discretion to determine whether a modification is warranted after considering the statutory factors. *Id.*

A petition to modify alimony must be filed prior to the termination of the award of alimony by any of the contingencies upon which the award is based, because the court jurisdiction to modify terminates upon the occurrence of a contingency when the award ceases to exist. For instance, if the alimony award is for ten years or until death or remarriage of the recipient, a petition to modify that is filed after the ten year period is too late, even if the recipient is still alive and unmarried, because the expiration of the ten year period terminates the alimony obligation and the court jurisdiction to modify. *Waddey v. Waddey*, 6 S.W.3d 230, 234 (Tenn. 1999).

The "live-in-lover" provision does not automatically terminate the alimony obligation. It merely gives rise to a presumption that alimony, in the amount previously ordered, is no longer needed, and shifts the burden of proof to the recipient to show a continued need. *Wright v. Quillen*, 83 S.W.3d 768, 772 (Tenn. Ct. App. 2002), *appeal denied.*

Insurance

The court can also order one spouse to pay the health insurance premiums for the other spouse, if the court deems it appropriate. The court may also order the obligor to obtain a life insurance policy and to designate the recipient as the beneficiary of that policy in order to secure the alimony obligation in the event of the obligor's death.

Enforcement

A divorce court may enforce its decree by equitable and legal means. The court can require the obligor to post a bond to secure payment; sequester rents and profits from the obligor's real estate and personal estate, if any; and impose a lien on the obligor's real and personal property. TENN. CODE ANN. § 36-5-103. Alimony obligations may also be enforced by executing on the obligor's property or garnishing the obligor's wages. TENN. CODE ANN. § 26-1-103 and § 26-2-201, respectively. A restraining order can be used to restrain the obligor from transferring or disposing of property. TENN. R. CIV. P. 65.07. The most often used enforcement tool is a petition to have the obligor held in civil contempt of the court's order to pay alimony. If the obligor is shown to have the ability to pay, the court may order the obligor to jail, indefinitely, until the alimony is paid. The obligor is said to "hold the keys to the jail." TENN. CODE ANN. § 29-9-104.

China*

Spousal Maintenance on Divorce and Compensation for Divorce Damage

In the Chinese mainland, besides economic compensation for housework when the marital property system terminates upon divorce, the property consequences of divorce to spouses also includes financial assistance on divorce and compensation for divorce damage. Hereinafter, on the basis of the current Marriage Law and relevant judicial interpretations, we'll give a brief introduction to the systems of financial assistance on divorce and compensation for divorce damage in the Chinese mainland, and analyze specifically the application of the two systems in the divorce case of *Lily v. Mario*.

Legislative Background

Financial assistance on divorce (hereinafter referred to as financial assistance) is called spousal support, alimony, or maintenance in some foreign countries. It is a legal system in which, when the spouses divorce, if one party has difficulty in self-support, the capable one should offer appropriate financial assistance payments by agreement of the parties or through the court's decision. Since the foundation of the People's Republic of China in 1949, Article 25 of Marriage Law 1950, Article 33 of Marriage Law 1980 and Article 42 of the current Marriage Law have described the provisions on financial assistance. The provisions concerned in the three marriage laws are set forth separately as the follows: "If one party does not remarry and has difficulty in self-support after divorce, the other one shall help maintain his or her living;" "Where one party has difficulty in self-support at divorce, the other one shall offer proper financial assistance;" "Where one party has difficulty in self-support at divorce, the other one shall offer the financial assistance from the personal property like residential houses etc." Article 14 of OPINIONS OF THE SUPREME PEOPLE'S COURT ON THE IMPLEMENTATION OF CIVIL POLICIES AND LAW, (1984) describes that "when divorce, if one party has living difficulty, the other one shall offer appropriate financial assistance. If one party is young with working ability but has temporary living difficulty, the other one shall offer the financial assistance of short-term or in a lump sum. In the marriage of long duration, where one party is old, or loses working ability and has no living incomes, the other one shall make proper arrangement on the residing

---

* This part is written by Chen Wei, Pi Xijun, and Ran Qiyu.

and living." Provision 27 of Judicial Interpretation I of the current Marriage Law describes that "at the time of divorce, one party rendering assistance with residential house from his/her own property to the other party with difficulty in supporting herself/himself may be in the form of the right to inhabit or of ownership of the house." Seen from these provisions, financial assistance is interpreted differently at different times in history, that is, from only helping maintain the living of the divorced party to proper financial assistance (not limited to basic living) and to offering proper assistance from the personal property such as residential house, etc. (expanding the separate property for financial assistance to residential houses, and paying attention to solving the difficulty in residential houses of the divorced women). The current Marriage Law and Judicial Interpretation 2001 provide for the new provisions, which are beneficial in solving the special difficulty that most divorced women have no residential houses, which reflects historical progress in legislation. *See* Chen Wei & Ran Qiyu, *A Study of the System of Spousal Maintenance on Divorce: A Comparison Between China and Russia*, 19 INT'L J. L. POL'Y & FAM. 322 (2005). In the Chinese mainland, during the times of planned economy regime in the past, mainly, residential houses were allocated to men in many enterprises. For example, the unit where the husband worked allocated the house to the husband on the basis of scores calculated according to the statistics of length of service of the married couple (even if the wife worked in another unit), the titles of a technical post, and current living houses of the married couple; then allocated the house to the husband and his wife was not entitled to require allocation of residential houses again from her working unit. So some divorced women had no residential houses in which to reside after divorce. A scholar once pointed out: "among the divorced women nowadays, 70% had no residential houses to live in." *See* Cui Li, *Wu Changzhen's Opinions on the Amendment of Marriage Law*, CHINA YOUTH, Jan. 15, 2001, at 7.

Compensation for divorce damage refers to civil liability where one of the spouses commits statutory wrongful acts resulting in divorce, entitling the innocent party, at divorce, to claim economic compensation from the separate property of the party at fault to compensate the innocent spouse. Compensation for divorce damage is a newly provided legal system in the current Marriage Law 2001. As a civil liability, this system performs three functions: "compensating for damage," "spiritual comfort," and "preventing and stopping illegal acts." The legislative purpose of compensation for divorce damage is to safeguard the lawful rights of the victim spouse and give civil punishment to the wrongful conduct by the party at fault which destroys marriages and families. Chen Wei, *A Study of the System of Compensation for Divorce Damage*, 6 MOD. LEGAL SCI., at 98–99, (1998). Although marriage Law 1950 and Marriage Law 1980 did not provide for the system after the foundation of PRC in 1949, with the development of society, the acts of bigamy, family violence, maltreating, or deserting family members increased. Before the amendment of Marriage Law 1980, according to statistics, about 0.4 million families disorganized in the Chinese mainland each year, among which, a quarter of the families broke down for family violence. Divorce caused by one party's bigamy continued unabated and became one of the main causes for divorce in some areas, constituting 60% of the divorce cases. In April 2000, a survey of public opinion on the amendment to Marriage Law carried out by the National Women's Federation of PRC in thirty-one provinces, municipalities, and municipalities directly under the Central Government in the Chinese mainland, showed that 94.2% of the people surveyed thought that bigamy, concubinage, and cohabiting with another of the opposite sex, while having a spouse, should be punished legally; 94.1% of the people surveyed thought that even though "maltreatment or desertion of any family member shall be prohibited" has been described in Marriage Law 1980, it is necessary to supplement the provision with the provision that "family violence shall be prohibited" in the current Marriage Law. *See* Sun Xiaomei, *Partners Sometimes are More Dangerous than Enemies*, CHINA WOMEN, June 26, 1998, at 3; Chen Min,: *Brief Discussion on the Characteristics and the Trial of Marriage and Family Cases*, 5 LEGAL REV., 82 (1997); LEGISLATIVE MATERIALS COLLECTION ON THE AMENDMENT OF MARRIAGE LAW OF PRC, 122,124 (Wang Shengming, Sun Lihai (chief editor) and Civil Law Office, Commission of Legislative Affairs of Standing Committee of the National People's Congress, China, eds. (2001). Hence, according to the urgent need and the strong appeal of the Chinese people, Article 46 was supplemented to the current Marriage Law to specify the system of compensation for divorce damage. This article provides that where one party commits bigamy, family violence, cohabitates with other opposite sex while having a spouse, ill-treats; or deserts family members which results in divorce, the innocent one is entitled to a claim for divorce damages. This system is significant for addressing three needs: first, is the need for improving the marriage law and strengthening the socialist legal system; second, is the need for safeguarding the lawful rights of marital parties in new situations; and third, is the need for the judicial departments to deal with cases according to the law and demand those who violate the law to shoulder the liability. *See* Chen Wei, RESEARCH ON LEGISLATION OF CHINA'S MARRIAGE AND FAMILY LAW, PUBLISHING HOUSE OF THE MASSES, 293–295 (2000).

In order to guide the people's courts to apply the systems of financial assistance and compensation for divorce damage in the current Marriage Law properly, some specific provisions on the application of these systems were stipulated in Judicial Interpretation I of Marriage Law by Supreme People's Court (2001). These provisions are discussed below.

Financial Assistance

The spousal support obligation shall be terminated after divorce in accordance with the legislative spirit of the current Marriage Law. However, where the statutory requirements are met, the divorced spouses are entitled to claim financial assistance, which right is also called the right for maintenance on divorce. Article 42 of the current Marriage Law describes: "if, at the time of divorce, one party has difficulty in supporting himself or herself, the other party shall render appropriate assistance with his or her own property such as his or her residential house. Specific arrangements shall be agreed upon by both parties. In case no agreement is agreed upon, the people's court shall make a decision." In the opinion of the authors, financial assistance is the continuation of the spousal support obligation existing during the marriage, which is one of the consequences of marriage, so it is a statutory obligation. The legislative purpose of this system is to relieve one party's difficulty in self-support after divorce, which reflects the doctrine and the spirit of protecting the interests of the disadvantaged in marriage and family laws. Of course, on the other hand, this system can help the party who has difficulty in self-support realize his/her freedom through divorce. *See* ChenWei & Ran Qiyu, *A Study of the Legal System of Spousal Support on Divorce—Comparison of Laws between Chinese Mainland and Russia*, 6 Yuedan Civ. & Com. L., 148 (2004).

Conditions for Seeking Financial Assistance

Like in the U.S., the recipient's need and the obligor's ability to pay are important criteria in determining alimony. In addition, as in the U.S., alimony must be awarded at the time of the divorce. It may not be claimed later. Under Article 42 of the current Marriage Law, a claim for financial assistance must meet the following three requirements:

> *One Party Must Have Difficulty in Self Support at the Time of the Divorce.* What is called difficulty in self support at divorce means that one's own property and property divided from community property at divorce is not sufficient to maintain the basic living conditions. Provision 27 of Judicial Interpretation I of the current Marriage Law provides: "One party has no residential house after divorce belongs to difficulty in supporting oneself." Where one party's personal property and property allocated from community property at divorce can

maintain his or her basic living needs, even if he or she is not employed or is suffering from serious diseases, it does not constitute "difficulty in supporting oneself" as defined in Article 42 of the current Marriage Law. Where one party is employed at the divorce and has economic income, but is unemployed soon after divorce, it does not constitute "living difficulty" in Article 42 of the current Marriage Law, either. If difficulty in supporting oneself arises after the divorce, it should be solved through the social security system.

The Other Party Must Have the Ability to Bear the Responsibility at the Time of the Divorce. Financial assistance is obliged only when one party can afford to offer it at the time of the divorce. That is, only when one party's personal property and the property divided from the community property at divorce can maintain his or her normal living, and in addition, can also help the other needy party, can he or she offer the financial assistance. Where the party has difficulty in self support at divorce without the ability to offer financial assistance to the other, he or she will not shoulder the obligation of the financial assistance.

Financial Assistance Must be Claimed at the Time of the Divorce. Where the statutory requirements are met, the entitled party shall exercise the right at the time of the divorce. Where one party does not claim financial assistance from the other spouse at the time of the divorce, it shall be deemed disclaimed. After divorce, the claimant is not entitled to claim financial assistance from the other party again.

The Way in Which Way Financial Assistance Is Offered

Under Article 42 of the current Marriage Law and Article 27 of Judicial Interpretation I of the current Marriage Law, there are two types of financial assistance. They include offering maintenance and residential house, each of which is discussed below.

Offering maintenance. Difficulty in self support means that one party's property after divorce is not sufficient to maintain one party's basic living standard of local places, hence, the capable other party should offer necessary maintenance to meet the basic living needs of the party with difficulty in self support.

Both parties shall seek an agreement on the amounts, duration, and ways to pay financial assistance at divorce. If the agreement fails, the people's court shall make a judgment.

As to the amount of the financial assistance payments, the people's court shall consider the following three factors comprehensively when making a decision, then fix on a reasonable amount: first, the basic needs for living of the party with difficulty in self support; second, the capability of the obligor to shoulder the obligation; third, the basic living standard of the local place. In short, because of the difference between living standards in rural and urban areas and the economic difference between different parties in our country, the people's court shall make a decision after considering needs for basic living, property, economic incomes, ages, health, ability to make a living of both parties, and the basic living standard of local places comprehensively.

With regard to the duration of the financial assistance, where one party has working ability but is not employed at divorce with interim difficulty, a short-term financial assistance payment can be awarded. Where the duration of marriage is long, and one party has no income for old age, illness, or losing working ability, it can be decided to pay a long-term payment, until the needy party dies, remarries, or has basic economic income because of regaining working ability.

As to the ways of paying the financial assistance payments, it may be paid in cash or in kind. To the difficulty in residential house, it may be determined to live in the house temporarily (not more than two years) or give the rent allowance in a lump sum. Where the financial assistance payment is determined to be paid in cash, it shall be paid monthly or quarterly according to the specific conditions of the needy party. Where the obligor is capable to pay the short-term payment in a lump sum, it can also be paid so.

Offering residential house. Provision 27 of Judicial Interpretation I of the current Marriage Law describes that "at the time of divorce, one party rendering assistance with residential house from his/her own property to the other party with difficulty in supporting herself/himself may be in the form of the right to inhabit or of ownership of the house."

It must be pointed out that, generally, financial assistance refers to economic help, and not daily life care to the other party. If one party can't look after himself or herself at divorce because of a disease or for other reasons, the claim for looking after the sick party shall not be supported by the people's court. However, voluntary care to the sick party is not prohibited by the law.

Termination of Financial Assistance

According to the current Marriage Law, financial assistance can be terminated for the following reasons:

Living Difficulty of the Claimant Has Disappeared. There are diverse reasons for the disappearance of the claimant's difficulty in self support, *e.g.*, the party who has difficulty in self support may become employed, may succeed another's property, win a prize in a lottery by chance, become supported by others, etc. No matter what the reasons are, it shows that the claimant does not need financial assistance, so the other one should end the payment.

The Claimant Remarries. If the claimant who can't support herself or himself remarries, the other one should end the payment. That is because where the claimant remarries, his or her new spouse shall assume the statutory obligation of maintenance.

The Obligor Has Lost Support Ability. As mentioned above, the prerequisite of financial assistance is the support ability of the other party. If the obligor has lost support capability for some reason, the financial assistance obligation shall be terminated.

As for the case *Lily v. Mario*, Lily meets the statutory requirements of financial assistance completely, so she is entitled to claim financial assistance from her husband Mario according to law. Firstly, Lily has difficulty in self support at divorce without enough property to maintain her basic living. From the angle of employment and income, Lily resigned her work since the birth of the first child Jade, and engaged in housework, and rearing the two young children for as long as nine years. Her employment skills have lagged behind times so that it is difficult for her to be employed in a short time, needing study and training for reemployment. Because Lily claims for the rearing of two minor children, she may be allocated the residential house, furniture, and articles of daily use, but the deposit and the cash may not be allocated to her. Furthermore, Lily has no other economic income or living sources to maintain her life, so she is the party who has difficulty in self support at divorce. Secondly, Mario has support ability at divorce. Mario works as a research biologist with a high salary at divorce, so he can afford the financial assistance. Thirdly, Lily has claimed financial assistance at the time of divorce. Hence, Lily meets the statutory requirements of financial assistance completely.

Mario asserted that, after divorce, Lily should become employed and complained that Lily had a close relationship with the neighbor Alex. Mario thought Lily had broken their marriage, so he was not willing to pay maintenance to her. However, according to the specific facts of this case, the five-year-old son Dino, who was born deaf, can't go to school now, and he still needs the care of his mother and follow-up recovery treatment, so it is reasonable for Lily to stay at home to look after Dino, and not to go out to work. In addition, the breakdown of the marriage of Lily and Mario was not caused by the relationship between Lily and the neighbor, but because of the parties' divergent views about matters such as child-rearing and education, Lily's going out to work etc., which has resulted in their sharp conflict so that Lily wants to divorce, as they can't live together harmoniously. Furthermore, even though Lily commits adultery with the neighbor Alex, this fault does not have an effect on Lily's claim for financial assistance from Mario if she meets the requirements of financial assistance, as the current Marriage Law does not preclude the party at fault from claiming financial assistance.

Both parties shall seek an agreement on the amounts, duration, and ways to pay the financial assistance. If an agreement fails, the people's court shall make a judgment. As to the amounts of the financial assistance, the people's court shall fix a reasonable amount after giving a comprehensive consideration of Lily's basic living needs, Mario's support capability, the basic living standard of local places, as well reference to the living standard during marriage when necessary. With regard to the duration and way of paying the financial assistance, Lily has working ability, but she can't go out to work for a time because of looking after the children and needing study and training for reemployment, so a short-term financial assistance payment can be decided (*e.g.*, a five-year payment), while Mario shall pay maintenance (*e.g.* 500–600 Yuan) monthly to Lily and shoulder the study and training fees for Lily to be reemployed after divorce. Of course, where Lily is reemployed after divorce, and the salary incomes can maintain her basic living, or she remarries, the financial assistance obligation of Mario should be terminated.

Compensation for Divorce Damage

Article 46 of the current Marriage Law provides that "in any of the following circumstances which has led to the divorce of husband and wife, the innocent party shall be entitled to claim compensation: bigamy; cohabitation with a third person of the opposite sex while having a spouse; family violence; maltreating or deserting any family member." This provision includes the prerequisites of compensation for divorce damage and the scope of damages, etc.

Statutory Prerequisites for Compensation for Divorce Damage

In accordance with Article 46 of the current Marriage Law and judicial interpretations concerned, the statutory requirements for compensation for divorce damage include three aspects: one party must have committed the statutory wrongful acts; the statutory wrongful acts must have led to divorce; the other party must be innocent.

One Party Must Have Committed the Statutory Wrongful Acts. According to Article 46 of the current Marriage Law, the innocent party may claim divorce damages not because of all wrongful acts done by the other one. Only when the statutory wrongful acts are committed can the innocent one claim damages. The statutory wrongful acts refer to the four acts which severely destroy marriage and family relationships, namely, bigamy, cohabitation with a third person of the opposite sex while having a spouse, family violence, and maltreating or deserting any family member. Other wrongful acts, *e.g.*, adultery, addiction to drugs, gambling etc., are not statutory wrongful acts, so they cannot constitute one of the statutory requirements for divorce damages.

The Statutory Wrongful Acts Must Have Led to Divorce. The fact that one party commits one of the above statutory acts does not, in itself, entitle the innocent spouse to divorce damage. The statutory wrongful acts must also be shown to lead to the breakdown of the marriage resulting in divorce. If the wrongful acts haven't led to divorce, or if there is a divorce, but the marriage breakdown was not caused by the statutory wrongful acts of one party, the innocent one cannot ask for the damages.

The Other Party Must Be Innocent. The third and final requirement is that the spouse asking for divorce damages must not have committed any of the statutory wrongful acts. If the claimant commits bigamy, cohabitation with other opposite sex while having a spouse, family violence, or maltreating or deserting any family member, he or she will not meet the requirement for divorce damages. For example, if the wife rents a house to cohabit with another person of the opposite sex during marriage, while the husband commits family violence to the wife, maltreats, or deserts the wife, neither the wife nor the husband shall be entitled to claim divorce damages for the reason that the other party commits the statutory wrongful acts at divorce. That is, the principle that the wrongful acts between husband and wife can be set off is not adopted because when both husband and wife commit illegal conduct, the nature of the illegal acts are the same, but only the amounts of the illegal acts are different. As it is difficult to find out the amounts of illegal acts, and one of the functions of compensation for divorce damage is to prevent and stop the illegal acts infringing upon the lawful rights of one party, it is inappropriate to set off the fault of the husband and wife. *See* Chen Wei, *Discussion on Several Problems on the Law Application of the System of Compensation for Divorce Damage*, 2 Law & Com. Res. 83 (2002)

The Scope of Divorce Damages

As a remedy system, compensation for divorce damage performs not only the function of compensating for damage and spiritual comfort, but also the function of punishing and preventing illegal acts. Article 28 of Judicial Interpretation I on the current Marriage Law states: "compensation" stipulated in Article 46 of Marriage Law includes compensation for material damage and compensation for spiritual damage," which shows that the scope of divorce damages consists of material damages and spiritual damages.

Compensation for Material Damage. Material damage compensation for divorce damage means that when the party at fault commits the acts of family violence, maltreating, or deserting any family member during marriage, and the innocent one suffers from physical damage, then the party at fault shall compensate for the material damage with economic compensation to the innocent party at divorce. Article 17 (1), (2) of INTERPRETATION OF SEVERAL ISSUES ON THE LAW APPLICATION OF CASES OF DAMAGES FOR PERSONAL INJURY (2003) "where the victim suffers from physical damage, the obligor shall compensate every medical fee for treatment and the income losses because of missing work, including the fees of treatment, missing work, care, transportation, accommodation, food allowance in hospital, necessary allowance for nutrition. Where the victim is disabled for damage, the obligor shall also compensate the necessary fees for living needs and the losses for losing working ability, including damages for disability, fees of aided apparatuses for disability, the cost of living of the dependent, as well the actual fees for the necessary recovery treatment, care, follow-up treatment because of the recovery care, continuous treatment."

Compensation for Spiritual Damage. The spiritual damage element of compensation for divorce damage includes two types of damage. One is based on actual physical damage carried out by the party at fault against the innocent one during marriage, causing spiritual damage such as bitterness, fear, sadness, etc., of the innocent party. In such a circumstance, the party at fault shall bear the liability of spiritual damage. The other type of damage does not require actual physical damage, as where the party at fault commits the statutory wrongful acts during marriage which has caused divorce, for which reason the innocent one suffers from spiritual bitterness. Under this circumstance, even though the party at fault does not engage in the act of physical damage, the divorce was caused by the statutory wrongful acts like bigamy or cohabitation with other opposite sex while having a spouse, which results in marriage breakdown. Divorce itself causes spiritual bitterness to the innocent party, for which the party at fault shall bear the liability of spiritual damage at divorce. *See* Chen Wei, *Discussion on Several Problems on the Law Application of the System of Compensation for Divorce Damage*, 2 LAW & COM. RES. 82,85 (2002).

As far as the case of *Lily v. Mario* is concerned, even though Mario claims for divorce damages in divorce proceedings from Lily, the claim shall not be supported because he does not meet the statutory requirements of divorce damages. Although Lily had a close relationship, even adultery with the neighbor Alex, Mario is not entitled to ask for compensation for divorce damages for the following two reasons: first, adultery is not one of the grounds for claiming divorce damages. Article 46 of the current Marriage Law only stipulates "bigamy" and "anyone who has a spouse cohabiting with another person of the opposite sex" as statutory faults, but does not stipulate that adultery is a statutory fault. This is because the nature of the three conducts are different. "Bigamy" and "cohabitation with another of the opposite sex while having a spouse" are crimes or illegal conducts which are prohibited by law, while adultery is conduct in breach of marriage morality. According to the current law and jurisprudence, "cohabitation with another of the opposite sex while having a spouse" and adultery are not the same concept. In accordance with Article 2 of Judicial Interpretation I of the current Marriage Law, "anyone who has a spouse cohabiting with another person of the opposite sex" stipulated in the current Marriage Law refers to anyone who has a spouse and cohabits with another person of the opposite sex out of wedlock continuously and stably, not in the name of husband and wife, which breaks the prohibited provision in the current Marriage Law publicly. Adultery, on the other hand, means anyone who has a spouse and has sexual conduct with other opposite sex willingly and secretly which conduct is regulated by morality but not by law. Further, even though Lily commits adultery, the marriage breakdown of Lily and Mario was not caused by Lily's adultery, which is expounded clearly in the case facts in Chapter 4. Lily wants to divorce Mario because of their divergent views about matters such as child-rearing and education, Lily's going out to work etc, which has resulted in their sharp conflict so that they divorce at last, as they can't live together harmoniously.

Italy

Background

Because of the sequential institutions of separation and divorce, spousal support in Italy comes in two distinct forms: a maintenance check during separation and a divorce check after marriage dissolution. If the conditions for eligibility are met, a maintenance check may be owed by the financially stronger spouse to the financially weaker spouse during separation, so that the financially disadvantaged spouse maintains, as much as possible, the same standard of living that she was accustomed to during marriage. On the other hand, a divorce check may be owed to the ex spouse who does not have adequate means. As is the case for many aspects of separation and divorce, even though there may be a purported substantial difference in purpose between the two support obligations highlighted by their respective eligibility rules, at the basis of both there is a common solidarity purpose extending beyond the crisis of the marital union. Also, factually, there are many similarities among the factors that judges consider in determining the amount of the check owed during separation and after divorce once the eligibility conditions have been met. The Supreme Court openly acknowledges that although there is a difference in purpose between the maintenance obligation during separation and the divorce check, in appropriate cases, the first can be a useful point of reference to decide on the second. Cass. Civ. Sez. I, 27 agosto 2004, n. 17128.

Eligibility for Spousal Support during Separation

The doctrine (respected legal scholarship) has adopted three different approaches in justifying the maintenance obligation during separation: 1) it would be a continuation of the duties flowing from marriage based on Art. 143 of the Civil Code, *i.e.*, the duty of reciprocal support and maintenance between spouses; 2) it would be a transformation of the duty of support and maintenance surviving in an attenuated form during separation; or 3) at separation, the duty of maintenance would be a new and different duty as it is based on a situation of disparity between the spouses, in contrast with the marital duty of maintenance which is grounded on the presumed equality of contribution of both spouses. SESTA, at 603.

The judge at the time of separation decides on spousal support unless it has been adequately addressed by the spouses by means of their agreement. C.c. Art. 156. The conditions for eligibility of a spouse to receive a maintenance check during separation are that: 1) the separation is not chargeable to the petitioning spouse; and 2) the petitioning spouse does not have adequate income of his own to maintain an adequate lifestyle similar to that enjoyed during marriage. *Id.*

The first requisite has to be satisfied by the petitioning spouse, while it is irrelevant as to the spouse against whom the petition is advanced. Because in practice a vast majority of the separation proceedings take the form of the consensual, in which by definition there is no imputability (charging one spouse with responsibility for the separation), the first prerequisite in most cases is moot, and the eligibility issue revolves around a condition of financial weakness of one of the spouses, coupled with an implicit condition of relative financial strength of the spouse charged with the maintenance obligation. However, before the judge can proceed to perform this comparative financial analysis, the first step is to ascertain the lifestyle maintained during marriage by the couple, particularly as it exists at the moment of separation. This analysis is not always based on factual reality, but looks at the economic potential of the couple during marriage. Indeed, in determining the needs and the expectation of the petitioning spouse the judge looks at the potential combined income and potential lifestyle either actually enjoyed or reasonably possible for the couple: thus, the judge will disregard a more modest lifestyle forced on or tolerated by the petitioner during marriage. Cass. Civ. Sez. I, 4 aprile 2002, n. 4800. Therefore, a spouse who acquiesced to a thrifty existence when the family nucleus had, in fact, more ample means is not penalized at separation. By the same token, the obligor spouse is not exonerated from the obligation of a maintenance check if the obligee spouse, during marriage, was relying on the financial support of the parents. Cass. Civ. Sez. I, 18 luglio 2003, n. 11224. On the other hand, the duration of the marriage is not a factor in deciding whether the petitioner is entitled to a support check, while at most it may be a factor to consider in determining the amount. Cass. Civ. Sez. I, 16 dicembre 2004, n. 23378.

Spousal Support or Maintenance Check during Separation

The Civil Code gives only broad brush guidance to judges deciding whether spousal support is due. In conducting the financial evaluation, the judge is directed by law to take into account not only the income of the obligor spouse but all the circumstances. C.c. Art. 156. However, the Code does not elaborate on what these circumstances may be, or on any method of analysis to be employed in carrying out the required evaluation. Faced with the silence of the black letter law, the courts have opined that, logically, the analysis is based on the relative financial weakness of one spouse, versus the comparative financial strength of the other spouse, so that in point of fact the judge has to evaluate both spouses' financial positions. This evaluation does not require mathematical exactitude: it merely has to be a credible approximation of the overall financial situation of both parties, including their ordinary income, justifying the obligation of one to contribute to the other, so that the other can maintain the prior marital lifestyle. See Cass. Civ. Sez. I, 19 marzo 2002, n. 3974. Some of the circumstances elaborated by the Supreme Court echo the statutory guidelines many states have enacted in the U.S. to provide guidance in deciding on spousal support. For example, the Italian judge considers the following factors as they apply in determining the weaker spouse's income for purposes of spousal support:

(1) The value of real estate owned by the spouse;
(2) The income generated by each parcel of real estate (The income is calculated taking into account the location of the real estate, its charac-

teristics and tax treatment even if in fact it may not be utilized to produce income. Once again, the judge looks at potential income, discounting the actual income when for example, a family member is renting an apartment and paying half of the rent that is customarily paid for an apartment of that kind in that location, or when the owner/spouse is not diligent about placing his real estate to use to produce income. If the petitioning spouse now does not own any real property because she just sold it prior to the separation, the proceeds of the sale are taken into account by the judge as they can now be invested to produce a return.);

(3) Account receivables, investments, extraordinary income, gifts from family members (as long as they were part of the habitual gifts which were bestowed during marriage and are completely voluntary, because the weaker spouse during separation should not burden her family of origin to the advantage of the financially stronger spouse. This is consistent with the rule of law that the obligation of "*alimenti*" (family support obligation based on the beneficiary's condition of need) falls on the spouse before it falls on the family of origin under C.c. Art. 433.);

(4) The contribution of the person who is living with the separated spouse *more uxorio* (common law marriage) as long as the relationship is characterized by sufficient certainty and stability (Cass. Sez. Civ. I, 4 aprile 1998, n. 3503. Although cohabitation does not, by law, determine a right to maintenance, it may objectively be a source of income, and, as such, it has to be taken into account. Cass. Civ. Sez. I, 22 aprile 1993, n. 4761. The burden of proof of this circumstance, which may reduce or even eliminate the obligation of maintenance of the other spouse, rests with the presumed obligor. Cass. Civ. Sez. I, 11 aprile 1986, n. 2569. The doctrine (respected legal scholarship) notes that this is an application of the principle of responsibility for oneself, because in creating a new unit by cohabitation *more uxorio* the separated spouse is demonstrating his intention of becoming independent from the other spouse, both emotionally and financially); and

(5) The petitioning spouse's ability and opportunity to work (This evaluation is based on the actual circumstances of the marriage, rather than in abstract terms, taking into account the common situation where during marriage, by mutual decision, one of the spouses stays home to care for the children, giving the other spouse the opportunity to pursue his career objectives. The consequences of decisions made during marriage relative to which spouse works outside of the house survive during separation. Cass. Civ. Sez. I, 19 marzo 2004, n.

5555. Because of these decisions, at the time of separation, the stay-at-home spouse may be at a disadvantage in seeking and finding employment commensurate to her abilities and her social position. To qualify for a spousal support check during separation, the weaker spouse is not required to seek or accept any job available because the purpose of the check is to maintain, as much as possible, the conditions that were present during marriage.

In any event, the determination of the amount of the spousal check is in the discretion of the court, and, as such, not subject to review by the Supreme Court unless the determination is not supported by the required reasoning. Cass. Sez. Civ. I, 8 maggio 1998, n. 4679. The spousal support check can be an overall periodic amount, or can be itemized in multiple expense items (i.e., mortgage, car payment) contributed periodically.

Alimenti

The financially weak spouse to whom the separation has been charged and who, through no fault of her own, is in a condition of need, is nevertheless entitled to petition for "*alimenti.*" C.c. Art. 433. When, as in the case of Lily, the spouse stayed home to care for the children, the separation places her in a situation of need. With respect to the amount of "*alimenti*" owed, the law makes no reference to maintaining a lifestyle comparable to the one enjoyed during marriage. Rather, it states that the check has to be commensurate to the needs of the petitioner to meet her living expenses, albeit taking into account her social position. The concept of *alimenti (basic maintenance)* is narrower than the concept of maintenance, and therefore the spouse who is denied maintenance in the first instance, can introduce the claim for *alimenti* on appeal. SESTA, at 625–626.

Lily will likely be entitled to a maintenance check during separation because she has not been working for some time, in order to take care of the children, and does not have a source of income. The only way that Mario, the breadwinner of the family, could avoid the maintenance obligation to Lily and be liable only for the more limited contribution of *alimenti* would be through a judicial separation (as opposed to consensual) if he succeeds in obtaining a decree that charges the separation to Lily. In a judicial seeking a charge, Lily's relationship with the neighbor Alex may become relevant, as well as Lily's firm position with respect to Dino's treatment. However, as we have seen, the judicial adds time and money to the process, provides no guarantees of outcome, and does not eliminate the eligibility of the financially needy spouse for *alimenti*. In practical terms, when the obligor spouse has relatively limited income, such as in Mario's case, while the obligee is without income like Lily, *alimenti* and maintenance check may not be that far apart in amount.

In pursuing her further legal education at the University of Bologna, Lily would be financially advantaged as compared to her U.S. counterpart, because that well recognized institution is part of the public education system, and tuition there as compared to any U.S. law school is more affordable. On the other hand, she may be disadvantaged as compared to her U.S. counterpart with respect to class and exam schedules which tend to be geared to the needs of full time students, while she may need to seek at least part time employment to supplement her spousal support check.

Revisions

The maintenance check is subject to periodic adjustment applying, by analogy, the rules specifically in force for automatic adjustment of the divorce check. *See* Law 1970/898 Art. 5(7) as modified by Law 1987/74, Art. 10; Cass. Civ. Sez. I, 2 marzo 1994, n. 2051. In addition, the maintenance check can be modified or revoked if justified reasons arise. C.c. Art. 156(5). Somewhat tautologically, the Supreme Court defines justified reasons as new circumstances occurring after the court's decision on the support check which change the parameters that originally formed the basis of the decision itself. Cass. Civ. Sez. I, 5 marzo 2001, n. 3149. The right to petition for revision is afforded by law and cannot be contractually disposed of or waived. There are no specific factors that give rise to an automatic revision, unless the changed factor affects the relative financial position of the spouses. For example, by itself, the mere acquisition or loss of real estate, or of another source of income by the obligor does not *ipso facto* constitute sufficient reason to modify the maintenance check, unless the effect of such change is such an increase or decrease in the relative financial position of the spouses that would alter the equilibrium existing at the time of separation. Cass. Sez. Civ. I, 1 agosto 2003 n. 11720.

One of the circumstances often presented to the courts is a financially stronger spouse who has created a new family unit whose needs and rights compete with the needs and rights of the former spouse. The Supreme Court recognizes that in these cases, an adjustment must be made, provided that the original family, at this point still in existence, although in separation, does not receive a lesser treatment financially than the new family which can only be at this stage a *de facto* family, without the legal sanction of a change of status. *See* Cass Civ. Sez. I, 24 aprile 2001, n. 6017. When there are children in this new *de facto* family, the constitutional principles of protection of the original legitimate family (COST. Art. 29) satisfied by the spousal support check compete with the equal protection constitutionally afforded to children born out of wedlock. *See* Cost. Art. 30. However, the spouse who owes a maintenance check is not entitled to a get a reduction of his obligation simply because he chose to form another family and assume additional financial obligations associated with it.

Another difficult question not uniformly resolved by the courts is whether the spouse who receives financial support during separation should benefit when the financial condition of the obligor spouse improves. Earlier decisions tended towards the negative, especially when the maintenance check was already sufficient to guarantee to the obligee a lifestyle similar to the pre-separation lifestyle. Cass. Civ. Sez. I, 24 novembre 1978, n. 5516. More recently, the opposite tendency has developed, based on the reasoning that if the bases for financial growth were established during marriage, both spouses should benefit proportionally during separation. Cass. Civ. Sez. I, 24 dicembre 2002, n. 18327.

Divorce Check: Eligibility and Criteria for Determination

As noted earlier, the Supreme Court acknowledges a correlation between the maintenance check during separation and the divorce check, stating that one of the reference points in deciding on the divorce check can be precisely what was established at the time of separation. However, that criterion applies only to the determination of the amount. Before determining the amount, at the time of divorce, the judge has to decide whether a check is owed in the first place. The letter of the law relative to the basis for a divorce check differs from the Civil Code eligibility rules for spousal support during separation. While at separation the key eligibility criterion is that the petitioning spouse lacks adequate income to maintain the lifestyle enjoyed during marriage, with the decision of dissolution of marriage or of the cessation of its legal effects, the tribunal disposes of the obligation of support that existed during separation. Law 1970/898 Art. 5(6).

There is a continuum in the eligibility rules of the three support obligations that may arise during marital crisis from the more liberal to the less liberal:

(1) The more liberal rules established by the Civil Code for the maintenance check owed during separation aiming at maintaining a financial *status quo* for the petitioning spouse and revolving around the concept of adequate means; (2) The less liberal wording of the marriage dissolution eligibility rules use the concept of lack of adequate means, and (3) The least liberal of the support obligations, "*alimenti*" is founded on the state of need of the petitioner and is the

minimum amount of support available to a spouse in need who has
been charged with the marriage failure.

For the amount of the divorce check, the black letter law provides more
guidance than with respect to the maintenance check at separation. The following factors must be considered by the judge in making the determination:

> (1) The condition of the spouses; (2) The reasons for the decision
> (that the check should be awarded); (3) The personal and economic
> contribution given by each spouse to the management and the accu-
> mulation of community or separate property and wealth; and (4) The
> income of each spouse.

The judge must evaluate the above factors also with respect to the duration
of the marriage. *Id.* Several of the factors to be considered in deciding the
amount of a divorce check may be duplicative when compared to the factors
considered by the courts in the calculus of the maintenance check during separation. However, the difference between the two checks stems from a fundamental difference in purpose as compared to the maintenance check during
separation, which as we have seen, is intended to prolong the financial status
quo existing between the spouses during marriage.

Initially, the Supreme Court and the doctrine (respected legal scholarship)
took the approach that the divorce check had a triple purpose: to assist, to in-
demnify, and to compensate the other spouse. This plurality of functions allowed judges to tailor the individual solution to the specific facts of the case,
but was soon sharply criticized as affording too much discretion to the courts.
SESTA, at 3281. The lore remains that the judges must be given detailed guidance, lest they display unbridled creativity in filling in the intended and un-
intended gaps the legislator (legislature) inevitably leaves open in the black
letter law. With the 1987 Reform, the law has been restated to specify, as indicated above, when the divorce check is owned, *i.e.*, when the petitioning
spouse does not have "adequate means." The Supreme Court has thereafter
clearly interpreted the phraseology of the law as indicating that the purpose
of the divorce check is primarily to assist, while the rest of the criteria, in-
demnification, compensation, and duration of marriage would come into play
only in the calculation of the amount. *Id.* at 3282.

One notable difference between the criteria for determination of the maintenance check as compared to divorce check is that the divorce check can take
into account the duration of the marriage, a factor explicitly excluded from the
calculus of the support check during separation. As we have seen, the duration
of marriage is one of the statutory factors to be considered in the U.S. as well.

The obligation of contributing a divorce check ends when the ex spouse marries again. Law 1987/74, Art. 5(10). The assistance obligation now falls on the new spouse. C.c. Art. 438. Here again, simple cohabitation does not mean that the ex spouse is no longer obligated to pay the divorce check unless the cohabitation results in an improvement in the financial position of the beneficiary spouse, but there can be a revision with respect to the quantum (amount) of the check.

The divorce check can be corresponded (paid) by agreement of the parties, in the form of a lump sum. Law 1970/898, Art. 5(8) as modified by Law 1987/74. If lump sum payment is chosen, then the beneficiary cannot ask for additional money later based on changed circumstances. The law reform introduced a judicial check on any lump sum agreement entered into by the parties by providing that such agreement will only be allowed if the court considers it fair. *Id.*

The method of proof of the parties' financial situation is their tax submissions which the parties must produce to the court for its evaluation. The court can utilize all methods of proof to ascertain the spouses' income, including enlisting the help of the Tax Police, the use of presumptions, and the court inquisitorial powers *sua sponte.*

As noted above, in Mario and Lily's case, Lily may be entitled to a maintenance check during separation, which will give her the opportunity to pursue her legal studies and acquire marketable skills, which would work like rehabilitative alimony. With divorce, Lily will likely be required to actively seek employment, affecting both Lily's eligibility for a divorce check, as well as the amount and duration of it.

Summary Chart—Spousal Support

	U. S. (Tennessee)	China	Italy
Consideration of marital fault in awarding spousal support.	Yes, in the court's discretion, although a number of states do not consider fault in setting support.	Compensation for divorce damages.	Maintenance check (based on marital standard of living) will not be awarded if the separation is attributable to the petitioning spouse. That spouse will be limited to *alimenti* (basic maintenance).
Most important factors in setting support.	Recipient's need, obligor's ability to pay and the length of the marriage.	Recipient's need, obligor's ability to pay and the length of the marriage.	Maintenance check —marital standard of living. Divorce check— recipient's need and length of marriage.
Basis for modifying spousal support.	Substantial and material change of circumstances (although *alimony in solido* is usually not modifiable).	A change in the recipient need or the obligor ability to pay.	Maintenance check is subject to periodic adjustment based on a change in the relative financial positions of the parties.
Modification possible based on decreased need or inability to pay.	Yes. A presumption in favor of modification usually arises if another adult lives with the recipient.	Yes	Yes and cohabiting may support a reduction in amount of support.
Spousal support generally terminates upon the death or remarriage of the recipient.	Yes	Yes	Yes
Spousal support is waived if not sought at the time of the divorce.	Yes	Yes	Yes
Recognition of both short term and long term spousal support.	Yes	Yes	No

CHAPTER 11

ADDITIONAL CONSIDERATIONS:
ANTENUPTIAL AGREEMENTS,
SETTLEMENT AGREEMENTS,
APPEALS, ATTORNEY FEES

United States

Overview

Previous chapters considered the major issues that arise in the typical divorce case. There are, however, several additional matters that deserve a least a cursory mention. These matters include antenuptial agreements, settlement agreements, appeals, and attorney fees and are addressed in this chapter.

Antenuptial Agreements

Antenuptial agreements used to be frowned upon by courts on the theory that they encouraged divorce. Increasingly, however, courts are giving parties greater autonomy to enter into these agreements as parties themselves are becoming more willing to negotiate these agreements in advance of the marriage. Antenuptial agreements are most likely to be used by engaged parties who have adult children from an earlier marriage. Knowing that their inheritance is protected can often go a long way toward softening relations between the adult children and the new spouse. Antenuptial agreements are often used by monied spouses to protect their considerable assets. These agreements may also be attractive to dual professional couples who are beginning their careers and marriage together.

Antenuptial agreements can address the rights of the parties in the event of death or divorce. Our discussion, however, will be limited to the provisions related to divorce. As states began to enforce antenuptial agreements, they were limited in many cases to division of property, and in some cases, only to division of separate property. Tennessee was such a state. The Tennessee statute authorized the parties to enter into antenuptial agreements concerning property owned by either spouse before the marriage. TENN. CODE ANN. § 36-3-501. We already know that property owned by either spouse before the marriage is considered separate property in Tennessee and not subject to equitable distribution at the time of divorce, so what is the purpose of this statutory provision? It allows the parties to contract concerning the income from and appreciation in value of separate property, which we learned was subject to statutory transmutation, causing it to be classified as marital property subject to equitable distribution at the time of divorce. Case law later extended the scope of antenuptial agreements to alimony waivers, *Cary v. Cary*, 937 S.W.2d 777 (Tenn. 1996), and division of marital property. *Bratton v. Bratton*, 136 S.W.3d 595 (Tenn. 2004). Issues involving child custody and support are still subject to the court's approval and the child support guidelines, although the parties are able to contract for support in excess of the guidelines amount and for post majority support.

Antenuptial agreements are governed by general contract principles, but, because the parties are deemed to share a confidential relationship, the procedural and substantive requirements are stricter than for other contracts. The contract must be entered into freely, knowledgeably, in good faith, and without exertion of duress or undue influence. TENN. CODE ANN. § 36-3-501.

Settlement Agreements

As mentioned earlier, the vast majority of divorce cases settle prior to trial. Even the cases going to trial usually are able to settle some issues prior to trial. The vehicle for recording those settlements is the settlement agreement, or Marital Dissolution Agreement (MDA), in Tennessee. The MDA may be reached through negotiations between the parties and their attorneys or through the use of a trained mediator. Once the MDA is presented to the court and accepted, it becomes an order of the court and may not be repudiated by one of the parties. *Ledbetter v. Ledbetter*, 163 S.W.3d 681 (Tenn. 2005). Prior to that point, if the MDA is repudiated by one party, it cannot be accepted by the court as a settlement of the divorce. If the MDA is signed, it may, nevertheless, be enforceable as a contract between the parties, assuming that the contract is otherwise valid. In such case, the court in the divorce proceeding may enforce the terms of the agreement in resolving the divorce issues between the parties. *Barnes v. Barnes*, 193 S.W.3d 495 (Tenn. 2006).

Appeals

If the parties enter into an MDA which is accepted by the divorce court, the parties will have no right to appeal. To the extent that the divorce is contested, however, the parties will generally have the right to appeal the court's findings of fact and conclusions of law within thirty days from the final judgment. In Tennessee, parties have an automatic right to appeal from the trial court to the intermediate appellate court, the Tennessee Court of Appeals, but there is no automatic right to appeal to the Tennessee Supreme Court. The parties must petition for permission to appeal to the Tennessee Supreme Court. Permission to appeal is granted in the court's discretion. While not controlling, the following are factors the court may consider:

(1) The need to secure uniformity of decision;
(2) The need to secure settlement of important questions of law;
(3) The need to secure settlement of questions of public interest; and
(4) The need for the exercise of the Supreme Court's supervisory authority. (TENN. RULES OF APP. PROC., Rule 11).

Not surprisingly, there are many court of appeals divorce decisions each year, but relatively few supreme court decisions.

On appeal, if the divorce is tried without a jury, the appellate court will review the case *de novo* upon the record with a presumption of correctness of the findings of fact by the trial court. Unless the evidence preponderates against the findings, the trial court must be affirmed, absent error of law. (TENN. RULES OF APP. PROC., Rule 13). If the trial court fails to make findings of fact regarding the factors considered in rendering its decision, no presumption attaches. In such cases, the appellate court will make an independent review of the record to determine where a preponderance of the evidence lies. *Crabtree v. Crabtree*, 16 S.W.3d 356 (Tenn. 2000). On the other hand, in nonjury cases where there are concurrent findings of fact, those findings are binding on the reviewing court if they are supported by any material evidence. *Aaron v. Aaron*, 909 S.W.2d 408 (Tenn. 1995). Trial court decisions are given a great deal of weight regarding the credibility of the parties and their suitability as custodians of the children because the trial judges have had the opportunity to see the parties and to listen to the evidence as it was presented and are, therefore, generally in a better position to judge credibility than is the appellate court, which must rely on the printed transcripts of that testimony. Insofar as the trial court's determinations are based on its assessment of witness credibility, appellate courts will not reevaluate that assessment absent clear and convincing evidence to the contrary. *Jones v. Garrett*, 92 S.W.3d

835, 838 (Tenn. 2002). The trial court's conclusions of law are reviewed *de novo* as well, but are not entitled to any presumption of correctness. *Taylor v. Fezell*, 158 S.W.3d 352, 357 (Tenn. 2005). The trial court's application of law to the facts are reviewed *de novo*, as well, with no presumption of correctness. *State v. Thacker*, 164 S.W.3d 208, 248 (Tenn. 2005).

Attorneys usually hire a court reporter to be present during the trial and to take down all of the testimony for purposing of preparing the record on appeal. If the parties do not have a transcript, the appellant can prepare a statement of the evidence. The appellee has an opportunity to object to the appellant's statement. Any differences regarding accuracy of the statement can be resolved by the trial judge, whose determination, absent extraordinary circumstances, is conclusive. (TENN. RULES OF APP. PROC., Rule 24(e)).

Costs on appeal are assessed by the court and are usually assessed against the losing party or split if the court's decision is split, affirming part of the trial court's decree and reversing and remanding other parts. The court may also award attorney fees for the appeal, where appropriate.

Attorney Fees

Each party is responsible for paying his or her own attorney fees. In very amicable divorces, the parties may choose to use the same attorney, but such cases are not the norm. If only one attorney is involved, it is usually because the parties cannot afford to hire two attorneys. Usually, that attorney will represent only one party. The other party will not be represented and may receive a bad result as a consequence. The American legal system requires the attorney to zealously represent his or her client. That attorney does not represent or owe an obligation to the unrepresented spouse, other than to tell the unrepresented spouse that the attorney does not represent him or her and to advise that spouse to get an attorney.

Attorney fees in divorce cases are usually for a lump sum or are based on hourly fees with a large retainer required up front. Contingent fees are rarely used in divorce cases. They are not per se unethical in divorce cases, but they are subject to careful judicial scrutiny. *Alexander v. Inman*, 903 S.W.2d 686 (Tenn. Ct. App. 1995), *appeal denied*. Contracts between clients and attorneys are governed by general contract law as well as by disciplinary rules which prohibit clearly excessive fees.

The parties may make provisions in their MDA for the payment of attorney fees. In some instances, the court has statutory authority to order one party to pay the other party's attorney's fees, particularly as a form of spousal support.

China*

Antenuptial (Premarital) Agreements

In China, under Article 19 of the current Marriage Law, before marriage, a man and a woman may come to an agreement in written form regarding whether the property acquired during the marriage or prior to the marriage will be owned by each party, will be jointly owned or will be partially owned by each party and partially owned by both parties. In other words, it is only the matrimonial property regime that the husband and the wife are entitled to choose. The agreement concerning the property obtained during the existence of marriage and premarital property shall be binding upon each party. At the time of divorce, both the husband and the wife or the judge should abide by the agreement concerned.

Settlement Agreements

Settlement Agreement Reached Prior to Divorce Proceedings

As mentioned above, where the spouses have become reconciled after mediation carried out by the relevant non-court organs or agencies, they do not have to go through any formalities with the marriage registration authority or the people's court. When the spouses reach a divorce agreement (marital settlement agreement) after mediation, both parties concerned must appear in person at the marriage registration authority and apply for divorce registration.

Settlement Agreement Reached during Divorce Proceedings

During the divorce proceedings of first instance, the people's court need not draw up a mediation agreement for divorce cases in which both parties have become reconciled after mediation. Any agreement that does not require a mediation agreement shall be entered into the transcript and become legally effective after the transcript is signed or sealed by the parties, the judge, and the court clerk. Once the mediation agreement is accepted, the conciliation statement shall become legally effective, and no appeal against it shall be admitted. Mediation is also an important approach to handle cases in divorce proceedings of second instance (appeals). When adjudicating an appellate case, the people's court of the second instance may offer mediation for the parties. If an agreement is reached through mediation, a mediation statement shall be made and signed by the adjudicating personnel and the court clerk,

---

* This part is written by Chen Wei, Pi Xijun, and Lai Wenbin.

and the seal of the people's court shall be affixed to it. After the mediation statement has been delivered, the judgment rendered by the people's court that originally tried the case shall be considered rescinded.

It should be noted that in a case in which the divorce was not granted in the first instance but the people's court of the second instance think it should be granted when hearing the appeals, the people's court of the second instance may carry out mediation under the principle of free will. If mediation fails, the case shall be remanded by an order to the original people's court for a retrial.

Appeals

In the Chinese mainland, the appeals in divorce cases are not regulated by the current Marriage Law, but are regulated by the CIVIL PROCEDURE LAW OF THE PEOPLE's REPUBLIC OF CHINA (1991) (hereinafter referred to as Civil Procedure Law), revised according to the DECISION OF THE STANDING COMMITTEE OF THE NATIONAL PEOPLE's CONGRESS ON AMENDING THE CIVIL PROCEDURE LAW OF THE PEOPLE's REPUBLIC OF CHINA (2008) and the judicial interpretation of OPINIONS OF THE SUPREME PEOPLE's COURT ON SEVERAL ISSUES CONCERNING THE APPLICATION OF THE CIVIL PROCEDURE LAW OF THE PEOPLE's REPUBLIC OF CHINA (1992) (hereinafter referred to Opinion on the Application of the Civil Procedure Law 1992).

Procedures and Time Limit for Appeal

When a party to a civil proceeding disagrees with the judgment rendered by the people's court, that party may appeal to the people's court at the next higher level within the statutory period for amending or rescinding the judgment which has not yet become effective. Presently, the system of third instance as the final (or three levels of court review) is the law in a great many countries in the world. That is, the party shall have the right to file an appeal against the judgment which has not come into effect of the first instance or the second instance. The third instance is the final instance. However, in the Chinese mainland, under the Civil Procedure Law, the system whereby the second instance is final has been put into practice. If a party disagrees with a judgment rendered by a local people's court of the first instance, he shall have the right to file an appeal with the people's court at the next higher level within fifteen days from the date when the written judgment is served. After the people's court of the second instance makes the judgments and rulings, the proceedings shall be terminated and the judgments and rulings shall become legally effective. Therefore, the second instance procedure is also called the final procedure. *See* Jiang Wei, Civil Procedure Law 3d ed. 378–379 (Beijing: China Penmin Univ. Pub. House) (2007).

Procedures of Appeal

The same procedures in ordinary civil cases apply to the appeal in divorce cases. In divorce cases of the first instance, the people's court may make a judgment or handle it through mediation. With regard to the divorce cases handled through mediation, once the mediation statement is accepted, the conciliation statement shall become legally effective, and no appeal against it shall be admitted. In the divorce case handled by judgment, if either party to a divorce proceedings disagree with the judgment on such matters as whether divorce shall be granted or not, property division, the repayment of joint debts, child rearing, compensation for divorce damage according to statutory reasons, financial assistance on divorce, or economic compensation for housework at divorce, he or she may file an appeal within the time limits for appeal. Generally speaking, the parties can only file an appeal before the people's court of the second instance in relation to the issues the people's court of the first instance has made a judgment or ruling upon. However, if the people's court of the first instance did not make judgment or ruling on the claims the parties pledged in the first instance, the parties may initiate proceedings before a people's court of the second instance. In accordance with Articles 182 and 184 of the Opinions on the Application of the Civil Procedure Law (1992) upon the claims the parties pledged in the first instance, if the original people's court did not make a judgment or ruling, the people's court of the second instance may carry out mediation under the principle of free will. If mediation fails, the case shall be remanded by an order to the original people's court for a retrial. In the procedures of the second instance, if the plaintiff of the first instance introduces independent new claims or the defendant of the first instance counterclaims, the people's court of the second instance may carry out mediation on the independent new claims and counterclaim under the principle of both parties' will, or inform the parties that they may bring a new lawsuit if mediation fails.

Time Limit for Appeal

The time limit for appeal in divorce cases is the same as that of ordinary civil cases. Article 147 of the Civil Procedure Law provides that, if a party disagrees with a judgment rendered by a local people's court of the first instance, he shall have the right to file an appeal with the people's court at the next higher level within fifteen days from the date when the written judgment is served. If a party disagrees with a ruling made by a local people's court of the first instance, he shall have the right to file an appeal with a people's court at the next higher level within ten days from the date when the written ruling is served.

Hearing of Appellate Cases

The hearing of the people's court of the second instance upon the appellate cases includes the hearing of facts and the hearing of laws. Under Articles 151 and 152 of the CIVIL PROCEDURE LAW, a people's court of the second instance shall review the facts and the law used in an appellate case. When handling an appellate case, the people's court of the second instance shall form a collegial bench (three judges) to adjudicate the case and hold a trial. After verifying the facts of the appellate case by consulting the files, making necessary investigations, and questioning the parties, if the collegial bench believes it is not necessary to hold a trial, a judgment or ruling may be made without a trial. A people's court of the second instance may try an appellate case in its own courthouse, or in the place where the case originated, or where the people's court that originally tried the case is located.

In accordance with Article 155 of the CIVIL PROCEDURE LAW, when adjudicating an appellate case, the people's court of the second instance may offer mediation for the parties. If an agreement is reached through mediation, a mediation statement shall be made and signed by the adjudicating personnel and the court clerk, and the seal of the people's court shall be affixed to it. After the mediation statement has been delivered, the judgment rendered by the people's court that originally tried the case shall be considered rescinded. Article 191 of the Opinions on the Application of the Civil Procedure Law (1992) provides that, if the parties become reconciled in the second instance, the people's courts may, at the request of the parties, examine the settlement agreement reached by the parties, accordingly make a written mediation statement and serve it to the parties concerned. If the parties desire to withdraw the case due to reconciliation, the people's court shall grant it after establishing that it meets the requirements of withdrawing the case.

Review of Facts and Review of Laws

"Review of facts" means that the people's court of the second instance reviews whether the facts the appellant disagrees with in an appellate case are correct and examines whether there is sufficient evidence to prove its truth. "Review of laws" means that the people's court of the second instance just reviews the application of laws rather than the facts in an appellate case, and then makes judgment accordingly. Here, "the application of the law" includes the application of substantive law and procedural law, the former refers to the law applied to the disputed issues of the parties, the later means the procedural laws applied by the people's court of the first instance in the proceedings. In short, the focus and function of "review of facts" and "review of laws" differ from each other. The former focuses on the discovery of facts and the protection of substantial rights of the parties, the latter concentrates on the uniform application of substantial laws and the legal protection of procedural rights of the parties.

Under Article 153 (1) of the CIVIL PROCEDURE LAW, after hearing an appellate case, the people's court of the second instance shall handle the case respectively according to the following circumstances: 1) if the facts were clearly found and the law was correctly applied in the original judgment, the appeal shall be rejected by a judgment and the original judgment shall be sustained; 2) if the law was incorrectly applied in the original judgment, the judgment shall be amended according to law; 3) if in the original judgment the facts were incorrectly found or were not clearly found and the evidence was inconclusive, the judgment shall be rescinded and the case remanded by an order to the original people's court for a retrial, or the people's court of the second instance may amend the judgment after investigating and clarifying the facts; or 4) if in the original judgment a violation of the prescribed procedure may have affected the correct judgment, the judgment shall be rescinded and the case remanded by an order to the original people's court for a retrial.

In addition, Article 185 of OPINION ON THE APPLICATION OF THE CIVIL PROCEDURE LAW (1992) provides that, where a divorce was not granted in the first-instance judgment and a party disagrees with the judgment and files an appeal, the people's court of the second instance, believing that a divorce should be granted, may carry out mediation together with the issues on child custody and property on a voluntary basis or the case shall be remanded by an order to the original people's court for a retrial if mediation fails.

Time Limit for Final Judgment and Effects of Judgments and Rulings

In accordance with Articles 158 and 159 of the CIVIL PROCEDURE LAW, when adjudicating an appeal from a judgment, the people's court shall make a final judgment within three months after the appeal was accepted for an adjudication of the second instance. Any extension of the term necessary under special circumstances shall be subject to the approval of the president of the court. When adjudicating an appeal from a ruling, the people's court shall make a final ruling within thirty days after the case was accepted for an adjudication of the second instance.

The judgments and rulings of a people's court of the second instance shall be final. That is, the judgments and rulings of a people's court of the second instance come into force immediately when they are made and the parties shall have no right to appeal.

The Burden of Appeal Costs

For the appellate cases tried by the people's court of the second instance or the cases remanded by an order to the original people's court for a retrial, the party concerned usually must pay the costs, according to law. Rates for the costs of accepting a case on appeal are the same as those of the cases of the first instance. For each divorce case, 50 Yuan to 300 Yuan shall be paid. If property partition is involved, and the total amount of property does not exceed 200,000 Yuan, no additional fee shall be paid; for property valued at more than 200,000 Yuan, the fee shall be paid at the rate of 0.5%. Whoever appeals in a property case shall pay the case acceptance fee in accordance with the claim amount in the appellate claim that he/she is dissatisfied with in the judgment of the first instance.

When the appellant submits the appeal to the people's court, he shall prepay the acceptance fee of an appellate case. If both parties appeal, they shall prepay the fee respectively. As to the litigation costs for a divorce case, both parties shall make agreement on it, if they fail to reach an agreement, the people's court shall make a judgment.

Attorney Fees

The situation about attorney fees for appeals is similar with that for the first instance.

First of all, who will bear the burden of attorney fees? In China's mainland, in principle, each party shall bear his or her own attorney fees, unless the appellant requested the respondent to assume his or her attorney fees in the complaint and finally won the case, at this time, the judge might order the respondent to bear the appellant's attorney fees in some cases.

Secondly, how much are the attorney's fees? In China's mainland, because economic levels differ in different regions, there is no national uniform criterion of attorney's fees so far. Competent lawyers' authorities, however, in some provinces or municipalities have promulgated local regulations on the standard of attorney's fees, requiring parties to reach an agreement on attorney's fees and specify it in a proxy contract. Therefore, each party's attorney's fees differ from each other based on such factors as regions, lawyers, and the subject matter concerned.

As to the divorce case of *Lily v. Mario*, if Lily desires divorce through action, she with Mario shall assume their respective attorney fees. As for the specific amount of attorney fees, it is generally charged in accordance with the relevant guiding price or bargained by either party with his/her lawyers. Of course, pursuant to relevant provisions, in the case of claiming child support or maintenance, where Lily needs an attorney and fails to entrust one due to economic difficulty, she may apply for legal aid to the legal aid institutions at the place where the person obliged to pay for the child support or maintenance is situated, and obtain free legal services including legal consultation, agency, etc.

Italy

Antenuptial Agreements

Antenuptial agreements are generally considered illegal because they are contrary to the principle that parties cannot dispose of rights they have not yet acquired, and because they are considered contrary to public order (*ordine pubblico*). Yet, recently, the U.S. experience with these tools spurred a lively debate on their admissibility and usefulness in the Italian system.

In the silence of black letter law, part of the doctrine (respected legal scholarship) and many legal practitioners, thinking that contractual arrangements would prevent future bitter disputes, argue that antenuptial agreements are not specifically excluded by any code provision, and actually can be considered an expression of the parties' contractual autonomy provided for by existing law. The contracting parties are allowed to freely determine the content of their contractual obligations even outside of the particular types of contracts specifically regulated by law, as long as the contracts are finalized to the realization of interests deserving legal recognition. C.c. Art. 1322. In this view, the only limitation would be to avoid stipulations in violation of specific rules such as establishment of a dowry, specifically precluded by Art. 166-*bis* of the Civil Code, and avoid stipulations that would run afoul of the principle of equality of each spouse in community property regime, mandated by Art. 210 of the Civil Code.

Based on the strength of these arguments, there have been legislative proposals to introduce antenuptial agreements as a specific expression of the spouses' contractual freedom with respect to specific aspects of their marriage, but these proposals, so far, have not been made into law.

Yet many ad hoc agreements are made by prospective spouses relative to certain items of property that, although not falling under the formal heading of antenuptial agreements accomplish similar goals under the general principle of contractual autonomy, and, as such, are generally enforceable.

Agreements before Divorce

Similarly, the question of whether the parties can enter into agreements with the object of disposing of their divorce check or to waive the same is open and is the subject of much doctrinal debate. *See e.g.*, Maria Claudia Andreini, *Gli Accordi di Separazione e di Divorzio*, [The Agreements of Separation and Divorce] IL FORO CIVILE 2008 *available at* http://www.diritto.net; SESTA, at 693-94 and 3308-10.

Indeed, during the protracted process of separation, many spouses may long to reach finality with respect to their financial arrangements sooner than the time frame imposed by the legal system. With respect to pre-divorce agreements, Italian doctrine (respected legal scholarship) and jurisprudence tend to share similar concerns as those prevailing in many states in the U.S. with respect to the content of antenuptial agreements, and primarily the need to protect the economically weaker spouse. The Supreme Court continues to carefully limit the nature and scope of these agreements and declares them null and void in specific instances citing to the principles of Art. 160 of the CIVIL CODE which states that a fundamental right connected to the status of spouse cannot be disposed of by contractual agreement prior to divorce; Law 1970/898, Art. 9 as modified which states that the divorce check cannot be disposed of before the divorce proceeding; or ruling that they are affected by an illicit purpose because these agreements violate the right of defense in the divorce proceeding yet to be initiated resulting in an act of disposition of the marital status. *See* Cass. Civ. Sez. I, 18 febbraio 2000, n. 1810.

Proponents of the validity of agreements regulating property distribution at divorce find their legal basis again in existing norms regulating contracts, in general contract principles, and in the very existence of divorce legislation. They see no obstacle in the principles of Art. 160 of the CIVIL CODE mentioned above arguing that that norm, once interpreted in light of its history and purpose, would be clearly directed towards the physiological phase of marriage (when the marriage is healthy), and not towards its pathological phase (when it breaks into separation and divorce). SESTA, at 694.

In practice, as in antenuptial agreements, doctrine (respected legal scholarship) and jurisprudence tend to give effect to the manifested intention of the parties in separation agreements. The reasoning is that language such as "the parties recognize that they are financially self sufficient" which have become relatively commonplace in separation agreements, are read to signify, as a matter of course, that the parties *merely recognize* they have no right to a maintenance check. *Id.* A mere recognition of having no right to a maintenance check is not substantially different than disposing of the check before divorce, which is what Art. 160 of the Civil Code prohibits. *Id.*

Appeals—Separation

With respect to separation, appeal relates only to the judicial. A partial decision of separation when the proceeding continues on economic issues and on custody of the children is susceptible of immediate appeal before it becomes final, but only through decision *in camera*, and is also subject to appeal after it becomes final. C.p.c. Art. 709-*bis*. In addition, the examining judge has the express power to revoke or modify the temporary and urgent orders adopted by the President of the Tribunal during the first hearing even though there may not have been a change of circumstances. C.p.c. Art. 709 4 cm. Against the temporary and urgent orders adopted by the President of the Tribunal at the first hearing, the aggrieved party can also file *reclamo* (limited appeal) to the Court of Appeal within ten days. C.p.c. Art. 708 4 cm.

The separation decision, once final, can be appealed like any other decision of the Ordinary Tribunal before the Court of Appeal of the same district where the Ordinary Tribunal which pronounced the decision is located. C.p.c. Arts. 339 and 341.

Appeals—Divorce

The divorce decree can have a negative content when it rejects the petition for divorce, upon finding that the conditions required by law for dissolution, or the divorce decree can have a positive content (granting the divorce) in which case it has a composite nature. First, a divorce decree with a positive content is of a constitutive nature as it changes the status of the parties; second, it may order one of the ex spouses to periodically pay a check to the other; third, it may include an assignment of the marital home, or render a determination with respect to the children. Based on Law 1970/898 Art. 4 11 cm. the decree is provisionally enforceable with respect to the economic issues.

However, the decree is subject to appeal, which follows the ordinary proceeding form *in camera*. Law 1970/898 Art 4 12 cm. The appeal is introduced by *ricorso* (a style of pleading) and must be filed within thirty days of the decree. C.P.C. Art 325 and 327. The appeal can be proposed by either of the spouses. In the doctrine (respected legal scholarship), the majority opinion is that only the losing party is entitled to appeal, while the minority opines that the principle of the losing party does not apply. Sesta, at 3269. The PM (Publico Ministero, representing the state), who is a necessary party even on appeal, can appeal the divorce decree as well. However, the PM's right to appeal is limited as compared to the rights to appeal of the spouses. The PM can only appeal with respect to issues affecting the rights of minors or legally emancipated children. Within those issues, a further limitation is that the PM can only appeal property issues affecting minor children as well as child support issues. The PM cannot appeal custody issues; only parents have a right to do so. Sesta, at 3269.

The preparation and discussion phase (*trattazione*) on appeal follow the format of ordinary civil proceedings, the decision phase (judicial deliberation) takes place *in camera* while the discussion phase (a summary of facts and legal arguments) can be either *in camera* or public. Sesta, at 3270. Evidence (yes, new evidence can be introduced on appeal) can be admitted until the discussion hearing as long as there is *contradditorio* which, with respect to evidence presentation, means that the parties or their counsel have to be present. *Contradditorio*, a basic tenet in all legal proceedings, related to the right of defense, refers to the maintenance during different stages of the legal process of the opportunity for the parties to be informed by notice or by means of a public hearing, of the development of the legal action against them or to be present during key steps of the process so as to present their arguments. *See* Cost. Art. 111. The final judgment is by *sentenza* (sentence).

Ordinarily, recourse to the Supreme Court is also permitted for the issues that are subject to final judgment, such as property division or whether a maintenance check is owed to one or the other spouse. Unlike in ordinary proceedings, third parties cannot oppose a divorce decision because the rights under dispute pertain exclusively to the spouses. Revocation by the PM is always admissible against decisions 1) that are reached without its participation, as required by law; or 2) that are the product of the parties' collusion to defraud the law. C.P.C. Art. 397.

Legal Expenses

As of March 1, 2006 as per Law 2005/80, the spouses need legal representation to access the court for separation or divorce. Many Italian attorneys charge a fixed rate for consensual separation and joint divorce whose procedural steps are predictable and whose content is negotiated with the parties. Instead, for the judicial separation and for contested divorces attorneys usually charge based on relatively uniform price lists itemizing each step of the process. Attorneys generally offer careful explanations with respect to the fact that the amount of legal fees in these types of proceedings cannot be estimated in advance.

Spouses whose income is below a minimum prescribed by law on a yearly basis can qualify for legal assistance free of charge. Assistance free of charge is offered by legal professionals who have their names listed in special rosters and who are committed to this type of pro bono activity. The client who qualifies for legal assistance free of charge from one of the listed professionals must indicate from the first encounter that he or she is accessing legal services of that attorney as part of the free of charge services (*patrocinio gratuito*) for which they believe they qualify.

Summary Chart—
Agreements, Appeals, and Attorney Fees

	U. S. (Tennessee)	China	Italy
Antenuptial agreements recognized.	Yes	The parties can agree only as to the type of property regime to be applied.	They are generally considered illegal.
Divorce settlement agreement allowed.	Yes, subject to court approval.	Yes	Yes, but may not dispose of maintenance check before divorce.
Right to first level appeal.	Yes, in contested cases.	Yes, in contested cases.	Yes, in contested cases for losing party (not as clear with prevailing party). PM can also appeal children's financial issues.
Time limit to appeal.	Thirty days.	Fifteen days for judgments, ten days for rulings.	Thirty days.
Right to second level appeal.	Subject to high court's discretion.	No	Yes
Evidence can be introduced on appeal.	Not ordinarily.	Yes	Yes
Legal representation required for divorce.	No, but it is advisable.	No, but it is advisable in complex or contested cases.	Yes
Attorney fees.	Each party responsible for his own attorney fees, but the parties may agree otherwise, or the court may order payment, as support or pursuant to statute.	Each party responsible for his own attorney fees, unless otherwise ordered by the court.	Each party responsible for his own attorney fees.
Legal representation available for indigent spouses.	Yes, in theory, but usually not in practice unless abuse is involved.	Yes	Yes

CHAPTER 12

CLOSING PERSPECTIVES—
THE FINAL DIVORCE DECREE

Now, that we have reviewed, compared, and contrasted the divorce law in the United States, China, and Italy, it is time, finally, to look at the final results of a divorce action between Mario and Lily in each country. How are the issues likely to be decided based on the facts of our case?

United States

As noted previously, the vast majority of divorce cases in the United States are settled between the parties prior to trial. That settlement may be reached between the parties representing themselves, without the benefit of an attorney; with only one party being represented by an attorney; or with each party being represented by an attorney. If there are minor children of the marriage, they may be represented separately by a guardian *ad litem* or attorney *ad litem*. In addition, the negotiations may be facilitated by a neutral party, as in the case of mediation or settlement conferences, for example.

Settlement agreements have been referred to as bargaining in the shadow of the law, because even though the parties are not bound by the law *per se*, it serves as a backdrop, or standard against which the negotiations occur. The attorney is very likely to counsel the client concerning how the attorney thinks the judge would likely rule on a given issue in order to assist the client in evaluating a settlement offer.

There are countless variations of settlement agreements that the parties could reach, which are influenced by many factors including the bargaining strength of the parties, each party's level of guilt, anger, or other emotion, as well as each party's desire to be divorced. A party may also be influenced by their financial need, or their desire to secure parenting time with minor children of the marriage.

In order to illustrate the variability of negotiations, the U.S. author set up mock negotiations of Mario and Lily's divorce with the students in her Family Law class. Each of the thirteen groups had two students who played the part of the clients and two students who played the role of attorney— each representing one party. Some groups also had a student who played the role of guardian *ad litem* for the children and/or a student who served as a mediator or judge.

Child Custody

On the custody issue, most groups (10) named Lily as the primary residential parent. Only three groups agreed to joint physical custody. Of those three, only one group agreed to equal time with each parent. The other two groups split the week with Lily receiving three days and Mario receiving two days during the week and alternating weekends between the parties. Joint legal custody (decision-making) was an easier sale. Nine of the groups agreed to joint legal custody. The other four gave sole legal custody to Lily. In the ten groups that agreed to make Lily the primary residential parent, each awarded Mario standard alternate residential parenting time of every other weekend, one night during the week, alternating holidays (rotating each year) and two weeks during the summer, with the exception of one group which split the school vacation periods. One group also agreed to allow Mario to pick up the children for church on the Sundays that they spent with Lily. In the four groups that went to trial, all four judges named Lily as the primary residential parent. One judge gave Mario parenting time each week from Friday after school until Saturday after 6:00 evening Mass. Another judge gave Mario six weeks in the summer. One group agreed that Lily would have decision making authority for extracurricular activities and education and that Mario would have decision-making authority regarding religious upbringing.

It is impossible to predict what type of custody arrangements might be reached by actual litigants or ordered by actual judges, but the norm under these facts would be for Lily to be named the primary residential parent and for Mario to be named the alternate residential parent and to receive standard parenting time of every other weekend, one night during the week, alternating holidays (rotating each year) and two weeks during the summer.

Other matters agreed to in the parenting plans included the following:

(1) Both parents agree to exchange time in the event one parent wishes to take the children on a vacation.

(2) Mario agrees to become proficient in sign language in exchange for Lily agreeing to make reasonable efforts for Dino to become proficient in lip reading.

(3) Lily's residence shall be the place of meeting for the exchange of the children, unless the children will be picked up at school for the exchange.

(4) Both parties agree they will not reside more than thirty miles away from the children's schools in an effort to maintain a close proximity to each other for the children's best interests.

(5) Paramour agreement is to be in place which prohibits overnight guests of the opposite sex in the presence of the children, except relatives or new spouses.

(6) Visitation is conditioned upon payment of child support.

(7) Both parents agree to attend parenting classes specifically targeted to parenting special needs children.

(8) Jade must play one sport a year of her choosing until she enters high school at which time she can decide whether to play sports.

(9) The parties must see a family counselor to resolve any disputes that arise concerning the children.

Child Support

All groups and judges deferred to the standard amount of child support, as calculated under the child support guidelines. In addition, Mario agreed or was ordered to maintain health insurance for the children and life insurance on himself with the children named as beneficiaries. One group also agreed that each parent would contribute 1% of their yearly income (including alimony income) to an educational trust fund for the children. Two other groups placed the burden of an educational trust fund only on Mario.

Most courts would also follow the child support guidelines and provide for health and life insurance. Most courts would not require an educational trust fund in the absence of a very high income obligor. The presence of the child support guidelines has decreased litigation over child support in most cases. There is still some litigation over the allotment of time with each parent, which can affect the child support obligation and there is litigation over the issues where the court has discretion to deviate from the child support guidelines, such as private school tuition, extracurricular activities that exceed the 7% amount incorporated in the child support guidelines, etc.

Property Division

Most groups agreed that Lily would keep her ring and that Mario would keep his watch and coin collection. All groups classified the ring, watch, and coin collection as separate property. Two groups agreed that Lily would sell the ring to Mario at fair market value and one group provided that Lily would keep the ring for her lifetime and then bequeath it to Jade. All other property was equally divided between the parties, including Lily's lottery winnings. Most groups gave the car to Lily, although two groups gave it to Mario. Most groups agreed to sell the house and split the equity, although three groups agreed that Lily would get full title to the house, along with the mortgage. Bank accounts were divided, 55% to Lily and 45% to Mario. Mario's pension was divided equally in most groups, but one group gave Mario all of his pension, but also required him to pay all of the marital debt. In all groups, Mario agreed to pay his educational debts. Some groups split the credit card debt unevenly with Mario paying as much as 75% of the charge card debts and as little as nothing. Other groups divided the credit card debt equally.

Each judge classified the ring as Lily's separate property and Mario's watch and coin collection as his separate property. All of the judges awarded the pension to Mario and the house to Lily, except for one judge who gave 25% of these two assets to the other spouse. All of the judges allocated all of the educational debt to Mario, along with most, if not all, of the other marital debt. Only one judge awarded the car to Lily.

Most courts would rule as our student judges did, classifying the ring, watch and coin collection as separate property. The courts might try to let Lily and the children remain in the home until the children are older, if it is economically feasible, with the home being sold and the equity being split at that time. The court would be inclined to divide the pension equally and would allocate most or all of the marital debt to Mario.

Spousal Support

Predictably, spousal support was the issue that resulted in the most diverse agreements and the most controversy, much like real cases. Unlike child support, there are no spousal support guidelines that can calculate a presumptive amount of support. There are several types of support and numerous factors that the court must consider in deciding whether to award alimony, and, if so, how much. Several of the negotiating groups could not reach an agreement on alimony. Among the groups who did reach agreement, most gave Lily rehabilitative alimony. The amounts ranged from 10% to 40% of Mario's earnings for a period of three years (four years for one group and six for another). One group agreed to 50% of Mario's earnings for a combination of spousal and child support with alimony *in futuro* continuing after Dino reaches majority, in the amount of 30% of Mario's current earnings. One group agreed only to short term transitional alimony. Several groups agreed that Mario would provide health coverage for Lily. The judges all gave Lily rehabilitative alimony (ranging from 20% to 50% of Mario's earnings) to permit her to go to law school, ranging from one to three years following the divorce.

Spousal support is one of the least predictable issues in a divorce for the reasons stated above. In this case, however, most courts would probably be inclined to award rehabilitative alimony to allow Lily to obtain her law degree. Doing so would increase the "financial pie" available to the children in the long term. In addition, the Tennessee legislature has stated a preference for rehabilitative alimony where feasible. Finally, the facts show that Lily helped Mario obtain an advanced degree, so courts are likely to think it reasonable for Mario to reciprocate.

As the results of the student projects demonstrate, there are many different outcomes possible, under the same facts, both in cases that are litigated and in cases that are negotiated or mediated.

China*

In the book, we introduced the divorce law of the PRC with its judicial interpretations and analyzed its practice using the divorce case of *Lily v. Mario* in the Chinese mainland. Now, the Chinese author shall make a short summary of the final results of the hypothetical divorce case of Lily and Mario. The summary covers divorce procedure, grounds for divorce, child custody and visitation, child support, property division, economic compensation at divorce for the value of housework, financial assistance on divorce, and compensation for divorce damage.

Divorce Procedure

In China's mainland, there are two approaches for the parties to divorce, divorce at a registry and divorce through action.

---

* This part is written by Chen Wei.

Procedure of Divorce at a Registry

In chapter 5, we explained that the vast majority of divorce cases in the Chinese mainland are settled through the procedure of divorce at a registry. If the parties, the husband and wife, both desire to dissolve their marriage and have reached an agreement on their children rearing and disposition of property after negotiation, they shall apply for a divorce at a marriage registration office with their written divorce agreement.

Based on the divorce case of *Lily v. Mario*, a divorce agreement may be drawn up, if Lily and Mario would divorce by means of registration, as follows:

Due to family disputes, the parties could not live together and both desire to divorce. A divorce agreement has been reached upon voluntary consultation in accordance with the current Marriage Law which states below:

(1) Both parties desire to divorce.
(2) Disposition of property and dealing with of debts as follows:

   The house including the value of room decorations in the ancillary facilities and the house appliances, furniture, and others (see list), totally evaluated by both parties, are allocated to Lily with the consent of the parties.

   The other property including the car, Mario's pension, and the ancient coins inherited from Mario's father, are allocated to Mario.

   No other creditor's rights or debts are jointly incurred by the husband and wife.
(3) Arrangements for children custody and support as follows:

   After divorce, Lily will have direct custody of the son Dino and Mario will pay child support of 500 Yuan (only including the son's living expenses, not his education expenses and medical expenses) monthly to Lily, on the tenth of each month until Dino can live on his own. Mario will direct custody and bring up the daughter Jade. Lily pays none of Jade's support because she has no job or other income. Mario shall pay Dino's education expenses and medical expenses, according to his demand for his study, training, and treatment of his disease.

   In addition, both parties, through consultation, should handle relevant significant issues such as the education, training, and medical care of their two children.
(4) Arrangement for child visitation as follows:

   After divorce, either of the parties has the right to visit his or her son or daughter and spend the weekend including the night of Friday, all day and night of Saturday and a day of Sunday with the child in Mario's or Lily's own family, but should send the son or the daughter back to the child's residence before 19 o'clock on Sunday. The visitation to a child by either party shall be in the interest of the physical and mental health of the child, and the other party shall have the duty to cooperate.

(5) Financial assistance (spousal support) on divorce as follows:

Due to no job, it is difficult for Lily to live independently after divorce. So Mario will afford Lily 1,000 Yuan monthly after divorce until Lily finds a job or remarries.

Then both parties Lily and Mario with the divorce agreement shall apply to the marriage registration office for divorce registration. After clearly establishing that both parties really desire divorce and the arrangements have been made for the care of their children and the disposition of property etc., the divorce shall be registered and the divorce certificate shall be issued by marriage registration office.

The procedure of divorce registration is not complicated, so that the parties can do a divorce registration without attorneys involved. However, as to the case in *Lily v. Mario*, the attorney may be required to offer services for the purpose of protecting lawful rights and interests of both parties better if the property relationship between the parties is very complex or either party is at fault that incurs divorce, etc.

Procedure of Divorce through Action

Under the current Marriage Law if one party desires a divorce, the organization concerned may carry out mediation or the party may appeal directly to a people's court to start divorce proceedings.

As to the divorce case of *Lily v. Mario*, where either party desires a divorce but the other party disagrees with him or her, he or she may require the relevant organization to carry out mediation. After the mediation, there may be three results. First, the parties may agree to an amicable settlement, in that Lily and Mario can become reconciled and Lily will abandon the request for divorce, or second, both parties agree to divorce. Under such circumstances, both parties shall go together to the marriage registration office to apply for divorce registration. Third, mediation fails. The party who desires a divorce may apply directly to the people's courts to start divorce proceedings.

After filing a lawsuit for divorce, if Lily has economic difficulty in life owing to living expenses and child support unpaid by Mario, she may petition to the people's court for advanced enforcement measures. After receiving the petition and making sure the relevant conditions are met, the people's court shall order the petitioner Lily to provide security, and accordingly make a ruling to enforce Mario to pay Lily a certain amount of spousal maintenance and child support in advance.

Owing to no job and income, if Lily really has difficulty in paying the litigation costs, according to relevant regulations, she may petition the people's court to postpone, reduce, or waive the costs. In addition, in the case of claiming for child support and maintenance, if Lily needs an attorney and fails to entrust one due to economic difficulty, she may apply for legal aid to the legal aid institutions at the place where the person obliged to pay for the child support or maintenance is situated, and obtain free legal services including legal consultation, agency, etc.

According to the current Marriage Law, the people's court shall carry out mediation in the process of hearing a divorce suit. As to the divorce case of *Lily v. Mario*, after mediation by the judge, if no agreement is reached through mediation or if both parties cannot be finally reconciled, the judge shall make a judgment timely. Divorce shall be granted if mutual affection no longer exists, or divorce shall not be granted.

Grounds for Divorce

In Chinese Mainland, the grounds for divorce vary in accordance with divorce at a registry or divorce through litigation.

Statutory Grounds for Divorce at a Registry

As introduced previously, As to the divorce case of *Lily v. Mario*, the statutory grounds for divorce registry is that divorce is desired by both parties and they have reached a written agreement on child rearing, division of matrimonial property, discharge of matrimonial debts, and financial assistance on divorce, etc.

Statutory Grounds for Divorce through Action

The statutory ground for divorce through action is that the mutual affection has broken down. In one of the following cases, divorce shall be granted if mediation fails: 1) where one party commits bigamy or cohabits with another person of the opposite sex; 2) where one party indulges in family violence, maltreats, or abandons family members; 3) where one party indulges in gambling, drug taking, etc. and refuses to reform after repeated persuasion; 4) where both parties have separated from each other for two full years for lack of mutual affection; 5) other cases which have led to the breakdown of affection between husband and wife. That is, where any of the five cir-cumstances occur, and the mediation fails, it is deemed that mutual affec-tion has broken down, so the people's court shall grant divorce according to the law.

As to the divorce case *Lily v. Mario*, if the condition is that the husband Mario brings an action against the wife Lily, but Lily does not agree to divorce, it is quite possible that the judge of the People's Court of Shaping Ba District, Chongqing may not support the claim of Mario in the first litigation if the agreement was not reached upon between both parties under mediation of the judge during the trial. Because of following reasons: first, the attitudes of the plaintiff and the defendant about child-rearing and education of the children conflict, which is only the cause for the crack of mutual affection of both par-ties, but their mutual affection has not broken down completely; second, eval-uating from the current situation of the mutual affection and the possibility of it to become reconciled, there are three main factors explained in chapter 6 for both parties to become reconciled; third, if the people's court grants di-vorce between the plaintiff and the defendant, it is the two minor children who may be harmed seriously, especially the five-year old son who was born deaf. The son may lose the common and careful care of his parents in the fu-ture, which may be adverse to the treatment and recovery of his hearing lost disease, and neither parent actually wishes to see this consequence.

The aforementioned facts and reasons demonstrate that mutual affection of the plaintiff and the defendant has not broken down, and there are some factors indicating the possibility that they could become reconciled. Hence, after examination, the judge holds the view that the grounds for divorce listed by the plaintiff are not sufficient, that is, the requirements of the breakdown of mutual affection to grant divorce in Article 32 of the current Marriage Law are not fulfilled. Hence, if mediation fails, the judge will not grant a divorce according to the law.

Child Custody and Visitation

After divorce, parents have the rights of his/her child custody and visita-tion according to the current Marriage Law. As regards the divorce case of *Lily v. Mario*, under the spirit of Article 36 of the current Marriage Law, the par-ents Lily and Mario shall seek an agreement through consultation at the time of divorce. If Jade or Dino were ages ten or older, their consent would be re-quired. If the parents fail to reach an agreement, the judge shall make a judg-ment in accordance with the rights and interests of the children and the ac-tual conditions of both parents.

If the judge decides that both the daughter Jade and the son Dino will live with their mother Lily and be under the mother's direct custody after divorce, the father, Mario shall enjoy the right to visit the children. However, the parents, Mario and Lily, must seek an agreement on how to exercise the right to visit, including the manner, time, place, and other issues on the exercise of the right to visit. If they fail to reach an agreement, the judge shall make a judgment in accordance with the law. And, when exercising the right to visit, Mario shall exercise the right properly in accordance with the agreement or the judgment. At the same time, Lily shall have the duty to assist Mario in exercising the right of visitation. If Lily fails to perform the obligation of assistance without reasonable reasons, Mario has the right to request the people's court to enforce the obligation. If the children refuse to be visited by their father Mario, the people's court shall not enforce the personal body and visiting act of the child.

Child Support

In the Chinese mainland, divorced parents' support to the child includes two methods, direct child support and indirect child support. Under the current Marriage Law and relevant judicial interpretations of the Supreme people's court, when parents divorce each other, the issue of child support should be dealt with properly on the principle of being conducive to the physical and mental health of the child, protecting the legitimate rights and interests of the child, and the specific conditions such as the rearing ability and actual conditions of both parents, etc.

As to the divorce case of *Lily v. Mario*, the two children of Lily and Mario both are above the age of two and both are post-breast-fed. Under the current Marriage Law, both parties Lily and Mario may seek an agreement on the support of the daughter Jade and the son Dino. If they fail to reach an agreement, the support shall be decided by the judge on the basis of the rights and interests of the children and the actual conditions of both parents. Based on the actual circumstances of the case, if the judge decides that the two children should live together with the mother Lily, it will be more conducive to the healthy growth of the children.

If the judge decides that the two minor children, Jade and Dino are under the custody of their mother Lily, under the current Marriage Law and relevant judicial interpretations, the father Mario shall pay the children support. The parents shall seek an agreement on the amount and the duration of child support payments. If they fail to reach the agreement, the judge shall make a judgment. Seen from the facts in the case, if Mario and Lily fail to reach the agreement, the judge shall decide that Mario should pay all the costs of up-bringing while Lily has no such obligation. The reason is that Lily does not work, so she has no salary or other sources of income. As to the specific amount of the support payments, it should be determined on the actual needs of the cost of living, educational expenses, medical expenses, and other ex-penses as well as Mario's actual paying ability and the actual local living stan-dards. Under Article 7 of SEVERAL OPINIONS ON HANDLING CHILD REARING ISSUES (1993), because Mario has a fixed income and pays for two children's support payments, a reasonable amount of the support payments shall be de-termined within the scope from 30% to 50% of his total monthly income. As the son Dino was born deaf, special costs such as the costs for recovery treat-ment and language training are in need, and the monthly wages of Mario is high enough to pay the support payments, so the above ratio can be increased. With regard to the duration of the support payments, the support payments to the daughter Jade shall be kept until Jade reaches the age of 18 with the ex-ception that she can't live independently. However, the support payments to the son Dino should not be limited to the time reaching the age of 18. After the son Dino reaches the age of 18, his child support payments shall be un-dertaken until he can maintain an independent life according to the actual re-covery of his hearing. Of course, the support payments of Mario to the two children should be paid monthly.

Property Division

According to the Marriage Law, at the time of divorce, the husband and the wife shall seek agreement regarding the disposition of their marital prop-erty. If they fail to reach an agreement, the people's court shall, on the basis of the actual circumstances of the property and on the principle of taking into consideration the rights and interests of the children and the wife, make a judgment.

Property Division at Divorce

As to the divorce case of *Lily v. Mario*, if the parties have no agreement on the property acquired by the spouses in duration of marriage, the system that property gained by one party or both parties during marriage belongs to mar-ital property shall be applied. Under the current Marriage Law and the judi-cial interpretations, for the ownership of the property gained during marriage by Lily and Mario, including the ownership of the housing and car, shall be determined based on whose property it is etc., rather than the registration name of one party of the housing and car. Thus, the ownership of the property acquired by the spouses during marriage shall be determined as follows:

(1) The ownership of housing, its ancillary decoration facilities, other attachments, and furniture etc. purchased after marriage. If they were purchased with marital property, they shall belong to jointly owned property. On the contrary, if they were purchased with the separate property prior to marriage of Lily or Mario, they shall belong to the separate property of the purchaser.

(2) The ownership of other assets acquired during the marriage. All other assets acquired by either or both spouses during the marriage, including cars and expectation benefits of the accumulated pensions of Mario belong to the statutory community property. However, if Lily or Mario alone before marriage purchased the car, it shall belong to the separate property of the party concerned.

(3) The property interests gained from health insurance and personal insurance. As to the health insurance and personal insurance of Mario offered by his employer, the ownership of the insurable interests shall be possessed by the person designated beneficiary, or by Mario himself or his statutory successor in accordance with the insurance agreements if there is no specific beneficiary. Therefore, all the property interests gained from health insurance and personal insurance do not belong to marital community property.

(4) The property inherited by Mario during the marriage. With regard to the ownership of ancient coins inherited by Mario from his father during the marriage, it should be determined based on whether there was a will of succession in which it appointed a party as the successor. If there was a will that said only Mario should inherit the ancient coins, it shall belong to Mario's separate property. Conversely, if no such a will designated that only Mario could inherit the ancient coins, it shall belong to the community property of Lily and Mario.

As for the divorce case of *Lily v. Mario*, if both parties desire to divorce at a registry, they may make the following arrangements by mutual consent in a divorce agreement on the disposition of marital property in accordance with Marriage Law 2001 and Regulations on Marriage Registration 2003: first, as to the house purchased with marital property, a value of 400,000 Yuan (including the value of ancillary decoration facilities of the room which is worth about 100,000 Yuan) belong to the wife. Second, household electronic appliances, furniture and others (see list) in the house, totally evaluated by both parties for 100,000 Yuan, also belong to the wife. Third, other assets acquired by them during their marriage including the car, Mario's pensions accumulated during their marriage, and the ancient coins inherited from Mario's father, a total value of 250,000 Yuan, belong to the husband. And the parties should state in the agreement clearly that there are no other creditor's rights or debts incurred jointly by Lily and Mario.

If Lily or Mario desires to divorce through action, both parties should seek agreement regarding the distribution of their marital property at the time of divorce. If they fail to reach an agreement, the judge shall, on the basis of the actual property and on the principle of equality between men and women and of taking into consideration the rights and interests of the child and the wife, make a judgment. From the specific facts of the case, Mario has a high-income job and growing wage in near future, on the contrary, Lily has no income because of long-time engaging in housework. For the rearing and healthy development of the children, the Judge shall decide that Lily directly brings up the two children and more marital property shall be allotted to her. And, for the convenience to living, she shall be granted the ownership of the housing, furniture and the car needed to pick up the child to school and hospital. Therefore, the judge may decide as follows:

(1) The house with two rooms and one hall purchased by the parties during the marriage, located on 3rd Floor, ×× Road, Shaping Ba District, Chongqing, China, a value of 400,000 Yuan (including the ancillary decoration facilities of the housing which is worth about 100,000 Yuan), and the furniture purchased during marriage (see list) in the house, totally evaluated by both parties for value of 100,000 Yuan, as well as the car with a value of 80,000 Yuan belong to the plaintiff Lily.

(2) The other property such as bank savings and stocks valued 20,000 Yuan acquired by either or both parties during the marriage; Mario's expected interests of pension accumulated during the marriage and valued 100,000 Yuan, as well as the ancient coins inherited from Mario's father valued 50,000 Yuan (no will designating Mario to succeed), belong to the defendant Mario.

If during the marriage, in order to maintain family living or repay the expenses of medical treatment for the son Dino or the education cost of daughter Jade, either Lily or Mario or both spouses owed a debt of 20,000 Yuan to a third person, the debt shall be community debts which will be paid off with marital property at the time of divorce. If marital property is insufficient to pay off the debt, both parties shall seek an agreement on the repayment, or the judge will make a judgment. On the basis of the specific circumstances of the case, taking into account the specific conditions of Lily who has less separate property and without other incomes at the time of divorce, the judge may decide that Mario should be responsible for all the marital debt.

Economic Compensation at Divorce

As to the divorce case of *Lily v. Mario*, Lily may require Mario to pay economic compensation for her housework during the marriage, if she meets the following three statutory requirements: first, both Lily and Mario must have agreed in writing that they adopt the separate property system after the marriage. Second, one spouse must have performed more household duties. Third, the party who performed more household duties shall claim for economic compensation at the time of divorce. Where Lily meets the requirements, she is entitled to claim the compensation at divorce from Mario. Both parties shall seek an agreement on the specific amounts and payment methods of the compensation, if they fail to reach an agreement, the judge shall enter a judgment. The judge shall undertake a comprehensive consideration of the following two reasons of Lily's claim for economic compensation at divorce; in particular, the second reason shall be paid more attention to. (a) The separate property respectively acquired by the husband and the wife during the marriage: the property acquired by Mario is six times as that by Lily. (b) The separate contributions of the husband and the wife to the family: as to the family and the children, Lily performed more household duties while Mario earned more wealth. However, Lily was mainly engaged in housework during the marriage, which had an adverse influence on her job, incomes, occupation in the future pension, expected economic interests, and so on. On the contrary, Mario's job, incomes and occupation in the future and pension expected economic interests and so on benefited from the assistance of Lily in housework.

Therefore, we believe that, based on the fairness principle of civil law and the opinion of recognizing the value of housework and protecting the legitimate rights and interests of women, under Article 42 of the Marriage Law in relation to the economic compensation at divorce, the judge may award the compensation offered by Mario to Lily, valuing 320,000 to 390,000 Yuan when granting a divorce. In other words, as to the property with a total value of 700, 000 Yuan acquired by Lily and Mario during the marriage, Lily may actually get 420,000–490,000 Yuan, accounting for 60% to70% of the total; Mario may actually get the property of value 280,000–210,000 Yuan, accounting for 30% to 40%. In addition, as Lily needs housing to reside, the judge in property division should give the consideration to her. The judge may decide that Lily shall be granted priority to such daily necessities as housing and furniture which shall be converted into money in the property distribution for maintaining the normal life of her and the children.

Finally, it is important to note that we theoretically analyzed the above-mentioned reasons for Lily to request for economic compensation at divorce and the application of relevant laws in the divorce case under the spirit of the Marriage Law. At the present time, what factors judges shall take into account on determining the amount of economic compensation at divorce is not clear. There are not any provisions in the Marriage Law. In judicial practice, the comprehension of judges may differ to some extent. For this reason, on the same case, judges may have different decisions.

Financial Assistance on Divorce (Spousal Maintenance)

As for the divorce case *Lily v. Mario*, Lily meets the statutory requirements of the financial assistance completely, so she is entitled to claim for the financial assistance from her husband Mario according to the law. Firstly, Lily has difficulty in self-support at divorce without enough property to maintain her basic living. Secondly, Mario has support ability at divorce. Thirdly, Lily has claimed for the financial assistance at the time of divorce. Hence, Lily meets the statutory requirements of the financial assistance completely.

Both parties shall seek an agreement on the amounts, duration, and ways to pay the financial assistance. If an agreement fails, the judge shall make a judgment. As to the amounts of the financial assistance, the judge shall fix on a reasonable amount after giving a comprehensive consideration of Lily's basic living needs, support capability of Mario, the basic living standard of local places, as well reference to the living standard during marriage when necessary. With regard to the duration and way of paying the financial assistance, Lily has working ability, but she can't go out to work for a time because of looking after the children and needing study and training for reemployment, so a short-term financial assistance payment can be decided (*e.g.* a 5-year payment), while Mario shall pay maintenance (*e.g.* 500–600 Yuan RMB) monthly to Lily and shoulder the expenses of study at a law school and the fees of training for Lily to be reemployed after divorce.

Compensation for Divorce Damage

The statutory requirements of compensation for divorce damage include three aspects: 1) one party must have committed the statutory wrongful acts; 2) the statutory wrongful acts must have led to divorce; 3) the other party must be innocent. The statutory four wrongful acts include bigamy, cohabitation with a third person of the opposite sex while having a spouse, family violence, maltreating or deserting any family member.

As to the divorce case of *Lily v. Mario*, even though Mario claims for the divorce damages in divorce proceedings from Lily, the judge shall not support the claim because it does not meet the statutory requirements of the compensation. Though Lily had a close relationship, even adultery with the neighbor Alex, Mario is not entitled to ask for the compensation for the following two reasons: first, adultery is not the statutory fault act claiming for the divorce damages; second, even though Lily commits adultery, the marriage breakdown of Lily and Mario was not caused by Lily's adultery.

Italy

In Italy, spouses are encouraged to work towards mutually agreeable practical solutions for their life after a marital crisis before accessing the legal system in separation-divorce cases. By and large, the Family Law Reform and its more recent developments favor pre-judicial convergence of interests between the spouses both by providing legal frameworks and support services where the spouses can play an active role in organizing their financial and personal interests in the pathological phase of marriage (such as mediation, consensual separation, and joint divorce), and by discouraging contentious approaches (by way of the additional time required to complete the respective procedural steps and the associated elevated costs). Looking at the consistent statistical prevalence of consensual separation and joint divorce in practice, these systems appear to be successful in keeping troubled spouses out of court until most issues have been narrowed or solved.

The legal profession is generally poised to favor the same approach. It seems that most family law attorneys double up as counselors and financial advisors and endeavor to help the spouses reach workable practical solutions, especially when children are involved, turning to the judicial system only for the required homologation (official recognition) or for as limited a number of issues as possible over which the parties can not agree. Conversely, especially after the introduction of divorce, the legal system shows relatively little interest in interfering with the spouses' decision relative to their status, as long as the requirements are met, and only intervenes on decisions affecting minor children.

Decisions pertaining to separation and divorce are as variable in Italy as they may be in the U.S. There are countless variations both in the content of agreements reached by the parties to be homologated by the judge in the consensual, and in the decisions reached by the judge in the judicial.

One key difference as compared to the U.S. is the stepping stone process of separation preceding the divorce petition. Although not all separations lead to divorce—the spouses may reconcile or decide to continue their journey as separated spouses—a separation is the most common predicate to a divorce petition. A vestige from the system predating the Family Law Reform which did not contemplate divorce, for better or for worse, separation continues to play a key role in Italian family law. Therefore, most of the issues to be broached at the point of marital crisis are broached at separation, which although not affecting the status of the spouses, sets out the parameters for the spouses' life apart from one another, provides for a temporary financial segregation of their assets, for custody of minor children, for child support, and for spousal support.

Child Custody

Joint legal custody is a given in a case such as Mario and Lily's. The issue to be resolved in the Italian system is whether an arrangement for shared parenting, favored by the most recent legislative changes tending towards favoring the maintenance after separation/divorce of a meaningful relationship of the children with both parents, would be possible in the case of Mario and Lily. Logistically, whether Mario and Lily continue to live within the same municipality after separation and divorce is likely to influence the decision relative to shared custody. Judges tend to allow the parents to develop workable mutually agreeable solutions which will be sanctioned by the court as long as the well being and the development of the children is safeguarded. Beyond that, judges use common sense to resolve the practical aspects of custody. For example, just like it may be the case in the U.S., religious instructions to Dino and Jade are likely to be the responsibility of Mario who is a practicing Catholic as opposed to Lily who is agnostic, yet would like for the children to receive a religious upbringing.

The recent legislative changes may not affect how the specific case is decided by the Tribunal if the parties do not reach a solution: the law prefers shared parenting, but does not make it mandatory. Therefore, Lily may still be awarded primary custody under the new norms.

If shared parenting is ordered, likely the children would alternate days with each parent to keep a routine whereby neither parent is absent from the everyday activities of the children too long. Also, in Italy, even if Lily gets exclusive custody, she will not be able to exclude Mario from visitation, as visitation is both a right-duty of Mario's with respect to his children and gives substance to Dino's and Jade's rights to maintain a meaningful relationship with both parents after separation and divorce.

Child Support

As we have seen, in Italy the minor child, or the child who having reached majority is unable to provide for himself financially and without fault, has a right to maintenance, which during divorce or separation generally gives rise to a maintenance check contribution to the custodial parent to take care of that obligation by the non custodial parent. The general factors indicated by Art. 155 of the Civil Code as guidance for the judge in determining child support in conjunction with the general principle of proportionality of contribution between the parents offer little practical help. Even the basic costs of food, clothing, books, and basic medical care vary significantly with the age of the child, inclinations and general health situation, as well as from place to place. Unlike in the U.S., there are no specific guidelines for child support. The judge will likely refer to local cost estimates for basic necessities. However, above that minimum, the Code indicates that the check should be determined taking into account the lifestyle that the child was accustomed to when living with both parents, opening the Pandora's box of diatribe as to what extent should the non custodial parent who has the financial resources be mandated to contribute to the custodial parent for her to continue "spoiling" the children as if nothing had changed. More relevant to the case of Dino and Jade are predictable expenses for specialty medical care not readily available through the National Healthcare System, orthodontic care, or for the costs associated with sports activities which Mario intends for Jade to join. Medical insurance, which is commonly offered to employees of larger corporations, supplements and complements the National Healthcare System, and may come in handy for specialty care for the children.

In general, not surprisingly, child support awards vary widely: from the equivalent of $200 per month to $1,000 for one child, while normally for more than one child the lowest awards are approximately $350 per month. It would be mere guesswork to estimate what award may be decided by a court in case Mario and Lily cannot reach an agreement.

Property Division

Just like in the U.S., in Italy, based on the code provisions and the direction of court decisions already touched upon in Chapter 9, it is likely that

Mario would keep his watch and the antique coin collection and that Lily would keep the diamond engagement ring. All other property will likely be equally divided between them.

The partition of the bank accounts would probably not fall in line with the equitable distribution identified in the U.S. as an Italian court may look at Mario as the chief contributor in making the deposits, and thereby rule in his favor. By the same token, with this approach, Mario would probably get the burden of the credit card debts, and most of the marital debt, not unlike in the U.S.

As for the car, it is part of marital property as it was acquired after marriage, and, as such, could be assigned to either Mario or Lily, offsetting half of its value against other items of marital property. The fact that the car is titled only in Mario's name by itself is not determinative, since all purchases during marriage automatically cause the items to fall within community property, the default regime, unless the couple has otherwise elected. In Bologna, both Mario and Lily are likely to have access to public transportation for most of their work, leisure and children's pick up and drop off to and from school and other activities.

In Italy, Lily's qualifying for a portion of Mario's pension resulting from the national Pension Fund is not discretionary, but predicated upon the existence of certain conditions when the pension becomes payable. The criteria for qualification are slightly different depending on whether the conditions giving rise to a pension arise during separation or after divorce. Private pension plans may follow ad hoc rules.

Lily's casino winnings are likely to escape community simply by her declaration that the bets were placed with her own cash, especially if the bets were not a substantial amount of money.

Most courts would probably let Lily keep the use of the marital home, whether she is granted exclusive custody or even shared custody, in order to facilitate a seamless transition for Dino and Jade until they are older, at least for several years until and unless Lily remarries.

Spousal Support

Just as for child support, spousal support is very hard to estimate given the broad directives of the black letter law on the subject. The discretion of the Italian judges is at its highest when, such as in this matter, Code provisions make reference to the equivalent of a totality of the circumstances analysis, without identifying any particular factors. In the determination of a maintenance check in favor of the economically weaker spouse by the comparatively stronger spouse, the key is maintaining as much as possible a standard of living comparable to that of prior to separation. This analysis, together with a consideration of all the sources of income of each spouse, and the potentialities of lifestyle of the couple during marriage (even when the weaker spouse accepted or tolerated a lower standard), makes it possible at least for the period of separation for the weaker spouse to get a measure of protection and equalization, as well as the opportunity to pursue training and schooling to eventually reenter the work force after having been home to care for the children, much like what is achieved through the instrument of rehabilitative alimony.

In the case of Mario and Lily, Mario could decide to pursue a judicial with the purpose of attaining a decision of *addebito (charging one spouse with responsibility for the separation)* against Lily based on her relationship with the neighbor Alex. A possible favorable outcome to Mario could mean a reduced liability limited to *alimenti,* for which more than likely Lily can qualify alleging and proving she is in a condition of need at separation. However, the time and expense involved in obtaining a judicial together with the fact that, for a relatively low income couple, maintenance and *alimenti (basic maintenance)* end up being not substantially different in amount may discourage Mario from pursuing that strategy.

The determination of the divorce check is based on factors besides the income of the ex spouse, such as the contribution of each to the marital property and the duration of the marriage, and is owed when one spouse lacks adequate means. Lily may indeed meet the qualifications for a divorce check at the time of divorce if she has not completed her studies while Mario continues to grow in his career.

Conclusion

Mario and Lily are now divorced. But how long the process took, how much it cost, and how the various issues like custody, support, and property division were decided depends very much, as we learned, on the situs of the divorce.

Most family law practices are single-state, and almost certainly, single-country oriented. This book, however, illustrates the advantage of having a broader comparative background when advising international couples like Mario and Lily about the costs and benefits of selecting the divorce forum.

We hope you enjoyed learning about the similarities and differences in divorce law and practice between our three countries as you read this book. We hope this brief introduction will encourage you to learn more about comparative family law.

Appendix — Case Law Reporting and Citation Style

One of the most interesting comparative law revelations of this book to students of the common law is likely to be the large impact of judge-made law in civil law countries. Case precedent is theoretically irrelevant in civil law systems. Consequently, judicial decisions are not as extensively and systematically reported in civil law systems as in the U.S. Researching Chinese and Italian case law, even apart from language barriers, can be challenging. Because we discuss case law from all three countries in this book, we offer a synopsis of how cases are reported and cited in the U.S., China, and Italy.

United States

The U.S. is unique among the three nations in having a uniform, easily accessible case reporting system for both federal and state judicial opinions. The National Reporter System, maintained by West Publishing Co., greatly facilitates case research in the U.S. Although the U.S. Supreme Court and some states continue to publish their own case reporters, standard practice is to cite to cases as they appear in the National Reporter System. Federal cases are reported in the Supreme Court Reporter (U.S. Supreme Court), Federal Reporter (U.S. Courts of Appeal), and Federal Supplement (U.S. District Courts). Separate federal topical reporters include the Bankruptcy Reporter, Federal Claims Reporter, Federal Rules Decisions, and Military Justice Reporter.

State decisions are reported in seven different regional reporters as follows: Atlantic Reporter (Connecticut, Delaware, Maine, Maryland, New Hampshire, New Jersey, Pennsylvania, Rhode Island, Vermont), North Eastern Reporter (Illinois, Indiana, Massachusetts, New York, Ohio), North Western Reporter (Iowa, Michigan, Minnesota, Nebraska, North Dakota, South Dakota,

Wisconsin), Pacific Reporter (Alaska, Arizona, California, Colorado, Hawaii, Idaho, Kansas, Montana, Nevada, New Mexico, Oklahoma, Oregon, Utah, Washington, Wyoming), South Eastern Reporter (Georgia, North Carolina, South Carolina, Virginia, West Virginia), Southern Reporter (Alabama, Florida, Louisiana, Mississippi), and South Western Reporter (Arkansas, Kentucky, Missouri, Tennessee, Texas). New York and California get their own reporters in the National Reporter system (New York Supplement and California Reporter). Not all, or even most, U.S. judicial decisions are published in the National Reporter System. Individual courts generally designate which cases are to be published.

U.S. cases follow a uniform system of citation style. Cases are cited by the names of the parties, followed by the volume of the reporter in which the opinion was published, the name of the reporter, the page on which the opinion begins, the page on which the specific material referred to appears (called the "pinpoint cite"), the court that decided the case, and the year the case was decided. Here's an example that explains the meaning of the following case cite, *Waddey v. Waddey*, 6 S.W.3d 234, 235 (Tenn. 1999):

> *Waddey v. Waddey*, [parties], 6 [volume] S.W.3d [South Western Reporter, 3d Series] 234 [first page of opinion], 235 [pinpoint page cite] (Tenn. 1999) [Tennessee Supreme Court and year of decision].

U.S. case law is widely available online through paid subscription services such as Westlaw and LexisNexis and also many free websites. Most federal and state court systems post their opinions and sometimes other court documents online. Legal resources sites such as washlaw.edu and findlaw.com maintain extensive collections of links to the law in all U.S. jurisdictions.

China*

As China is one of the civil law countries, Chinese judges have no right to "make law" like judges in common law countries, where case law is regarded as the main source of law in some instances. When the judges in common law countries adjudicate cases, if there are no relevant laws, regulations, and precedents to refer to, they may exercise discretion to handle the cases. However, in China, the judicial interpretations of the Supreme People's Court, the Opinions of local High Court on the application of relevant laws, and the local

---

* This part is written by Chen Wei and Lai Wenbin.

regulations, rules, and measures enacted by local People's Congress are legally binding when judges hear cases. Although the cases handled by the higher court are not legally binding when the judges in the lower courts adjudicate cases, judges of the lower courts usually make reference to those relevant cases handled by the people's court at a higher level or at the same level.

Books entitled, *Selected Cases,* selected and compiled carefully by the research organs of people's court play an important role in guiding the judges of people's court at all levels to hear cases. Take the book, Selected Cases in People's Court for example. It is compiled and written by the Institute of Research on Chinese Practical Law, charged by the Supreme People's Court of PRC, with four volumes published every year, including the typical cases handled by the basic People's Court, Intermediate People's Court, Higher People's Court throughout our country, and the Supreme People's Court. As Chen Min, an associate researcher of the Institute of Research on Chinese Practical Law said in her speech entitled "Gender Equality in Judicial Cases" at the "International Seminar of Gender Equality and Law Reform" held in Beijing, on May 17–18th, 2008, Selected Cases in People's Court (No. 2 of 2007, volume 60) published some typical cases regarding domestic violence and female crime, involving such issues as determining the commission of domestic violence, the due considerations in the case of counter-violence when the victims of domestic violence killed the offender, as well the impact of the murdered person's fault on sentencing, etc. Also, in every volume of Gazette of the Supreme People's Court of the People's Republic of China, some typical cases are published as a reference for the judges of people's courts at all levels. In addition, such online databases as the judicial cases database in the website called law 863 (http://www.law863.com/) and the judicial cases database in the website called Law-information-of-china (http://www.Lawinfochina.com) provide a specialized database of judicial cases, most cases handled by the people's court at all levels may be accessed through these channels. Some of the cases are available in English.

Most of the Higher People's Court of provinces, municipalities, and autonomous regions publish periodicals such as Sichuan Trial sponsored by the Higher People's Court of Sichuan province and Chongqing Trial sponsored by the Higher People's Court of Chongqing Municipality etc. They provide the people's court at the local all levels with guidance and reference in adjudicating cases. Take Chongqing Trial for example. It is published quarterly by the Higher People's Court of Chongqing Municipality and contains some typical cases with the viewpoints of the court as to the grounds for the decisions and the application of law in every volume, which serves as a reference for judges to hear similar cases in the future. Typically, cases in Chongqing

TRIAL, follow a four-step approach. The first step is to introduce the circumstances of the case briefly, and the second step is to examine several controversial views of the judges who hear the case and their reasoning. The third step is to comment on the application of the relevant law and the judgment, and the last step is to analyze and comment on the grounds for decision, the application of the rule of law, the choice of relevant legislation, and the judicial experience, based on the practice by other judges and legal experts.

Some of the basic People's Court and intermediate People's Court also have their own websites. For example, the website of Supreme People's Court of PRC is http://www.court.gov.cn/. Also, the Higher People's Court of Chongqing Municipality, the No.1 Intermediate People's Court of Chongqing and the People's Court of Shaping Ba District, Chongqing are available online respectively at http://www.cqcourt.gov.cn/, http://www.cqyzfy.gov.cn/, and http://www.cqspbfy.gov.cn/. The establishment of these sites is very convenient for allowing the parties concerned to understand the proceedings of the case and to obtain legal knowledge. The sites also assist the judges in learning about the laws and regulations applicable in the cases concerned.

Italy

Family Law in Italy is contained in the Constitution, the Civil Code, the Civil Procedure Code, the Penal Code, and in Special Laws. Particularly, the Civil Code deals with separation at length providing substantive guidance, while divorce is regulated by special law.

There are several publishers who publish the four codes in print. Some include just the code provisions and are supplemented by the constitution, the most important international conventions, and supplemental laws. Other publications are the Codes Annotated which include maxims from the Supreme Court and other Courts interpreting a specific code provision. Several noted publishing houses, such as Giuffrè and LaTribuna publish Codes of both types. The Codes are published every year, as laws are consistently enacted which update, modify, add, or eliminate Code provisions more or less substantially. These recognized annotated codes can be consulted during the bar exam, the exam for judgeship, the consular admission exam, and other contests for posts in the public sector.

On line there are several non-subscriber sites which provide access to the Codes and other laws (e.g., www.senato.it; www.altalex.com; www.diritto.it). These sites are available and free. However, they are not very user friendly for research purposes.

For Codes there is a uniform system of citation as follows:

Civil Code is cited as c.c.
Code of Civil Procedure is cited as c.p.c.
Penal Code is cited as c.p.
Code of Criminal Procedure is cited as c.p.p.

For laws and decrees the citation formats include the date of enactment, and the number.

There is no national uniform system of reporting decisions. Supreme Court decisions are published on the site of the Supreme Court, going back several years. In addition, the Supreme Court publishes maxims of its own decisions containing the principle of law the opinion focuses on.

In civil law countries the role of the judge is confined in principle to the interpretation and application of the black letter law contained in codes, laws, and decrees, while judges' decisions, including the Supreme Court's decisions, are not law. However, court decisions influence law making in many ways, as well as interpretation and application of the law. The importance of court decisions to the legal process in a civil law country may have come as a surprise to some students. First, lower courts look to Supreme Court rulings, their own prior rulings, and sister court rulings as persuasive in formulating their decisions. When the law or code provision is terse or does not address the issue at hand, i.e. in most cases, precedent, although not binding, tends to be looked at closely. Decisional trends thus develop, with different tribunals following different patterns, and certain tribunals forging new grounds, not unlike some courts do in the U.S. Second, the "doctrine" (which could be defined as an authoritative analysis of the law, fleshed out through the analysis of the Codes, Constitution, and special laws and decrees in light of their history and purpose) picks up certain decisions as more reasoned and in line with the intent of law, endorses them as the acceptable interpretation of the law, thereby conferring scholarly clout to this or that ruling, which then tends to be utilized by attorneys and picked up by judges in rendering subsequent decisions. Hence, decisions endorsed by doctrinal blessings thus become "more persuasive." Third, many times the rulings of the Supreme Court become law by subsequent enactment by the legislature.

Yet dealing with court decisions in Italy is still a daunting task. Although Supreme Court decisions are reported consistently, lower court decisions, are not published as systematically as in the U.S. Although specific decisions are cited in briefs and in opinions, both attorneys and judges often refer to this or that doctrinal opinion in their writing without more.

Decisions are cited in various formats including the issuing Court, the date and the number. For the most part, the parties' names are omitted. When the parties are listed, the plaintiff and the defendant are separated by a c.

Selected Bibliography

Many of the sources listed below proved helpful in composing this book. The bibliography focuses on the U.S., China, and Italy, and except as otherwise noted, is limited to sources available in English. Some online sources are listed in the preceding appendix.

General Comparative Law and Legal History

Nigel Foster & Satish Sule, German Legal System and Laws (Oxford University Press 2002).

Lawrence M. Friedman, A History of American Law (Touchstone 3d ed. 2005).

Mary Ann Glendon, Michael W. Gordon & Paolo G. Carozza, Comparative Legal Traditions in a Nutshell (West Group 2d ed. 1999).

Vivian Grosswald Curran, Comparative Law: An Introduction (Carolina Academic Press 2002).

Leslie J. Harris & Lee E. Teitelbaum, Family Law (Aspen 3d ed. 2005).

Frederik G. Kempin, Jr., Historical Introduction to Anglo-American Law in a Nutshell (Thomson West 3d ed. 1990).

John Henry Merryman, The Civil Law Tradition: An Introduction to the Legal Systems of Western Europe and Latin America (Stanford University Press 2d ed. 1985).

John Henry Merryman, David S. Clark & John O. Haley, The Civil Law Tradition: Europe, Latin America, and East Asia, Cases and Materials (LexisNexis 1994).

M.C. Mirow, Latin American Law: A History of Private Law and Institutions in Spanish America (University of Texas Press 2004).

Robert E. Oliphant & Nancy Ver Steegh, Family Law, Cases & Explanations (Aspen 2d ed. 2007).

Robert E. Oliphant & Nancy Ver Steegh, Work of the Family Lawyer (Aspen 2d ed. 2008).

RUDOLF B. SCHLESINGER, HANS W. BAADE, PETER E. HERZOG & EDWARD M.
WISE, COMPARATIVE LAW (Foundation Press 6th ed. 1998).
D. KELLY WEISBERG & SUSAN FRELICH APPLETON, MODERN FAMILY LAW
(Aspen 2006).

Comparative Marriage and Divorce Law

D. MARIANNE BLAIR & MERLE H. WEINER, FAMILY LAW IN THE WORLD COM-
MUNITY: CASES, MATERIALS AND PROBLEMS IN COMPARATIVE AND IN-
TERNATIONAL FAMILY LAW (Carolina Academic Press 2003).
ANN LAQUER ESTIN & BARBARA STARK, GLOBAL ISSUES IN FAMILY LAW (West
2007).
THE INTERNATIONAL SURVEY OF FAMILY LAW (DR. ANDREW BAINHAM, ED.)
(Jordan Publishing Ltd.) (Published annually on behalf of the Interna-
tional Society of Family Law).

U.S. Divorce Law

DOUGLAS E. ABRAMS, NAOMI R. CAHN, CATHERINE J. ROSS & DAVID D. MEYER,
CONTEMPORARY FAMILY LAW (Thomson West 2006).
JUDITH C. AREEN & MILTON C. REGAN JR., FAMILY LAW (Foundation Press 5th
ed. 2006).
HOMER H. CLARK, JR. & ANN LAQUER ESTIN, CASES AND PROBLEMS ON DO-
MESTIC RELATIONS (Thomson West 7th ed. 2005).
HOMER H. CLARK, JR., THE LAW OF DOMESTIC RELATIONS IN THE UNITED
STATES (Thomson West 2d ed. 1988).
IRA MARK ELLMAN, PAUL M. KURTZ, ELIZABETH S. SCOTT, LOIS WEITHORN &
BRIAN BIX, FAMILY LAW: CASES TEXT, PROBLEMS (LexisNexis 4th ed. 2004).
W. WALTON GARRETT, TENNESSEE PRACTICE, TENNESSEE DIVORCE, ALIMONY
AND CHILD CUSTODY VOL. 19 (Thomson West 2d ed. 2007).
JOHN DE WITT GREGORY, JANET LEACH RICHARDS & SHERYL WOLF, PROPERTY
DIVISION IN DIVORCE PROCEEDINGS: A FIFTY STATE GUIDE (Aspen 2003
& 2005 Supp).
JOHN DE WITT GREGORY, PETER N. SWISHER & SHERYL L. WOLF, UNDER-
STANDING FAMILY LAW (LexisNexis 3d ed. 2005).
HARRY D. KRAUSE, LINDA D. ELROD, MARSHA GARRISON & J. THOMAS OLD-
HAM, FAMILY LAW: CASES, COMMENTS AND QUESTIONS (Thomson West
6th ed. 2007).

Harry D. Krause & David D. Meyer, Family Law in a Nutshell (Thomson West 5th ed. 2007).

Principles of the Law of Family Dissolution (American Law Institute 2002).

Janet Leach Richards, Richards on Tennessee Family Law (Lexis Nexis 2nd ed. 2004, 2007 Supp.).

Carol Sanger, Family Law Stories (Foundation Press 2007).

Carl Schneider & Margaret F. Brinig, An Invitation to Family Law: Principles, Process and Perspectives (Thomson West 3rd ed. 2006).

Mark Strasser, Questions & Answers: Family Law (LexisNexis 2003).

Walter Wadlington & Raymond C. O'Brien, Family Law in Perspective, (Foundation Press 2nd ed. 2007).

Walter Wadlington & Raymond C. O'Brien, Domestic Relations, (Foundation Press 6th ed. 2007).

Chinese Law—General

Series A: Laws & Regulations (including laws, regulations, rules and judicial interpretations)

China's Laws, Regulations, Rules and Judicial Interpretations

Marriage Law of the People's Republic of China 1980 (Adopted on September 10, 1980, effective as of January 1, 1981, amended on April 28, 2001 and effective as of April 28, 2001).

Constitution of the People's Republic of China (Adopted for effect as of December 4, 1982 and amended respectively on April 12, 1988 & March 29, 1993 & March 15, 1999 & March 14, 2004).

Organic Law of the People's Courts of the People's Republic of China (Adopted on July 1, 1979 and effective as of January 1, 1980; and revised for the first time on September 2, 1983; for the second time on December 2, 1986; and for the third time on October 1, 2006).

Decision of the Standing Committee of the National People's Congress Regarding Perfecting the System of People's Assessors (Adopted on August 28, 2004, and effective as of May 1, 2005).

Law on Lawyers of the People's Republic of China (Adopted on May 15, 1996, and effective as of January 1, 1997; amended on December 29, 2001; and revised on October 28, 2007).

General Principles of the Civil Law of the People's Republic of China (Adopted and promulgated on April 12, 1986, and effective as of January 1, 1987).

MARRIAGE LAW OF THE PEOPLE'S REPUBLIC OF CHINA 1950 (promulgated for enforce as of May 1, 1950, and invalidated by Marriage Law 1980).

LAW OF SUCCESSION OF THE PEOPLE'S REPUBLIC OF CHINA (Adopted and promulgated on April 10, 1985, and effective as of October 1, 1985).

ADOPTION LAW OF THE PEOPLE'S REPUBLIC OF CHINA (Adopted on December 29, 1991, and effective as of April 1, 1992; amended on November 4, 1998, and effective as of April 1, 1999).

CIVIL PROCEDURE LAW OF THE PEOPLE'S REPUBLIC OF CHINA (Adopted for effect as of April 9, 1991; revised on October 28, 2007, and effective as of April 1, 2008).

LAW OF THE PEOPLE'S REPUBLIC OF CHINA ON THE PROTECTION OF WOMEN'S RIGHTS AND INTERESTS (Adopted on April 3, 1992, effective as of October 1, 1992; and amended on August 28, 2005).

LAW OF THE PEOPLE'S REPUBLIC OF CHINA ON THE PROTECTION OF MINORS (Adopted on September 4, 1991, and effective as of January 1, 1992; amended on December 29, 2006 and effective as of June 1, 2007).

LAW OF THE PEOPLE'S REPUBLIC OF CHINA ON PROTECTION OF THE RIGHTS AND INTERESTS OF THE ELDERLY (Adopted and promulgated on August 29, 1996, and effective as of October 1, 1996).

LAW OF THE PEOPLE'S REPUBLIC OF CHINA ON MATERNAL AND INFANT HEALTH CARE (Adopted and promulgated on October 27, 1994, and effective as of June 1, 1995).

LAW OF THE PEOPLE'S REPUBLIC OF CHINA ON POPULATION AND FAMILY PLANNING (Adopted and promulgated on December 29, 2001, and effective on September 1, 2002).

NATIONALITY LAW OF THE PEOPLE'S REPUBLIC OF CHINA (Adopted on September 10, 1980, and effective as of September 10, 1980).

REGULATIONS ON MARRIAGE REGISTRATION (Adopted on July 30, 2003, and effective as of October 1, 2003).

MEASURES FOR REGISTRATION OF ADOPTION OF CHILDREN BY CHINESE CITIZENS (Approved on May 12, 1999, promulgated and for effect as of May 25, 1999).

MEASURES FOR REGISTRATION OF ADOPTION OF CHILDREN BY FOREIGNERS IN THE PEOPLE'S REPUBLIC OF CHINA (Approved on May 12, 1999, promulgated for effect as of May 25, 1999).

INTERPRETATION OF THE SUPREME PEOPLE'S COURT ON SEVERAL ISSUES IN THE APPLICATION OF MARRIAGE LAW OF THE PEOPLE'S REPUBLIC OF CHINA (I) (Effective as of December 27, 2001).

INTERPRETATIONS OF THE SUPREME PEOPLE'S COURT ABOUT SEVERAL PROB-
LEMS CONCERNING THE APPLICATION OF THE MARRIAGE LAW OF THE
PEOPLE'S REPUBLIC OF CHINA (II) (Effective as of April 1, 2004).

PARTICULAR OPINIONS OF THE SUPREME PEOPLE'S COURT ON HOW TO DE-
TERMINE THE PROPERTIES DIVISION IN THE DIVORCE CASE UNDER THE
TRIAL OF THE PEOPLE'S COURT (Issued for implementation as of Novem-
ber 3, 1993).

PARTICULAR OPINIONS OF THE SUPREME PEOPLE'S COURT ON HOW TO DETER-
MINE THE CHILD REARING IN THE DIVORCE CASE UNDER THE TRIAL OF THE
PEOPLE'S COURT (Issued for implementation as of November 3, 1993).

PARTICULAR OPINIONS OF THE SUPREME PEOPLE'S COURT ON THE ESTAB-
LISHMENT OF THE SHATTERING OF AFFECTION BETWEEN HUSBAND AND
WIFE IN THE DIVORCE CASE UNDER THE TRIAL OF THE PEOPLE'S COURT
(Issued for implementation as of November 21, 1989).

OPINIONS OF THE SUPREME PEOPLE'S COURT ON IMPLEMENTING THE CIVIL
POLICY AND LAW (Issued for implementation as of August 30, 1984).

SOME PROVISIONS OF THE SUPREME PEOPLE'S COURT ON EVIDENCE IN CIVIL
PROCEDURES (passed on December 6, 2001, and promulgated for effect
as of April 1, 2002).

MEASURES ON THE PAYMENT OF LITIGATION COSTS (Adopted and promulgated on December 8, 2006, and effective on April 1, 2007).

REGULATION ON LEGAL AID (Adopted on July 16, 2003, and promulgated for
effect as of September 1, 2003).

LAW OF THE PEOPLE'S REPUBLIC OF CHINA ON THE CONTRACTING OF RURAL
LAND (Adopted on August 29, 2002 and effective as of March 1, 2003).

INTERPRETATION OF THE SUPREME PEOPLE'S COURT ON SOME ISSUES CON-
CERNING THE APPLICATION OF LAW FOR THE TRIAL OF CASES ON COM-
PENSATION FOR PERSONAL INJURY (Adopted on December 4, 2003, and
promulgated for effect as of May 1, 2004).

INTERPRETATION OF THE SUPREME PEOPLE'S COURT ON PROBLEMS REGARD-
ING THE ASCERTAINMENT OF COMPENSATION LIABILITY FOR MENTAL
DAMAGES IN CIVIL TORTS (Adopted on February 26, 2001, and promul-
gated for effect as of March 10, 2001).

OPINIONS OF THE SUPREME PEOPLE'S COURT ON SOME ISSUES CONCERNING
THE APPLICATION OF THE CIVIL PROCEDURE LAW OF THE PEOPLE'S RE-
PUBLIC OF CHINA (Adopted and promulgated for effect as of July 14, 1992).

Relevant Laws of Foreign Countries

FRENCH CIVIL CODE (Luo Jiezhen trans, Beijing: Law Press) (2005).

GERMAN CIVIL CODE (Chen Weizuo trans, Beijing: Law Press) (2004).

LATEST CIVIL LAW OF JAPAN (Qu Tao trans, Beijing: Law Press) (2006).

Series B: Chinese Books
(authors' last names appear first)

CHEN WEI, RESEARCH ON LEGISLATION OF CHINA'S MARRIAGE AND FAMILY LAW (Beijing: the Masses Press) (2000).

CHEN WEI, THE SETTLEMENT OF DISPUTES ON MARRIAGE AND NULLITY (Beijing: Law Press) (2001).

CHEN WEI, LEGAL SCIENCE OF MARRIAGE, FAMILY AND SUCCESSION (Beijing: Law Press) (2002).

CHEN WEI, LEGAL SCIENCE OF MARRIAGE, FAMILY AND SUCCESSION (Beijing: the Masses Press) (2005).

CHEN WEI: A COMPARATIVE STUDY OF FOREIGN MARRIAGE AND FAMILY LAW (Beijing: the Masses Press) (2006).

A COMPILATION OF FOREIGN FAMILY LAW (Family Law Society of China Law Society eds.) (Beijing: the Masses Press) (2000).

DU JUN, ON DIVORCE (Beijing: the Masses Press) (2000).

FAMILY VIOLENCE AND LEGAL AID (Research Center for Women's Law and Legal Service of Peking University ed.) (Beijing: China Social Sciences Press) (2003).

HU KANGSHENG, INTERPRETATION OF THE MARRIAGE LAW OF THE PRC (Beijing: Law Press) (2001).

JIANG WEI, LAW OF CIVIL PROCEDURE, 3d ed. (Beijing: the Press of China Renmin University) (2007).

THE JUDGMENT OF CONTEMPORARY CHINA, Vol. B, (Editorial Office of Contemporary China Series, ed.) (Beijing: Contemporary China Press) (1993).

LAW YEARBOOK OF CHINA Vol. 2001–2004 (The editorial board of China Law Yearbook ed.) (Beijing: the Press of China Law Yearbook) (2004).

LEGISLATIVE MATERIALS COLLECTION ON THE AMENDMENT OF MARRIAGE LAW OF PRC, (Wang Shengming, Sun Lihai & Civil Law Office, Commission of Legislative Affairs of Standing Committee of the National People's Congress China eds.) (Beijing: Law Press) (2001).

LIANG SHUWEN, A NEW EXPLANATION ON MARRIAGE LAW AND RELATIVE PROVISIONS (Beijing: Publishing House of the Chinese People's Security University) (2001).

Liguxinyi [Japan], SOCIOLOGY OF DIVORCE LAW, (Chen Mingxia & Xu Jihua, trans.) (Peking University Press) (1991).

LIU SHIJIE & LIU YALIN, RESEARCH ON DIVORCE TRIAL (Chongqing: Chongqing University Press) (1998).

RONG YIYI & SONG MEIYA, NO FAMILY VIOLENCE AGAINST WOMEN—THE THEORY AND PRACTICE OF CHINA (Beijing: China Social Sciences Press) (2003).

WU CHANGZHEN, YANG DAWEN & WANG DEYI, INTERPRETATIONS AND AN EMPIRICAL STUDY OF THE MARRIAGE LAW OF PRC (Beijing: the Press of China's Legal System) (2001).

WU CHANGZHEN, A SURVEY OF THE IMPLEMENTATION OF MARRIAGE LAW (Beijing: the Central Literature Press) (2004).

XU XIANMING & CAO YISUN, SITUATION OF CHINA'S LAW EDUCATION (Beijing: China University of Political Science and Law Press) (2006).

ZENG YI, RESEARCH ON DIVORCE IN 1980S CHINA (Beijing: Peking University Press) (1995).

Series C: Articles

Journals

Chinese Journals

Chen Min, *Brief Discussion on the Characteristics and the Trial of Marriage and Family Cases*, 5 LEGAL REV. (1997).

Chen Wei, *Research on Parents' Rights to Child Custody after Divorce*, 3 CHINA LEGAL SCI. (1998).

Chen Wei, *A Study of the System of Compensation for Divorce Damage*, 6 MOD. LEGAL SCI. (1998).

Chen Wei, *Discussion on Several Problems on the Law Application of the System of Compensation for Divorce Damage*, 2 LAW & COM. RES. 83 (2002).

Chen Wei, *Research on Some Issues in the Application of Divorce Compensation*, 2 RES. ON LAW & BUS. (2002).

Chen Wei, *On the Amendment and Perfection of Marriage Law*, 4 MOD. L. SCI. (2003).

Chen Wei & Ran Qiyu, *A Study of the Legal System of Spousal Support on Divorce—Comparison of Laws between Chinese Mainland and Russia*, 6 YUEDAN CIV. & COM. L, (2004).

Chen Wei & Xie Jingjie, *On the Establishment of the Paramount Principle of the Best Interests of the Child in Marriage and Family Law of China*, 5 RES. ON L. & BUS. (2005).

Xia Yinlan, *On the Protection of the Interests of Divorced Women*, INVESTIGA-TION ON THE IMPLEMENTATION OF THE MARRIAGE LAW (Wu Changzhen ed.) (Beijing: Central Literatures Press) (2004).

English Journals

Chen Wei, Ran Qiyu, *A Study of the System of Spousal Maintenance on Divorce: A Comparison Between China and Russia*, 19 INT'L J. OF LAW, POLICY AND THE FAMILY 3 (2005).
Chen Wei, *Recent Developments in the Marital Property System of the People's Republic of China*, INT'L SURV. OF FAM. L. (2006).

Newspapers

Cui Li, *Wu Changzhen's Opinions on the Amendment of Marriage Law*, CHINA YOUTH, Jan. 15, 2001.
Sun Xiaomei, *Partners Sometimes are More Dangerous than Enemies*, CHINA WOMEN, June 26, 1998.

Internet Materials

Gu Xiulian, *Lawyers Playing a Significant Role in the Building of Harmonious Socialist Society*, at: http://politics.people.com.cn/GB/1026/6204995.html.
Jian Chun'an, *An Analysis of Emotional Fuels of Marriage Problems*, at: http://cc.msnscache.com/cache.aspx?q=72748635718333&mkt=zh-CN&lang=zh-CN&w=e480c6d2&FORM=CVRE.
L Guohua, *The Gap between Lawyers and Enterprisers in China*, at: http://www.wn315.com/shop_info_view.asp?id=2598.
Song Jianchao, Sun Changshan, *Comprehension of the People's Assessor System*, at: http://www.xrfw.com/Article/ShowArticle.asp?ArticleID=213.
The Statistics of the Chinese National Bureau (2006), at: http://www.stats.gov.cn/tjsj/ndsj/2006/indexch.htm.
Wen Zhe, *People's Assessor: A System Shows the Feature of Chinese Trial*, at: http://npc.people.com.cn/GB/28320/101761/101765/6221919.html.
Ye Wenzhen, Lin Qingguo, *Analysis of the Divorce Trend and Its Reasons in Contemporary China*, at: http://www.hunyu.net/3/detaindex.asp?page=1&id=15554.

Italian Law

Italian Law—General

(ITALIAN) IL CODICE CIVILE[THE CIVIL CODE], I Codici Commentati con la Giurisrudenza, (La Tribuna 2005).

(English) BELTRAMO, M. (1993). *The Italian civil code and complementary legislation: release 93-1, issued July 1993.* Roma, Oceana Publications.

(English) (2003). *Italy—Constitution.* http://www.oefre.unibe.ch/law/icl/it 00000%5F.html.

(English) PEGORARO, L. (2003). *The Italian Constitution: text and notes.* Centre for constitutional studies and democratic development lecture series, 4. Bologna, Libreria Bonomo.

(ITALIAN) IL CODICE DI PROCEDURA CIVILE [THE CIVIL PROCEDURE CODE], I Codici Commentati con la Giurisrudenza, (La Tribuna 2005).

(ITALIAN) IL CODICE PENALE [THE PENAL CODE], I Codici Commentati con la Giurisrudenza, (La Tribuna 2006).

(Italian) ITALY, & BRAGHÒ, G. (2008). *Codice penale e leggi complementari: con esplicitazione dei rinvii normativi e sintesi delle novità: 2008.* Milano, Giuffrè.

(English) ITALY, WISE, E. M., & MAITLIN, A. (1978). *The Italian penal code.* The American series of foreign penal codes, 23. Littleton, Colo, F.B. Rothman.

(ITALIAN) IL CODICE DI PROCEDURA PENALE [THE CRIMINAL PROCEDURE CODE], I Codici Commentati con la Giurisrudenza, (La Tribuna 2006).

(ENGLISH) MAURO CAPPELLETTI, JOHN H. MERRYMAN, & JOSEPH M. PERILLO, THE ITALIAN LEGAL SYSTEM: AN INTRODUCTION, (Stanford University Press, 1967).

(English) Leroy G. Certoma, THE ITALIAN LEGAL SYSTEM, (London Butterworth 1985).

Italian Divorce Law

(Italian) Michele Sesta, Codice della Famiglia, [The Family Law Code] (Giuffrè Ed. 2007).

(English) Francesco Parisi & Gianpaolo Frezza, *The Evolving principles of Italian Family Law*, 9 Digest 1 (2001).

(ITALIAN) NEW CONCORDAT, TREATY BETWEEN THE ITALIAN REPUBLIC AND THE HOLY SEE, February 18, 1984 (specifically, Art. 8 Law 25 marzo 1985, n. 121 (ratifying the agreement 18 febbraio 1984, modifying the Concordato Lateranense 11 febbraio 1929, between the Italian Republic and the Holy See) and Art. 4 of the Additional Protocol).

(English) Mario Ventura, *The Permissible Scope of Legal Limitations on the Freedom of Religion or Belief in Italy*, 19 EMORY INT'L L. REV. 913 (2005).

(ITALIAN) SEPRAZIONI E DIVORZI IN ITALIA ANNO 2005 [SEPARATIONS AND DIVORCES IN ITALY 2005], (ISTAT, Giustizia 2007) *available at*: http://www. istat.it/salastampa/comunicati/non_calendario/20070626_01/ testointegrale.pdf (last visited 12/16/2007).

(Italian) ISTAT, Matrimoni Separazioni e Divorzi [Marriages Separations and Divorces] (2003), *available at* http://www.istat.it/societa/struttfam.

(Italian) ISTAT, Separazioni e Divorzi in Italia [Separations and Divorces in Italy], (2005), *available at* http://www.istat.it/societa/struttfam.

(Italian) ISTAT, La Violenza e i Maltrattamenti Contro le Donne Dentro e Fuori la Famiglia [Violence and Mistreatments against Women Inside and Outside the Family] (2007) *available at* http://www.pariopportunita.gov.it/ DefaultDesktop.aspx?doc=1058.

(Italian) Matteo Santini, *L'Assegnazione della Casa Conuigale in caso di Separazione*,[The Assignment of the Marital Home in Separation] *available at*: http://judicium.it/news/ins_04_07_07/Symp/Symposium%20Santini.html

(Italian) Maria Claudia Andreini, *Gli Accordi di Separazione e di Divorzio*, [The Agreements of Separation and Divorce] Il Foro Civile (2007).

(English) Andrew Bainham, *The International Survey of Family Law*, Family Law 2002.

(English) DE FRANCISCIS, M. E. (1989). *Italy and the Vatican: the 1984 concordat between church and state.* Studies in modern European history, v. 2. New York, P. Lang.

SEYMOUR, M. (2006). *Debating divorce in Italy marriage and the making of modern Italians, 1860–1974.* Italian and Italian American studies. New York, Palgrave Macmillan. http://site.ebrary.com/lib/sfu/doc?id=10167451.

English Translations of Chinese and Italian Codes

English translations of Chinese codes are available online at:
http://english.gov.cn/
http://www.lawinfochina.com/
http://en.chinacourt.org/
These internet sources contain information about Chinese Marriage Law:
http://www.helplinelaw.com/law/china/marriage/mlaw.phphttp://newyork.chi na-consulate.org/eng/lsqz/laws/t42222.htm
English translations of Italian codes can be found at:

BELTRAMO, M. (1993). *The Italian civil code and complementary legislation: release 93-1, issued July 1993.* Roma, Oceana Publications.

ITALY, WISE, E. M., & MAITLIN, A. (1978). *The Italian penal code.* The American series of foreign penal codes, 23. Littleton, Colo, F.B. Rothman.

ABOUT THE AUTHORS

Janet Leach Richards, Cecil C. Humphreys Professor of Law at the University of Memphis, has authored two books on family law: RICHARDS ON TENNESSEE FAMILY LAW and PROPERTY DIVISION IN DIVORCE PROCEEDINGS: A FIFTY STATE GUIDE (with Gregory and Wolf), five CALI (Computer Assisted Legal Instruction) family law lessons, and numerous law review articles. A member of the American Law Institute's Consultative Group for the ALI Principles of the Law of Family Dissolution, and past chair of the Family Law Section of the Association of American Law Schools, she currently serves on the Tennessee Supreme Court Advisory Commission on Rules of Practice and Procedure, the Tennessee Family Law Code Commission of the Tennessee Bar Association, and is a contributing author for the TBA's Alimony Bench Book.

Chen Wei, professor of law and a supervisor of doctoral candidates at Southwest University of Political Science and Law in China, has been working at the university for twenty-one years and is the director of the Research Center on Foreign Family Law and Women's Theory. She teaches Marriage and Family Law, Law of Succession, and Comparative Law of the Family. As an expert on family law, she participated in the session in March 2001 held by the Law Committee of the Standing Committee of National People's Congress to amend the Marriage Law of PRC 1980 and at the convention held jointly by the Society of Marriage and Family Law of China and the Research Society of China Women for the purpose of amending Law of the People's Republic of China on the Protection of Women's Rights and Interests 1992. Since 2004, she has been the vice-president of the Society of Marriage and Family Law of China. She also serves as a professional consultant on family law of the United Committee of Women of Chongqing Municipality and of the Station Researching on Judicatory System Regarding Protecting Children, in the People's Court of the Shapingba District, Chongqing Municipality, China. She has edited more than ten books on family law and succession and has written about fifty papers on family law as well.

Lorella dal Pezzo graduated from the University of Bologna, Italy with a degree in Jurisprudence in 1981, was fully admitted to the Bologna bar in 1984, and has been a member in good standing ever since. She was in private practice in her native Imola (Bo) for several years, focusing on the areas of family and business law. After moving to the United States, she attained a Master in Business Administration at Florida International University (FIU), Miami, Florida in 1987, and then worked in business management for many years. Most recently, in 2007, she   graduated from the FIU College of Law in the top 5% of her class and was admitted to the Florida Bar the same year. Ms. dal Pezzo is now in private practice in Miami, where she continues to study and work in family and business law as well as to publish comparative law essays and articles.

INDEX